Standing before the Shouting Mob

STANDING BEFORE THE SHOUTING MOB

Lenoir Chambers and

Virginia's Massive Resistance to

Public-School Integration

Alexander Leidholdt

The University of Alabama Press

Tuscaloosa and London

∞

The paper on which this book is printed meets the
minimum requirements of American National Standard for
Information Science—Permanence of Paper for Printed
Library Materials, ANSI Z39.48-1984.

Library of Congress Cataloging-in-Publication Data

Leidholdt, Alexander.
Standing before the shouting mob : Lenoir Chambers and
Virginia's massive resistance to public-school integration /
Alexander Leidholdt.
       p.   cm.
Includes bibliographical references (p. 161) and index.
ISBN 0-8173-0858-X (pbk. : alk. paper)
1. School integration—Virginia—History.   2. Chambers,
Lenoir, 1891-1970—Views on school integration.
3. Journalists—Virginia—Biography.   I. Title.
LC214.22.V8L45   1997
370.19′344′09755—dc20   96-19043

British Library Cataloguing-in-Publication Data available

To my mother and father:
for their
love.

Contents

Preface

THIS BOOK EXAMINES the life of the *Norfolk Virginian-Pilot*'s editorial-page editor Lenoir Chambers, with particular emphasis on the role he played in influencing public opinion during Virginia's "massive resistance" to public-school integration. The book also attempts to fill a historical vacuum with a detailed account of the exemplary journalism practiced by the major southern newspaper he edited at a critical time in our nation's history and the impact of that paper's stance on the resolution of a bitter controversy.

This study also examines a pivotal moment in our nation's racial history. The peaceful reopening of Norfolk's public schools portended the collapse of Virginia's massive resistance and considerably advanced the momentum of the civil rights movement on a national level.

In 1958 the nation's attention was focused on Virginia. In an attempt to stymie judicially mandated integration, Virginia's Governor J. Lindsay Almond, supported by the powerful political machine of United States Senator Harry Flood Byrd, Sr., ordered Norfolk, Charlottesville, and tiny Warren County to close their public schools. During the previous year, mob violence had erupted when the Little Rock, Arkansas, school board had unsuccessfully attempted to comply with the Supreme Court's decision in *Brown v. Board of Education of Topeka.*[1]

Almond's order displaced only two thousand students in Charlottesville and Warren County, and these small school systems quickly and effectively improvised educational arrangements. Norfolk, however, was a major urban area. Nearly ten thousand students were displaced by the state action; and four months after the closing, nearly three thousand students were still receiving no education.

Massive resistance, the coordinated attempt by southern legislators to resist public-school integration, transformed Norfolk into a battleground where resisters were pitted against pro-school forces and the courts. The outcome of this battle had national implications. Byrd warned Virginians that the forces of integration were "working on the theory that if Virginia [could] be brought to her knees, they [could] march through the South singing Hallelujah."[2]

In February of 1959, Norfolk's schools reopened and Virginia's policy of massive resistance crumbled. Although the process by which Norfolk's schools were integrated was far from orderly, the transition was characterized by debate, political maneuvering, and judicial action—not violence.

The *Virginian-Pilot* served as an important influence in facilitating this peaceful integration. The *Pilot,* alone among Virginia's white newspapers, urged compliance with the Court's mandate to desegregate public schools. Lenoir Chambers, who as the *Pilot*'s editor-in-chief set its editorial policy, was later awarded the Pulitzer Prize for his five-year campaign opposing massive resistance.

Although editorials are read by a minority of newspaper readers, they are read by a stratum that is educated, articulate, and of an elevated social standing. Editorial readers often serve as opinion leaders and influence the thinking of members of their social groups. Opinion pages are particularly followed by politicians who read on a daily basis the newspapers published in their districts.

The *Virginian-Pilot*'s editorial page may have had a limited readership among the general population of Norfolk, but an influential elite regularly read and was influenced by Chambers's editorial campaign, and these opinion leaders, in turn, influenced their followers.

Four decades later, the arguments of Lenoir Chambers and his associate editors—Harold G. Sugg, William Shands Meacham, Robert Mason, and Robert Smith—seem restrained, reasonable, indeed ordinary. Yet during the South's reckless and emotional opposition to the Supreme Court's mandate, the *Pilot*'s editorial policy was viewed by many as a betrayal of deeply ingrained beliefs and sacrosanct tradition.

C. Vann Woodward wrote that during massive resistance a man who dared open his mouth was a "moderate," and one who advocated eventual compliance with the law was an "extremist." Compliance was seen as treason.[3]

Throughout the emotionally charged period of massive resistance, the *Virginian-Pilot* influenced public opinion by arguing against the excesses of the time. "Accurate news coverage and editing were never more important," wrote Harold Sugg. "Editorials were never more read, praised and damned. Letters to the editor flowed like rivers."[4]

Acknowledgments

M ANY FORMER *Virginian-Pilot* reporters and members of its editorial staff such as Alonzo T. Dill, Harold Sugg, Bob Smith, and Luther Carter gave freely of their time and provided vital information that informed my research on this book. Robert Mason, Lenoir Chambers's successor as editor of the *Pilot*, deserves special mention. Mr. Mason consented to many interviews, corresponded with me throughout my research and writing, and read and critiqued several drafts of this manuscript. I could not have completed this book without his support and guidance. Frank Batten, Sr., former publisher of Norfolk Newspapers—now chairman of Landmark Communications—took time from his busy schedule to discuss his recollections of Chambers and his own important role in Virginia's massive-resistance crisis.

The *Virginian-Pilot* and the *Ledger-Dispatch* editorials in this book are reprinted with the generous permission of the *Virginian-Pilot* and the *Ledger-Star* (formerly the *Ledger-Dispatch*).

I am deeply indebted to the many reference librarians and archivists who assisted me in my research on this book. In particular I am very grateful to Richard Shrader, Reference Archivist at the Southern Historical Collection at the University of North Carolina Library, and his staff. Michael Plunkett, Director of Special Collections and Curator of Manuscripts at the University of Virginia Library, and his staff also rendered crucial assistance. Other librarians such as Lawrence Mykytiuk, Assistant Professor of Library Science and Reference Librarian at Purdue University; Frances Wilhoit, Librarian at the Journalism Library at Indiana University; Ann Johnson, Director of the *Virginian-Pilot* library; Daniel Bowell, Director of the Library at King College and student intern Tamara Moore; Conley Edwards, Acting State Archivist for the Library of Virginia; Anne Rees, Reference Librarian at Old Dominion University; and the staff of the News Library at the *Greensboro News and Record* graciously provided guidance and access to their collections.

I have been very fortunate to have had faculty mentors who served as role models for me throughout this project. Professor Bentley Anderson at Virginia Wesleyan College and Professor Carmen S. Fellicetti at Clarion University instilled in me an appreciation for learning and a strong work ethic. Professor Maurice Berube at Old Dominion University energetically and knowledgeably directed my dissertation on Lenoir Chambers and never wavered in his support over the past four years in my many additions and changes to that early work. I am extraordinarily grateful to Professor Berube for his guidance and his friendship.

Lenoir Chambers's daughter, Elisabeth Burgess, and his stepson, Robert Glenn, provided invaluable help. They shared their memories with me and directed my attention to important sources that greatly informed my research.

I must acknowledge the tremendous assistance provided by my mother, Louise Leidholdt, a gifted writer and a clear thinker. She meticulously examined, proofread, and suggested many changes to each of the many drafts of this manuscript. My respect for my mother's wisdom grew with each iteration of this book.

I also wish to express my deep appreciation to Malcolm MacDonald, Director Emeritus of The University of Alabama Press, for supporting me throughout this project. He expressed an interest early in my work, and his support never flagged. The anonymous readers at the Press greatly strengthened this book with insightful criticisms and constructive comments. Suzette Griffith, Assistant Managing Editor, patiently worked with me in the preparation of this manuscript.

Standing before the Shouting Mob

1

Closing of the Schools

IN 1958 NORFOLK was a major metropolitan area and the state's largest city, with a rapidly increasing public-school enrollment. With 32,163 white pupils and 15,171 black pupils enrolled in the city's thirty-six white and twenty black schools, the public schools received $6,000,000 in local funding, $2,439,000 in state money, and $1,240,000 from the federal government.[1] Norfolk's school system required the administrative services of a superintendent, three assistant superintendents, and twelve directors of departments.[2] The September 29, 1958, closing of six formerly white secondary schools by Governor Lindsay Almond displaced 9,950 students and portended the displacement of thousands more as the federal government ordered desegregation of their schools.

In the first few days following the closing, few voices in Norfolk, other than that of *Virginian-Pilot* editor Lenoir Chambers, were raised in objection. An unnatural quiet pervaded the city as a stunned citizenry attempted to come to terms with what had happened. Although the crisis had been clearly foreshadowed by the political and judicial events of the preceding several years, many of Norfolk's citizens never really believed that public schools could be closed. Some thought, as did Joseph Leslie, the editor of the afternoon newspaper, the *Ledger-Dispatch,* that even if the schools were shut down, they would reopen in a few days.[3]

Although many of Norfolk's citizens favored the immediate reopening of the city's public schools, few were willing to speak out. This was especially true of business and community leaders. Many of these leaders feared economic repercussions, social ostracization, and harassment by the Defenders of State Sovereignty and Individual Liberties (a white citizens' council organized to oppose school integration) and other hard-line segregationists.[4]

As the numbing sense of disbelief of the first few days of the closing wore off, tempers began to rise. Citizens were bitterly divided over the closing. Benjamin Muse writes that in the fall of 1958, Norfolk was not "a pleasant city in which to live."[5]

Observers of this period believe that the closure stirred feelings and divided the population to a degree not equaled in their lifetimes. Sam Barfield, a prominent local political figure, described a climate of high emotion. "The only thing that has come close to it in my lifetime has been the abortion issue; [and] I think it was even more emotional than the abortion issue. The city was split wide open."[6]

"People who write about it today," said Frank Batten, who was then the publisher of the co-owned *Virginian-Pilot* and *Ledger-Dispatch,* "have a difficult time in understanding the climate and emotions of the times. The people didn't talk about anything but that, literally. . . . It was a very passionate subject. . . . People who had been close friends—even families— broke apart. They just formed these hatreds over the subject."[7]

The most profound effects of the closing were felt by the ten thousand students and their teachers. Students in the last year of their secondary-school education were frustrated. Those who planned to attend college were particularly disappointed. City officials feared a wave of juvenile delinquency would sweep through Norfolk.[8]

Informal "tutoring groups," usually conducted by teachers of the closed schools, sprang up across the city. Many of these groups were organized by students' mothers, who gathered half a dozen to two-dozen students in improvised classrooms in private homes and twenty-seven churches and synagogues that made rooms available, and recruited a teacher. The teachers were often qualified to teach only a single subject. Normally parents paid twenty dollars a month for tuition.[9]

Prior to the closing, Norfolk's school teachers had received the lowest salaries in the country in cities of over three hundred thousand residents, and they were understandably grateful for the twenty dollars or so they received from parents for tuition.[10]

The facilities of the tutoring groups were clearly inferior to those of the public schools. Card tables often replaced school desks; cafeterias were nonexistent; and libraries, laboratories, and educational equipment were totally lacking. Additionally, the quality of the teaching was spotty.[11]

Other parents attempted to transfer their children into private schools or public schools in other districts. During the closing, Norfolk's students were scattered over twenty-nine states. Ironically, some displaced students who attended out-of-state schools were educated at integrated facilities.[12] The educational arrangements developed by Robert Stern, a professor at the Norfolk branch of the College of William and Mary, and his wife were not unusual. One daughter was sent to live with relatives and attend school in Glens Falls, New York. Another daughter attended private school in Virginia Beach, and a son was enrolled in a tutoring group. "It's a strange experience we're undergoing in Norfolk," Stern is quoted as having said, "a little like something out of Jonathan Swift."[13]

Some students continued their schooling in the neighboring city of South Norfolk, where the superintendent of schools, arch-segregationist

William Story, was particularly supportive of the state's defiant stand. Classes for Norfolk's displaced students were held from 4:00 to 9:00 P.M., after the schools' regular hours.

A small number attended school at the Tidewater Academy, which was founded by the Tidewater Educational Foundation (TEF). The TEF encountered great difficulty in attracting a teaching staff. As a result, the opening of its only school was delayed until October 21. Retired teachers taught the academy's classes, which met in a Norfolk church.[14] Financing for the school was generated by a twenty-dollar monthly tuition fee. Although this would not raise sufficient revenue to support the academy, the school expected also to receive assistance from the Virginia Educational Fund (VEF), a statewide segregationist foundation closely linked to the Defenders of State Sovereignty and Individual Liberties. The VEF was headed by former governor Thomas B. Stanley and received only the most marginal backing in its fund-raising efforts.[15]

The number of Norfolk's displaced students who would be unaccounted for and presumably receiving no schooling during the closing—2,700 out of 9,950—was startling. It constituted a much higher percentage than the corresponding figure in either Warren County or Charlottesville.

The closing would end the educations of many of Norfolk's students. Some would drop out. Others would join the military or the work force. Many would marry and begin families. A number would drift into unemployment. The extent to which the closing may have contributed to delinquency will never be known.

2

Divergent Views

THE SCHOOL CLOSING did not surprise Lenoir Chambers and his staff. The *Pilot* had anticipated the possibility that the inflexibility of the state's massive-resistance policies would result in such a crisis. Chambers wrote,* "The *Virginian-Pilot* is the only newspaper in Virginia which has opposed from 1954—because of their impracticality, unconstitutionality, general lack of wisdom, and inevitable arrival at educational dead-ends—virtually everything that has been attempted in Virginia."[1]

The *Virginian-Pilot* held that the school closing was the logical result of the state's policy of resistance to the Supreme Court order. Chambers contended that massive-resistance legislation ultimately would be overturned by the courts and would do nothing to stave off integration. Massive resistance, he wrote, was the irresponsible invention of a "small coterie of political leaders" (the Byrd organization) and was based on a number of false clichés and shibboleths.[2] Arguments by segregationists that the Supreme Court's order could legally be disobeyed, that states' rights must be defended or forever lost, and that outsiders were to blame for Virginia's racial problems were dismissed by the *Pilot* as specious and misleading.[3]

The editor decried the destruction of the state's system of public education and cautioned that newly created private schools and informal tutoring groups would be grossly inadequate substitutes for public schools. Trained teachers would be difficult to locate, the acquisition of facilities and educational equipment would be problematic, and accreditation of the substitute schools would be difficult to obtain.[4]

The *Pilot* refused to endorse the segregationist Tidewater Educational Foundation and recommended that parents enroll their children in tutoring groups, despite their obvious shortcomings. The editorial staff wrote that the Tidewater Educational Foundation's "political coloration strip[ped] its

---

*Although Chambers did not personally write every editorial herein ascribed to him, he set the *Virginian-Pilot*'s editorial policy, outlined and assigned the editorials, and exercised complete control over the results of the process. He usually wrote the lead pieces and eventually took upon himself the task of writing all of the paper's rebuttal to massive resistance.

prospective schools of the free atmosphere which most educators [considered] essential to learning."[5]

Chambers questioned the commitment of the state's political leaders to its young people. He feared that students would pay the price of the legislature's irresponsibility. As a result of the school closings, he predicted, many students would lose their "educational stride." Others would drift into unemployment or delinquency. "The memory of . . . this stupidity . . . will never fade," the editor warned. "It will be like the memory of depression or war. It will press young attitudes into permanent shape."[6]

In a lead editorial, "The Schools Must Be Opened," Chambers implored citizens and educational and political leaders to work cooperatively to reopen the schools. The school board had delayed long enough and should provide leadership. The city council had a special responsibility to the community to work to develop a solution to the school problem. Citizens should speak out and lend their support to responsible policies. The state "has no moral right—," Chambers wrote, "and probably no legal right—to punish [Norfolk's schoolchildren]."[7]

The closing of the schools took Joseph Leslie by surprise, as it did most of Norfolk's citizens. Harold Sugg, an associate editor at the *Virginian-Pilot*, sounded out the *Ledger-Dispatch*'s editor shortly before the closing. "I found Mr. Leslie alone, and the conversation ran something like this: 'Joe, I know you are in favor of the public schools. You just can't be in favor of their closing down.' 'Harold, that isn't going to happen; they may close for a few hours or a few days, but they will reopen quickly in other forms.' "[8]

The *Ledger-Dispatch* responded to the school closing by encouraging readers not to waver in their support of resistance to integration. "Massive resistance will come to nothing," Leslie wrote, "if it turns into weak-kneed resistance."[9] The *Ledger* maintained that the overwhelming majority of the city's electorate had demonstrated their support for massive resistance by selecting Lindsay Almond over Ted Dalton in the recent gubernatorial election and that although Norfolkians would be confronted with trying times, the school closing was to be preferred over the "Pandora's box of trouble and anguish" that would be opened should schools be integrated.[10]

Leslie and his staff stated that the legislature was not responsible for the crisis. The paper blamed, instead, the "NAACP's recklessness" and "judicial absolutism."[11] Leslie wrote that it was naive to believe the Supreme Court was incapable of error and that it was well within the rights of citizens to challenge the Court's decisions.

The paper urged readers to support the segregationist Tidewater Educational Foundation. "It is more than ever imperative," the editor wrote, "that steps for improvising educational facilities to meet this problem be advanced. Only one agency, the Tidewater Educational Foundation, is organized for this purpose."[12]

Throughout Virginia's massive resistance to public-school desegregation, the editorial staffs of the *Virginian-Pilot* and the *Ledger-Dispatch* took opposing positions. The *Pilot* urged a good-faith compliance with the Supreme Court's decision, whereas the *Ledger* generally supported the actions of the Byrd organization.[13] It is likely that this phenomenon—co-owned papers taking opposite positions on the issue—was a unique occurrence in southern journalism.[14]

The two papers' editorials were markedly different in style. On the whole, the *Pilot*'s writing was and would remain more involved and analytical; editorials were longer, sentence structure was more complex, and more evidence was set forth for conclusions. The *Ledger*'s writing seemed primarily to summarize the views of its editorial staff, whereas the editorials of the *Pilot,* while certainly reflecting the opinions of Chambers and his staff, appear to have been written with the intent of educating readers. As a result of this disparity in style, the *Ledger*'s editorials were likely more readable, and the *Pilot*'s more informative, intellectual, and convincing.

Some observers believed the divergent editorial stances of the two papers were contrived in an attempt by the owners of Norfolk Newspapers to increase readership and advertising revenues. "[Frank Batten] ran a newspaper to make money," explained Sam Barfield, "and he often said, 'I want my newspapers to be opposite each other.' Now I laugh about that. That's so people can't bring in another newspaper, won't want to bring in other newspapers. How sincere the editors were I don't know."[15]

Regardless of perceptions such as this, the differences between the *Pilot*'s and the *Ledger*'s editorials were not contrived. The opposing editorial positions of the two papers were entirely the result of the conflicting beliefs of the two papers' editors. Throughout Chambers's editorial career he had argued for political moderation and racial tolerance. Leslie was much more a traditionalist in racial matters; and because of this and his relationship with his father-in-law, Byrd-intimate Ebbie Combs, he tended to align himself closely with the state's powerful political machine directed by U.S. senator Harry F. Byrd. According to Robert Mason, who was then an associate editor of the *Pilot* under Chambers, the difference between the two papers' policies was simply a matter of the two editors' following their lifelong convictions.[16]

Chambers himself bristled at allegations that the differences between the papers were not genuine. In response to a reader's insinuation that the papers were more concerned with profit than responsible journalism, the editor wrote: "There is no purpose to make 'better business' in the sense you appear to intimate out of the natural, normal, and historical differences in the views of the *Virginian-Pilot* and the *Ledger-Dispatch*. I should appreciate it if you should repeat as much to any persons you may hear suggesting that there is. . . . Those who know the history, traditions, and principles of the *Virginian-Pilot*, for which I have some right to speak, or who know the editors of this newspaper, know better."[17]

The editorial autonomy afforded the two senior editors by their young publisher helped to create an environment in which the editors' views on integration could be expressed without reservation. Frank Batten endorsed the long tradition of independent editorial policy on the part of the two papers and the wide editorial latitude that extended back through the tenure of several of his predecessors.[18]

Some observers believed that the different perspectives espoused by the two papers' editorials had a positive effect and stimulated thinking and debate on integration. In the opinion of Elisabeth Burgess, Chambers's daughter, the exposition of the differing points of view was healthy for the city and its people. She believed that was Batten's philosophy, and she did not think her father objected.[19]

Nevertheless, the appearance of the ownership of the two papers trying to pander to readers was disturbing to Robert Mason: "I was pained that there was another paper under the same roof that was taking an opposite view. I don't think that would ever happen again. . . . I think [it] was a mistake. . . . At the time, I never heard anyone at the newspapers or editorial offices object to it. I did."[20]

Mason believed that had Batten been more experienced, he would have unified the papers' editorial policies: "He had no doubts at all about his ability to run that business, but he had great respect for his editors. He had little urge for editorial work and so he let them alone. If he had been thirty-five at the outset, I think he would have gone to them and said, 'Look, it's too bad you feel differently, but we aren't going to give the appearance of working both sides of the street. We've got to agree on a course on this thing, and there's going to be unity.' Certainly the time would come when [Batten] wouldn't blink at a transfer or early retirement."[21]

Had Batten taken such a course, there is little doubt which side would have prevailed. Frank Batten surely would not have risked losing his star editor, who would not have budged from his position. Joseph Leslie would have had to reverse or drastically modify his stand or relinquish his editorship with Norfolk Newspapers. And consistency in the message from Tidewater Virginia's two leading papers would have magnified its effectiveness manifold.

Chambers could not have been persuaded even to restrain his opposition to Virginia's recalcitrance because it so integrally conflicted with his core values. He objected to massive resistance primarily on the grounds that it violated fundamental precepts of our system of government, especially the authority of the Supreme Court to interpret the Constitution. He explained:

> My personal views and those of the *Virginian-Pilot* editorially do not extend as far as the views of many of my brethren to the south of us—or in Virginia for that matter. This does not mean that we have preached integration or that we are unaware of the magnitude and complexity of the problems. It does mean that we have more respect for a unanimous Supreme Court opinion than some others do, and that we have been critical of intransigence on a universal scale, and stupid ideas, and political exploitation of the emotionalism of the times, and various other current phenomena.[22]

What he perceived as the obfuscation and dishonesty practiced by the Byrd organization disturbed and keenly disappointed the editor. In a letter to his close friend Gerald Johnson, Chambers wrote that the curse of this period in the South was not the wish of most southerners to retain segregation—a wish that he understood—but the preposterousness of their reasons, which he felt had no basis in fact. He saw their arguments as inconsistent, hypocritical, and dishonest.[23]

He was particularly perturbed by the unwillingness of respected leaders in the state's academic, professional, and business communities to challenge massive resistance openly. "It is depressing to have to add," he continued in his letter to Johnson, "that most college faculty and administrative leaders, nearly all doctors, and absolutely all businessmen dived into their holes four years ago and have not stuck their heads out except to estimate the force of the winds and thereafter to retire again."[24]

Although Chambers based his editorials primarily on his deeply held beliefs regarding the sanctity of American democracy and the duty of public officials to practice responsible leadership, the legacy of former editor Louis Jaffe certainly played a part in shaping the *Virginian-Pilot*'s editorial response to *Brown v. Board*. Chambers wrote, "The *Virginian-Pilot* has a long record of trying to do what it could for justice and opportunity for Negroes. My predecessor, Louis I. Jaffe, won a Pulitzer Prize in 1928, for editorial work directed for the control of lynching. . . . This is not a wildcat newspaper. It does not crusade. But it does try to appeal to reason and to encourage all educational processes that overcome prejudice in the end. It was doing so before May, 1954."[25]

Chambers was not a social activist as Jaffe had been. "He never took the attitude that [*Brown v. Board*] was long overdue after all these years of oppression," said Robert Mason.[26] Chambers did not openly embrace integration. In many ways he was a product of the segregated South and a privileged upbringing, and his personal experience with blacks and racial issues was limited. With few exceptions, the only blacks he had known were menial and janitorial workers. He was removed from the masses by birth, education, and position.[27] To his credit, he was conscious of this shortcoming and how it had shaped his thinking and attitudes. "Chambers didn't know many blacks," confirmed associate editor and fellow University of North Carolina graduate Robert Smith. "He was very aware of that. He more than anyone I have ever known had gone to his heart to explore what he was about. I saw him struggle with himself on it, and I saw how he wrote about it."[28]

What impelled Chambers to target massive resistance and racial prejudice in his editorials was not foremost a desire to advance social justice. He was motivated primarily by a deep belief in the precepts of American democracy and orderly and responsible government. For the editor, the decisions of the Supreme Court were truly the law of the land. Massive resistance further affronted him because of its intellectual dishonesty, its lack of manners, and its emotionalism.

And ever figuring as a vital factor in Chambers's philosophy stood the Tarheel state, more specifically the liberalizing influence of the University of North Carolina, which had indelibly stamped him, many of the members of his staff for whom he felt the most affinity, and his mentor and peer Gerald Johnson. Chambers frequently corresponded with and regularly visited Frank Porter Graham, the president of the University of North Carolina; Louis Graves, editor of the liberal *Chapel Hill Weekly;* and Louis Round Wilson, the university librarian. All of these men had fought the good fight, educating the state's students and readers about the injustices and prejudices of their region and taking on a wide range of foes: fundamentalists who nearly managed to outlaw the teaching of evolution, textile-mill owners who grossly exploited their workers, and the Ku Klux Klan.

Under the charismatic and enlightened leadership of Frank Porter Graham, the university had become a shining exception to the mediocrity that prevailed in southern higher education at the time. What had been during Chambers's student years an unexceptional southern university in a sleepy backwater town had been transformed into an institution of national prominence, unquestionably then the leading university in the South. The University of North Carolina Press, begun by Louis Wilson, had become the region's only press of any real merit. Under W. T. Couch's management, it had achieved national renown by publishing books on contemporary political, social, economic, and racial topics; a number of them were written by black authors. The Sociology Department and the Institute for Research in Social Science, employing modern techniques, systematically and energetically investigated southern society and culture.[29]

Interestingly, then, the university, which one might expect to have exerted the most influence over Chambers during his years of residence there, served to a greater extent as a moral and intellectual anchor later in his life. Linked to the university by the ties of loyalty many feel to their alma maters, by his two years there as university publicist, by continuing service in a variety of alumni organizations, and by regular attendance of university and professional functions in Chapel Hill, Chambers remained a part of the community of the progressive and controversial institution that was playing such an important role in transforming the Southland.

For some, Chambers's editorial stance on the implementation of the *Brown* decision must have seemed incongruous with his relatively advanced age. Many observers of Norfolk's school closing perceived older residents as more conservative than their younger neighbors with regard to racial matters. Although research conducted by the University of North Carolina's Institute for Research in Social Science, focusing on the Norfolk school closing, did not support this hypothesis, scholars examining the southern intelligentsia during Chambers's era have concluded that age figured prominently in their subjects' ability to come to terms with changes in the South's racial landscape.[30] Daniel Singal writes, "For those who came of age in the 1930s . . . it would be a relatively easy task; for others . . . just a few years older, it would take a long and hard struggle."[31]

Chambers, who earned his Pulitzer at sixty-nine, might have been expected to take a more traditional position on school desegregation, one similar to that of Virginius Dabney of the *Richmond Times-Dispatch*. But age did not stifle Chambers's voice during his editorial campaign. He was not a recent convert to the position he staked out during massive resistance. His upbringing, education, life experiences, and journalistic career propelled him on the course he chose and galvanized him for his life's crucible.

3

Lenoir Chambers

The Formative Years

JOSEPH LENOIR CHAMBERS, JR., was born December 26, 1891, to a distinguished and affluent family in Charlotte, North Carolina. Davidson College named the Chambers Building for his grandfather, and the names of a city and county in North Carolina and a building at the University of North Carolina commemorate other members of the Chambers family. His father, a graduate of Davidson College, had worked for five years as city editor and editorial writer for the *Charlotte Observer* before going into business as a manufacturer of cotton gins, steam engines, boilers, and sawmills. The elder Chambers, who served as the president of Charlotte's public library board, was active in civic affairs and was one of the city's most influential leaders. Grace Singleton Dewey Chambers, the mother of Lenoir Chambers, Jr., was a graduate of Presbyterian College in Charlotte. Her mother had been the librarian of the city's first public library.[1]

Lenoir Chambers, Jr., was born only a generation after the Civil War, and the history and aftermath of the conflict loomed large in his childhood. His great-grandfather, the Reverend Dr. Drury Lacy, had performed the marriage of Anna Morrison to Confederate General "Stonewall" Jackson. Some of young Lenoir's earliest recollections were of the general's widow, who was a close friend of his grandmother. Clad in black and wearing a widow's cap and veil, the great lady seemed to young Chambers the embodiment of the lost struggle. The general would become the subject of Chambers's acclaimed two-volume biography, *Stonewall Jackson.*[2]

Lenoir, the youngest child and the only boy of the four Chambers children, suffered painful shyness.[3] If noticed too closely, he would erupt into tears. He received his early schooling in Charlotte's public schools, from which he graduated with honors in 1907. At his graduation, Lenoir read an original essay entitled "The Probability of War with Japan."[4] Indications of the regionalism and the cultural climate of the day appear in the graduation address, which, according to a local newspaper, the speaker "devoted to a masterly analysis of Southern life [and] Southern thought."[5]

For three years Lenoir attended high school at the prestigious Woodberry Forest School in Orange, Virginia, where he would later teach. At Woodberry he participated in sports and achieved some distinction playing baseball. The *Washington Post* noted that in the University of Virginia's victory over its only preparatory school opponent, Lenoir's fielding was one of the bright spots for Woodberry: "Chambers put up a clever game at short stop."[6]

Sports continued to be an important part of Chambers's student life during his years at the University of North Carolina. There he earned three letters, playing varsity football and basketball for two years and varsity tennis for three. However, a clipping from the campus newspaper, the *Tar Heel*, suggests that other forces sometimes competed for his attention at game time. "Coach bawled for Chambers to take the left half. No response. Coach searched the sidelines, but no Lenoir did he find. The game went on without him. Where was the young Mr. Chambers? Why, he sat in the grandstand with all his war togs on, surrounded by admiring bunches of calico."[7]

Although his gridiron performance was not outstanding, he was a gifted tennis player. Later in life Chambers, with characteristic modesty, dismissed his athletic accomplishments, claiming that he had played "without distinction."[8] He would retain a lifelong interest in sports. He continued to play tennis, as well as golf, and he was an avid baseball fan.

As a student at the University of North Carolina, Chambers also displayed an interest in writing and journalism. For three years he served as the editor of the university newspaper, the *Tar Heel*. He also wrote for the college periodicals, the *University Magazine* and the *Yackety Yack*. A talented student, he graduated third in his class and Phi Beta Kappa.

Upon his graduation in 1914, he accepted a position teaching English and history and assisting in coaching the football and basketball teams at his previous alma mater, Woodberry Forest preparatory school. Chambers taught there—"learned, really," in his view—for two years.[9] He would later play an active role in the affairs of the school for many years by serving as a trustee. In 1968 he received Woodberry Forest's J. Carter Walker Award for distinguished service.

Chambers attended Columbia University School of Journalism as a member of the 1916–17 junior class. Although little is known about this year of his life, studying at Columbia and living in New York City must have been stimulating, indeed eye-opening for the young southerner. In the period just prior to America's entry into World War I, Columbia's journalism program attracted a particularly imaginative and rebellious student body. Students attended closely to literary trends and political thought, and many embraced pacifism and socialism. Max Eastman (editor of the soon-to-be-banned *The Masses*) and even John Reed were lionized. Student journalists were among the most strident members of a group known as the Anti-Militarism League at the university. Chambers could hardly have gone unaffected by the ferment.[10]

Upon America's entry into the war in April, Chambers worked briefly with a faculty member, Walter B. Pitkin, and several fellow students, including Max Schuster, later of the publishing house that bears his name, to organize the New Republic News Service in Washington, D.C. They intended to secure the government information work that eventually went to George Creel and the Committee on Public Information.[11]

Although Pitkin had newspaper experience and was a prolific author with a canny sense of public moods and popular opinion, he lacked the administrative talent, political contacts, and financial backing to succeed in such an ambitious undertaking. The effort was a disastrous flop.[12]

Chambers's colleagues and friends would one day look back on his career and remark on its seamless progression, but the young man now well into his twenties must have felt anxious about his future. Teaching had not proved satisfying, and now the youthful news-service venture had failed. Many students at Columbia, several years younger than he, were regularly contributing to New York presses. With the rosy years at the University of North Carolina behind him, Chambers naturally would have questioned whether he would fulfill the bright promise he had displayed there. By his account, he "fled" Washington several weeks later for officers' training school in Tennessee; and there he earned a commission as a first lieutenant in the Army.[13]

Having completed additional training at Fort Oglethorpe in Georgia, Chambers and the other members of the 52nd Infantry of the Sixth Division sailed for Europe from New York City on July 6, 1918. After brief stops in Glasgow and Southampton, he arrived in Cherbourg, France.[14]

The Sixth Division took part in minor skirmishing with German troops in Alsace, and Chambers briefly commanded a company in trench combat. His unit was shelled, and it repelled an enemy advance. Thereafter, his division marched and was transported throughout France but did not engage in further fighting.[15] Chambers bemusedly wrote that his outfit, which was composed of soldiers from across the nation, earned the name of the Sight-Seeing Sixth, "because it went everywhere and did nothing of moment."[16] Although he felt that he had earned the respect of his men by treating them humanely, Chambers expressed in a letter to his mother his impression that his colonel did not like him.[17]

Throughout his military service he recorded his experiences in letters to his family, with the intention of drawing upon them for a book on the war.[18] Chambers's correspondence with his parents was especially candid. He reported on the alluring nature of French women, mentioned his wine bill, described his newly grown mustache, and expressed uneasiness over his post-war future. The openness with which he spoke about his personal life suggests an exceptional familial closeness.

Later in his life, Chambers would reminisce about the war in decidedly unromantic terms. His viewing of a photographic history of the conflict sent to him by Max Schuster brought back the carnage. It evoked in him, he said in his response to Schuster, "the angry, choking feeling that is aroused by human stupidity and blindness and cruelty and the arrogant ordering of men's lives."[19]

After the armistice Chambers remained in Europe and served as the division's recreation officer, organizing a football team and a horse show, and booking and transporting entertainment acts throughout the division. He also established and edited a newspaper for the unit. He found the new position unexciting and thought he was a much better company commander than recreation officer.[20]

Although demanding, Chambers's new responsibilities allowed him the freedom to travel and the time to lead an active social life. Ruth Draper, who would later become America's most acclaimed character actress, fell in love with him. The relationship began in February 1919, when Ruth entertained the Sixth Division at Montigny-Sur-Aube and Aignay-le-Duc in France soon after the armistice.[21] As the division's recreation officer, Chambers would have been charged with arranging Draper's performances.

At thirty-five, Ruth was seven years older than Chambers. She performed frequently in France—often two or three times a night—with her friend, singer Harriet Maple. Ruth's grandfather, Charles Dana, would have been well known to the aspiring journalist. Dana had been editor and part-owner of the *New York Sun* and had been a renowned leader in journalism and a strong defender of liberal causes.[22]

For the next seven years, in her letters to Maple, Draper would voice her frustration with the desultory romantic interest of a mysterious "N.C.," a reference to North Carolina. "No word comes from the mountains (N.C.) and nothing appears to take its place—no one really interests me and tho' I get a surfeit of praise and admiration, I seem not to touch a spark, except for passing moments, and I see it veiled by a strange awe and embarrassment and then go out."[23]

Chambers found Europe intriguingly different from North Carolina and even from New York and Washington. His experiences there opened his eyes to a more sophisticated world. He called France "the most civilized and cared-for country" he had ever seen.[24] And the young first lieutenant was captivated by the women he encountered there. "I hope you don't mind my writing frankly about these girls," he wrote to his mother. "You can't ignore them any more than you can ignore the sea. They are just a part of the place. France is different from America."[25]

Perhaps Chambers would one day draw from his own experiences in France, when, in his biography of Stonewall Jackson, he described young Jackson's encounters with the opposite sex in Mexico City: "It would have been remarkable indeed if a healthy, vigorous young man did not seek to know more about these alien and strangely alluring girls and young women who were beginning to make his blood tingle."[26]

In France, Chambers observed that blacks enjoyed freedoms unavailable to them in the segregated South. "In my hotel lives an American Negro prize-fighter, a fine-looking figure of a man, very well dressed. He eats . . . where I eat sometimes, and he talks very pleasurably and intimately with the French."[27] Chambers also was struck by the multinational and multiracial nature of the Allied troops: "Great numbers of them. Every nationality, race, color, and variety of uniform."[28]

While on liberty for two weeks, Chambers became engaged to a young American woman who was working for the YWCA canteen service with the American Expeditionary Force. It was by far the most serious romance of his life to date. Nell Lewis, at twenty-six, was two years his junior. She was the daughter of Dr. Richard Henry Lewis, a Raleigh physician; and she was the half sister of Ivey Lewis, a prominent member of the faculty of the University of Virginia, and Kemp Plummer Lewis, the owner of a prosperous textile mill.[29]

Nell had graduated from Smith College and worked in New York City for a year. She returned to Raleigh "filled with liberal ideas," according to her niece.[30] Thereafter, women in her duly alerted family would not be allowed to attend Smith and other eastern colleges but would be enrolled securely at either Sweet Briar in Virginia or St. Mary's College in North Carolina.

Chambers and Nell almost certainly had become romantically involved prior to Europe. Although the relationship likely began in North Carolina, the two lived in New York at the same time, and probably dated there. Arriving in France, Nell was stationed in Nice; and Chambers arranged to spend his liberty with her.

The YWCA's strict standards for leave in Nice would have made courtship difficult: "Girls must not lunch or dine with men without permission. . . . They must not smoke or drink in public. . . . They must have a chaperon if looking on at hotel dances." Undeterred by the ever-vigilant supervision of Nell's superior, a Mrs. Williams, Chambers could report to his mother that he and Nell were together "every second she was not on duty."[31]

The two planned their marriage and their future, and Nell's father sent her the money to buy a trousseau. "Both of us want the date fixed with some degree of accuracy," Chambers wrote to his father, "so that at the very least it will be a mark to shoot at, and both of us want it to be soon."[32]

In spite of her engagement to Chambers, Nell had no shortage of male admirers among the troops. "I was in love with you and I am more so now that you are engaged," one soldier pined. "Somehow I knew that Lieutenant Chambers was your fiance. If I ever see him, I shall tell him he is the luckiest man in the world."[33] Another love-struck doughboy gushed, "I'm perfectly wild about your eyes and that merry little laugh. Nobody but that somebody from Raleigh NC could do it."[34]

Chambers worried about his prospects for post-war employment and his ability to support a wife. "I have no illusions about the difficulties," he confided to his father. "I know my own standing financially and I know that so far as being assured of a living competence for myself goes, nothing in my achievements thus far gives me any assurance about anything. And so far as having anything like a profession or any standing in a recognized line of work, again there is nothing."[35]

His fiancée shrugged off these concerns. A "modern" woman, by Chambers's definition, she planned to work, either as a stenographer or as a commercial artist. She had worked previously as a stenographer for National City Bank in New York City and cared little what folks in Charlotte might think. "It's the twentieth century," Chambers quoted her to his father. "Don't you know you are robbing me if you don't let me share the struggle with you?"[36]

Chambers viewed his responsibility more conventionally. As he considered potential livelihoods, he was certain of one thing: journalism was the only career that interested him. And he was willing to start from the bottom so that he would learn the newspaper business thoroughly enough to someday edit his own paper.[37]

With his father acting on his behalf, the younger Chambers learned that the University of North Carolina was seeking a publications director. Although he hoped to find "straight newspaper work" and worried that Chapel Hill was too secluded, he saw much to recommend the position. He asked his father to hedge with the university until he returned that summer.[38]

The love affair came to an unhappy ending in late December of 1919 when Nell's overbearing father, intolerant of her independence and liberal attitudes, insisted that the couple break off the relationship. One of Lewis's nieces recalls that Dr. Lewis told Chambers his daughter had a "mental weakness."[39] After her breakup with Chambers, Nell did in fact receive treatment for a nervous condition. It is unclear whether she suffered actual instability or whether her father created the condition as a means of reining in his free-thinking daughter. Chambers's thoughts regarding the broken engagement and Nell's mental state, while interesting as matters of speculation, unfortunately must remain just that.

Throughout the rest of her life, Nell would seek a variety of cures for her nervous condition in sanatoriums and from faith healers and Christian Science practitioners.[40] She also received treatment for alcoholism.[41]

Despite her ostensible instability, Nell Lewis went on to develop a notable career as a crusading journalist for the *Raleigh News and Observer,* where in her weekly column, "Incidentally," she relentlessly campaigned for women's rights; academic freedom; penal, legal, and labor reform; and a wide range of other social improvements. Mentored and encouraged by H. L. Mencken, like so many other southern writers and journalists, she published widely in national magazines, including the *Nation* and *American Mercury.*[42] Lewis ran for state legislature in the Democratic primary of 1928, read law and was admitted to the bar in 1929, and from 1937 to 1944 taught English and Bible studies at St. Mary's College in North Carolina. Later in life, following World War II, she grew increasingly conservative and renounced many of her earlier positions. Convinced that Communists had infiltrated reform movements and the University of North Carolina, she turned on many of her former allies in her newspaper column.[43]

Chambers and Lewis would spend their entire careers working in the same region for the area's major newspapers. They met again on at least one occasion, and they must have closely followed each other's columns. Another of Lewis's nieces says that her aunt never fully recovered from the breakup with Chambers or forgave her father for his interference. Nell Lewis never married.[44]

Had Chambers and Lewis's betrothal not been thwarted, would the union have enhanced their careers and journalistic impact? There would be a precedent for a relationship of this sort; Julian and Julia Harris, vital members of the small coterie of southern liberal journalists in this era, worked in concert, courageously editing the *Columbus Enquirer-Sun.*[45] Would the history of southern journalism differ markedly if Chambers and Lewis had joined together in a similar partnership? It seems unlikely. Chambers would never lack stimulation or encouragement for his work in his future marriage, and Lewis would fill the void in her personal life with a fierce dedication to her causes.

4

The Emergence of an Editor

AFTER THE ARMISTICE, Chambers returned to Chapel Hill. There he served as director of the University of North Carolina News Service for two years. His duties consisted of publicity work and reporting, and many of his newspaper articles were published by presses throughout the state.

Then in 1921 he resigned to join the staff of the *Greensboro Daily News.* Chambers had conducted a thorough and critical search for his first real newspaper job and had chosen the *Daily News* because of its reputation as a highly literate and nonpartisan paper. He worked briefly as a reporter and quickly rose to the position of city editor.[1]

Only four years after joining the *News,* Chambers was appointed associate editor (editorial writer) and worked in that position for another four years. His apprenticeship in the rough-and-tumble world of the newsroom had been brief, and his rapid promotion into the scholarly atmosphere of the editorial office removed him from the day-to-day workings of the paper. Although he would display a reporter's curiosity throughout his career, Chambers would remain better suited by dint of professional background and temperament to working intimately with a few close colleagues in an editorial suite than to managing a reporting staff.

His predecessor as associate editor of the *News* was Gerald W. Johnson. The two remained close friends and regularly corresponded throughout their careers. Although Chambers would encounter little support among his peers in the Virginia press for his opposition to massive resistance, other prominent journalists south of the Mason-Dixon Line, such as Johnson, helped sustain him during his five-year editorial campaign.

Johnson, upon reading Chambers's first editorial, offered only faint praise but strongly worded advice:

> You are under the most solemn obligation to speak as much of the truth as you are able to speak . . . [and] to use all the brains God gave you all the time, even when it is likely to be highly unpleasant and even dangerous to use them. . . . The newspaper editor who is afraid to stand up to be laughed at, or sworn at, is . . . a slacker.
>
> By shouting with the mob you gain a fat pay-check and a soft job; the chamber of commerce and the Rotary Club may call you a great editor,

but the good God who gave you the brains to be an editor will know you for a louse.[2]

Johnson left the paper in 1924 to accept a faculty position in the University of North Carolina's journalism department. A gifted essayist, critic, and historian, he later wrote for the Baltimore "Sunpapers," where he earned the appellation "Baltimore's second sage." (H. L. Mencken was acclaimed the city's first savant.) Johnson went on to devote his considerable talents to freelance writing and the authorship of over twenty-five books, including biographical studies of Andrew Jackson, Woodrow Wilson, and Franklin Roosevelt.[3] There is much in Chambers's career to suggest that he took Johnson's early advice to heart.

Although most North Carolina newspapers at the time served as party vehicles, the *Greensboro Daily News,* under the editorship of Earle Godbey, practiced a policy of genuine independence.[4] The *News*'s tradition of responsible journalism nurtured Chambers's development of his own editorial philosophy.

Reflecting on the paper's role in encouraging moderation, Chambers later wrote that in the early decades of the century, courage had been required in order to be politically independent, to represent minority views fairly, and to print unpopular news. Chambers and his colleagues had set about determinedly to "lift the state not only from the mire of its old roads but from the clinging habits of allegiance that had lost their validity."[5]

In Greensboro, while he was city editor, Chambers met the woman who would become his wife. Roberta Strudwick Glenn, a graduate of North Carolina College for Women (now the University of North Carolina at Greensboro) and the daughter of Greensboro attorney Robert Cincinattus Strudwick, was the society editor of the *Daily News.*[6]

Her mother, Sally Patterson Lewis Strudwick, had died when Roberta was thirteen, and Roberta lived with and kept house for her father. She was divorced and the mother of a young son, Robert. The marriage and separation had been painful; and throughout her life, even among her closest friends, Roberta never discussed her first marriage. She had given little thought to marrying again.[7]

During the early stages of his courtship of Roberta, Chambers continued to correspond with and visit both Nell Lewis and Ruth Draper. Apparently in spring 1926, while visiting Ruth, Chambers told her that their relationship would best remain platonic; and after a period of wounded pride, she acquiesced. "Friendship is too precious for egotism to destroy," she wrote Chambers. "I pray Heaven to guard against that danger. If I can know that my faith in you helps you to grow, gives you happiness and courage, then I am happy."[8] Despite the fact that Draper's prospects for a romantic relationship with Chambers had ended, she still attended closely to his mention of Lewis. "I wish you had told me more of your meeting with her," Draper wrote. "She must be an interesting person. I sometimes think you two may drift together again."[9]

Although Lewis lived nearby in Raleigh, and Chambers followed her column in the *News and Observer,* there is no evidence to indicate that he retained any romantic interest in her; his attention was becoming more and more directed toward Roberta.

On the surface Nell, Ruth, and Roberta had little in common, but all displayed conspicuous intelligence and exceptional independence. That Chambers found these qualities attractive in a potential mate suggests progressive views on women's roles for a southern male of his era.

Chambers and Roberta dated for four years before marrying on September 15, 1928. Her father was ill, and the ceremony took place in his bedroom. A small reception followed downstairs.[10]

In 1929 another momentous event occurred in Chambers's life when Louis Jaffe offered him the position of associate editor of the *Virginian-Pilot,* Norfolk's prominent morning newspaper. Jaffe's personal and editorial campaign against lynching and his racial activism had earned the editor acclaim and the *Virginian-Pilot*'s editorial page a national reputation.[11] In Tidewater, Virginia, the *Pilot* and its journalistic ancestors had also long enjoyed a reputation for strong advocacy of Norfolk's public school system. Indeed, former editors of the Norfolk *Virginian* and the Norfolk *Landmark* had served as school superintendents, and their newspaper offices frequently had hosted school-board meetings.[12]

When Jaffe's associate editor, John Newton Aiken, left the *Pilot* for the *Baltimore Evening Sun,* his departure placed the full weight of the *Pilot*'s editorial responsibilities on Jaffe and whatever freelance support he could muster. Anxious to identify a replacement, he initiated a search for "a budding Gerald Johnson—Grover Hall—Julian Harris—a well-educated, level-headed liberal who can write intelligently, vigorously, and attractively about the things the editorial page holds out to discuss and illumine, and can do it without alienating the customers. That . . . is no mean trick."[13] The hunt for Aiken's successor reveals Jaffe's and Chambers's connectedness to a small but vital circle of southern liberal journalists.

Gerald Johnson strongly recommended Chambers to Jaffe. "He has the stuff—education, intelligence, a graceful style, intellectual balance, liberal spirit, and as for personality he is simply marvelously equipped," Johnson wrote.[14]

Grover Hall, editor of the *Montgomery Advertiser,* seconded Johnson's recommendation, although he had never met Chambers: "It strikes me that whoever is helping Godbey . . . is fit to be on any paper."[15] Hall also suggested W. J. Cash, who was in the early stages of writing what would become arguably the major book on the region, *Mind of the South*. Hall said that he believed Cash had recovered sufficiently from a recent nervous breakdown to return to work.[16] While the brilliant but erratic and tortured Cash would undoubtedly have added much to the *Pilot*'s editorial page, it is difficult to imagine anyone less suited to facing the deadlines of daily journalism and to working with the brusque and demanding Jaffe.[17] (Tragically, Cash, who suffered from depression his entire life, would commit suicide in 1941, the same year Knopf published *Mind of the South*.)[18]

The *Pilot*'s editor was familiar with the liberal viewpoint of the *Daily News*'s editorial page and Chambers's work there, but he despaired of ever dislodging Chambers from the paper.[19] Johnson had tried mightily to persuade Chambers to join the *Baltimore Sun* but to no avail: "What's the matter with the damn fool I don't know—too much married, I fear—but he seems to be afflicted with an inertia that will hold him in Greensboro the rest of his days."[20]

But unknown to Jaffe and Johnson, Chambers was becoming increasingly frustrated with the politics of the Greensboro News Company, owners of the *News* and the *Greensboro Daily Record*. Chambers perceived editor Godbey's influence as waning and managing editor A. L. Stockton's power increasing with President E. B. Jeffress. A textile strike in Marion, North Carolina, which occurred simultaneously to Jaffe's search for an associate editor, provided the impetus for Chambers to consider leaving his comfortable position in Greensboro.

Marion mill workers toiled in appalling conditions, commonly receiving wages of less than ten dollars for a fifty-five- to sixty-hour work week. On October 2, 1929, a local sheriff and his heavily armed, heavily drinking, and hastily sworn-in deputies fired into the backs of a crowd of striking workers, killing six and seriously wounding twenty-five.[21]

Stockton's story on the shooting appeared on the *News*'s front page the following day. The lead sentence of the report set the tone for what was to follow: "The community building, erected by the Marion Manufacturing company for the pleasure and comfort of its [workers], . . . was tonight an armed camp with military companies from Salisbury and Winston-Salem quartered there."[22] (Stockton omitted mention that workers were charged ten cents each time they bathed, swam in the pool, or bowled in the community center—a substantial sum, given their low salaries—or that tomorrow's wages too frequently were spent purchasing today's groceries at the company store.)[23] "The battle was between officers and strikers," Stockton continued, "but the opinion was expressed tonight that unquestionably some of those wounded, if not killed, were hit by bullets from strikers' pistols."[24] The remainder of the story was overwhelmingly devoted to presenting the viewpoints of the mill's president, R. W. Baldwin, and the sheriff, Oscar F. Adkins.

The *Nation*'s account of the shooting differed substantially from Stockton's. It called the living conditions in the mill village "morally and humanly, almost indescribably degrading."[25] It quoted Baldwin as applauding the marksmanship of the law officers and portrayed him as heartless and ignorant regarding the operations of his mill. The *Nation* depicted Adkins as a flunky and a simpleton.

The day following Stockton's report, an editorial appeared in the *News* that in all likelihood was written by Chambers. Identical in style and in voice to the editorials Chambers would one day write attacking massive resistance, it castigated law officials and urged the state's lethargic legislature to act to prevent future tragedies.

> Surely it must have sunk in to the state . . . that in no instance of disorder anywhere in the state these months has any sheriff, deputy sheriff or policeman handled any situation confronting him in a manner to create confidence in him or in what he stands for. The state has little truth about this Marion killing; perhaps it will never have the full truth. But it knows a squad of officers thrown face to face with a real problem not only did not solve it but so acted that the end was tragedy.
>
> . . . The tragedy behind this tragedy is that no wise leadership has developed, no voice has been heard to which men will listen, no man has loomed large before the combatants to whom they look with confidence and assurance. That is the state's failure. It is the state's disgrace. It is the state's most serious problem and strongest need.[26]

The sheriff and his deputies ultimately were exonerated.[27] Johnson reported to Jaffe that Stockton, who "always believed in better and more murders," had given Chambers "a sharp case of spiritual and dam [*sic*] nigh physical vomiting."[28] Johnson advised Jaffe to make Chambers an offer.

Chambers interviewed with Jaffe in Norfolk in October, and the editor, who normally was not given to flattery, was overwhelmed. "I am enormously attracted to you," Jaffe declared, "both as a person and an intellect. . . . We have the makings of a great team. . . . This team, for the good of both of us, ought to be consummated." Jaffe went on to quote Shakespeare and to implore Chambers to accept the position: "There is a tide in the affairs of men, which taken at flood leads on to fortune." These lines, he said, had been stirring in his mind all morning. "I do powerfully believe that this tide now waits on you. Don't let it give you the slip! Cast out fear. Come. The time will come, I do believe, when you will regard this as a historic letter."[29] Chambers accepted the position largely because of his high regard for Jaffe's ability as an editor.[30]

Jaffe, who wanted Chambers to start work immediately, grew increasingly frustrated by what followed. Johnson had confided in him Chambers's current salary of $3,900, and Jaffe based his five-thousand-dollar offer on that figure. First, Chambers bargained for more money; and Jaffe, after a meeting with his publisher, raised the offer to $5,200, with a promise of a raise to $5,500 within a year.[31] Then Chambers, concerned that he not inconvenience the *News*, asked for a series of extensions before reporting to Norfolk, so that his successor could be found. A search for an apartment further delayed his arrival.

Chambers arrived in Norfolk and began work in December. Johnson cautioned the brusque Jaffe to handle his new associate with "kid gloves" for the first few weeks: "Should you find him a trifle touchy during the first week or so . . . it is a passing phase, without significance. . . . Under his surface enamel, the fellow is shy. But under that is a substratum of hard, common sense, which is the real Lenoir. Once he has got his feet under him and knows where he stands, you can give it to him and as hot as you know how, and he won't bat an eye."[32] A few weeks later Jaffe wrote to Johnson that he had "ordered [his] deportment accordingly," that everything was running smoothly, and that Chambers was measuring fully up to his expectations.[33] Chambers would serve as Jaffe's associate for fifteen years.

Louis Wilson, a prominent faculty member at the University of North Carolina, was disappointed by Chambers's departure. (The university's library, named after Wilson, would one day hold Chambers's papers.) Four years after assuming his position as associate editor of the *Greensboro Daily News*, Chambers had become, in Wilson's view, North Carolina's most liberal editorial writer. "All the liberal forces in the state will miss you," Wilson lamented.[34]

At the *Pilot*, the work between Chambers and Jaffe was divided evenly, with Chambers doing a little more writing than the editor. The associate editor averaged three editorials a day and, although much of his writing focused on national and international issues, he wrote extensively on the South and racial topics, including lynching.[35]

Although Chambers was nearly as experienced a journalist as Jaffe, the *Pilot*'s editor undoubtedly exerted an important intellectual influence upon him. Jaffe's championship of fair play, honed by the devastation and racial prejudice he had witnessed as an Army officer and journalist in Europe during and after World War I, undoubtedly augmented Chambers's own liberal views. And Jaffe's insistence that his editors keep abreast of a broad spectrum of opinion through the arch-conservative to ultra-liberal reading matter he brought in each day in his dark-green linen book bag provided invaluable editorial training. Chambers admired Jaffe tremendously.[36]

In addition to his writing for the *Pilot*, Chambers contributed articles and editorials on an occasional basis to the *Baltimore Evening Sun,* the *New York Herald Tribune,* and the *New York Times Watch-Tower* section. The *Watch-Tower* focused on regional news stories and editorials and was edited by eminent journalist Arthur Krock and, later, Harold A. Littledale. Virginius Dabney, the editor of the *Richmond Times-Dispatch,* was the regular *Watch-Tower* correspondent for the three-state region, which consisted of Virginia, North Carolina, and West Virginia. In Dabney's absence Chambers substituted, and Littledale seemed to prefer his reporting and writing: "There has been none better in the section, and I say that feeling that the best in the *Watch-tower* is of an exceptionally high order."[37]

Chambers also found time to participate in a range of integrated activities intended to advance race relations, serving on both the Norfolk and the Virginia Commissions on Inter-Racial Cooperation.[38]

Although Chambers and Jaffe shared professional values and a similar social consciousness, they differed greatly in their personal styles. Jaffe could be brusque, demanding, and intimidating in his interactions. A longtime city legislator once confided that when he answered his telephone and heard "This is Jaffe," invariably any information the editor requested immediately vanished from his mind.[39] Many people were "put off" by Jaffe, according to Alonzo Dill, who served as Jaffe's associate editor throughout the 1940s. "He was rough. He could not suffer fools, [but] if you knew him, he was very, very warm."[40]

Jaffe reluctantly participated in the civic and social activities expected of a newspaper editor, but he was reclusive and revealed himself best in his editorials. Some of his introversion may have been due to the alienation he experienced because of his Jewish heritage. If Jaffe took controversial stands—as he did with regularity—he was aware that some readers would say behind his back, "That's what you get from a Jew editor."[41] (Jaffe, who converted to Episcopalianism in the early 1920s, felt little affinity for organized religion, even the Jewish faith of his upbringing.)[42]

Chambers was more genteel and less aggressive than Jaffe. "Lenoir came from the gentlemanly precincts of Woodberry Forest and the gentle atmosphere of the University of North Carolina, and Louis probably wouldn't have gone to a fine college unless he'd lived in the shadow of one," explained Dill.[43] Chambers, who was confident of his place in Norfolk society and displayed a graceful and natural courtesy, was uncomfortable with personal conflict. Still, the associate editor was more than willing to express unpopular and critical opinions in his writing.[44]

Their differing personalities notwithstanding, the two men worked well together, as close friends. Jaffe was "a tip-top man to work with," Chambers wrote to Gerald Johnson. "I respect . . . and like him immensely."[45]

Despite the associate editor's overall satisfaction with his work at the

Pilot and his closeness to Jaffe, he actively sought positions with other newspapers. Jaffe, only three years older than Chambers, would likely remain the paper's editor until his retirement. And Chambers was dissatisfied with his salary; ten years after being hired, he had not received a raise in pay.

He was, however, unwilling to serve as editor of a newspaper whose editorial policy conflicted with his own deeply held liberal beliefs. Asked by the publisher of the *St. Louis Star-Times* to consider accepting a position there as editor, Chambers based his decision on the editorial policy of the paper, explaining that regardless of the attractiveness of the offer, he felt he could be neither effective nor happy in an atmosphere incompatible with his deeply ingrained liberal philosophy.[46]

While on the *Pilot*'s staff, Chambers received an attractive offer of an associate editorship in Pittsburgh. As a consequence he secured a promise from the management of Norfolk Newspapers, Inc., the owners of the *Ledger-Dispatch* as well as the *Virginian-Pilot,* that he would receive the next editorial appointment.[47]

5

A Fish Out of His Pond

IN 1944 THE elderly editor-in-chief of the *Norfolk Ledger-Dispatch*, Douglas Gordon, died, and Chambers assumed the editorship. Chambers's seniority and ability made him the obvious choice for the opening, and the opportunity to assume editorial leadership and receive a concomitant salary increase held great appeal for him.

Nevertheless, the move had serious drawbacks. The *Ledger-Dispatch*, the afternoon paper, which did not publish a Sunday edition, was considered the lesser of the two papers both in reputation and in circulation. Moreover, the relationship with his associate editor was sensitive. Joseph A. Leslie, Jr., Douglas Gordon's associate editor and a future editor of the *Ledger*, resented Chambers's appointment. He had served loyally under Gordon for many years, working six days a week—often under trying conditions—and deeply desired to be appointed editor.[1] Frustrated by perpetual number-two status and a perception that his contributions to the paper were unappreciated, he had become cynical. He resented that a contemporary, Chambers, was viewed by both staff and management as an editor of national caliber, while he was not.[2]

Leslie was an experienced journalist who had served on the staffs of several prominent Virginia newspapers besides the *Virginian-Pilot* and the *Ledger-Dispatch*. A native of southwestern Virginia and a graduate of the University of Richmond, he held the stereotypical political and social views of the South. Leslie was connected by marriage to the state's ruling political machine, the Byrd organization. His wife, Nell, was the daughter of long-time clerk of the state senate, E. R. ("Ebbie") Combs, Senator Harry F. Byrd's closest associate and chairman of the State Compensation Board. Leslie was somewhat ingenuous regarding tokens of fealty Combs regularly received from state employees concerned about their jobs and salaries. Alonzo Dill marveled, "Joe used to say rather naively, 'My father-in-law is so lovable they send him hams and Scotch whiskey.' "[3] Leslie was a member of the Fraternal Order of the Masons, as were Byrd and Norfolk mayor W. Fred Duckworth.[4]

Regardless of his personal feelings concerning Chambers's promotion, Leslie had to work closely with him and, to his credit, developed a friendly relationship with the new editor. "Leslie and I team up all right," Chambers wrote. "He is steady and reliable and full of common sense, and I count him a good friend."[5]

Because of the *Ledger*'s secondary rank vis-à-vis the *Pilot,* Chambers's six years as editor of the *Ledger* often disappointed him. His editorials were much less widely read than they had been at the *Pilot,* and they received scant notice from his friends and colleagues. What was more important, *Pilot* staffers, perhaps unfairly, considered the *Ledger* inferior. The position as editor of the lesser paper would not have been an illustrious one in which to end a career. Many of Chambers's friends felt that he was "a fish out of his pond."[6]

Chambers, however, persevered, and with Leslie as his only associate editor, established an editorial philosophy very similar to that of the *Virginian-Pilot.*[7] White readers who embraced traditional racial attitudes routinely complained to the management of Norfolk Newspapers, Inc. "There is plenty of discussion among your readers concerning your new policy of pro Negroism," one subscriber complained. Chambers refused to identify people by race in the paper's reporting and editorials—a common practice in many southern newspapers.[8] Additionally, he declined to publish letters he considered likely "to incite emotionalism and have an inflammatory effect rather than to contribute thoughtfully to the solutions of extremely difficult [racial] problems."[9]

Many of Chambers's years as editor of the *Ledger* were anxious and worrisome for him on a personal level. Previously always vigorous, he had recently developed some health problems. Two years prior to assuming the editorship, he had experienced three incidents of paroxysmal tachycardia, a condition marked by a rapid heart rate. His physician had prescribed a capsule of quinidine a day.[10] Although the ailment was not life threatening, it likely created some distress.

The wartime military service of his stepson, Robert, caused great anxiety. A Marine Corps lieutenant, Robert participated in several combat operations in the Pacific. He was slightly wounded on Guam and, as a naval gunfire spotter, was the only officer in his company to survive the invasion of Iwo Jima, where he was awarded the Navy Cross for heroism.[11] Chambers, from the time of his marriage on, had viewed Robert as his own son and was deeply devoted to him.

The children, Robert and Elisabeth, were raised by their parents to be respectful of blacks and to be sensitive to the racial injustices that were common in Norfolk. Elisabeth told of a time her brother was incensed over the treatment of a black man by a city streetcar driver. Drivers often treated blacks discourteously. Public transportation was segregated, and although trolleys and buses had front and rear doors, blacks had to board from the front and squeeze past whites to reach their seats in the back. Robert had watched a black man show his pass to a driver and gesture as if to ask if he could board the crowded trolley from the rear. The driver nodded his approval; and as the man walked toward the rear door, the trolley drove away.

Robert wrote to his father's paper about the incident and signed his letter "Irate Citizen." The day after the letter was printed, the manager of the transit company complained to Chambers in person, insisting that the incident had not taken place and demanding to know the identity of the author of the letter to the editor. The interaction came to an abrupt halt when Chambers revealed that his son was the writer.[12]

In 1947, while serving as editor of the *Ledger,* Chambers began work on his biography of Stonewall Jackson. Chambers had originally intended to write a book about World War I, but William Morrow and Company editors Helen Brinkley King and Frances Phillips urged him to write about Jackson. Although writing the book was a labor of love, it was also an arduous experience. When he began the project, Chambers knew little about Jackson, and Phillips set an unrealistic writing schedule for him. Morrow had hoped to bring the book out in the fall of 1950, but by the summer of 1949 Chambers was still painstakingly researching his topic and had not written a word.[13] Chambers's biography would be particularly comprehensive and critical, focusing on much more than military history. He would explore and document in detail minutiae including Jackson's dietary habits, his obsession with his health, and his many eccentricities.[14]

Some of Chambers's reasons for writing the book were pragmatic. He confided to a Morrow editor that he was motivated in part by "the high cost of living."[15] Chambers was also stimulated by the desire to enhance his professional standing as a journalist and historian. Gerald Johnson, Chambers's former colleague and mentor at the *Greensboro Daily News,* urged him on, citing other prominent regional editors—Douglas Freeman and Virginius Dabney of Richmond and Jonathan Daniels of the *Raleigh News and Observer*—who had "solidified" their professional standing with outside publications.[16]

Daniels himself was less optimistic about Chambers's ability to complete such a mammoth undertaking. He once confided to Robert Mason that Chambers would never finish the book. "He said a man [Chambers's] age would come to the place where he could not proceed. He was wrong about that, but I think [Chambers] came pretty close to [giving up] once or twice."[17]

6

Liberal Journalism in the South

THE *Virginian-Pilot*'s editorial stance on racial issues and that of the *Ledger-Dispatch* during Chambers's editorship were atypical for white southern presses but not anomalous. Other newspapers in the region had similar histories of advocating racial understanding and cooperation. School desegregation was to become a signal event for southern liberal journalists, and the heady and confrontational politics of the time metamorphosed many. It is illuminating to consider Chambers within the context of the era's journalistic ferment and to explore the influences and forces that formed the crucible of the times.

For the South, the United States Supreme Court's 1954 decision in *Brown v. Board of Education* constituted nearly as tumultuous a watershed as the Civil War. The outlawing of segregated public schools impacted with explosive force on the region's politicians, its private citizens, and its press.

Still in the 1950s the primary dispenser of current news and opinion, the print media held enormous potential for swaying popular opinion. Variously employing the devices of slanting, candid advocacy, and outright agitation according to the zeal and scruples of the individual publications, the southern press had long taken sides on civil-rights issues. Its reaction to the *Brown* mandate would be a powerful factor in the debate that followed.

Shortly after the *Brown* decision was announced, the widely respected moderate editor of the *Raleigh* (North Carolina) *News and Observer,* Jonathan Daniels—sounding much like Lenoir Chambers—hopefully predicted that the South would respond to the Supreme Court's mandate "with the good sense and good will of the people of both races in a manner which [would] serve the children and honor America."[1]

Throughout the century many of the South's major cities had liberal newspapermen who, like Daniels and Chambers, campaigned for improved racial relations. For thirty-five years Louis Jaffe had played that role in Norfolk. Other leading liberal southern editors included Julian LaRose Harris of the *Columbus Empire-Sun;* Grover Hall of the *Montgomery Advertiser;* John Temple Graves II of the *Birmingham Age-Herald;* Hodding Carter II of the *Greenville* (Mississippi) *Delta-Democrat Times;* W. J. Cash of the *Charlotte News;* Ralph McGill of the *Atlanta Constitution;* Virginius Dabney of the

Richmond Times-Dispatch; Mark Ethridge of the *Macon Telegraph and News* and later the *Louisville Courier-Journal;* and Barry Bingham, also of the *Courier-Journal.*[2]

The racial views of many liberal southern newspapermen had been shaped by their experiences while stationed overseas during World War I. "In Europe," John Kneebone writes, "these newsmen encountered new sets of values and behaviors that they inevitably compared with those of their South. At the beginning of their careers, then, they had gained an awareness to the southern way of life."[3] This was the case with Chambers and to a larger extent with Jaffe, whose experiences in wartime Europe and following the war, as a member of the Red Cross News Service in the Balkans, had served to create in him an acute and lifelong sensitivity to injustice. After returning from Europe, Jaffe had translated this awareness into pioneer advocacy for racial justice in the South.

During the first decade of Jaffe's editorship of the *Virginian-Pilot,* a rash of racial violence and Ku Klux Klan activity had erupted in Virginia. Newport News, across the harbor from Norfolk, had become a center of Klan doings, and it was alleged that Norfolk's chief of police was an active member.[4]

In August of 1926 a mob of fifty men—some disguised in women's clothing—entered Wytheville's jail, where Raymond Bird, a black man accused of criminally attacking a young white woman, slept. (The woman had brought charges some months after the offense allegedly occurred.) The mob shot Bird to death, beat his head to a pulp, dragged his corpse behind a car for nine miles, hung his body in a tree in the woman's yard, and riddled it with bullets. Local law authorities arrested no one.[5]

Within little over a year's time, a number of other violent racial incidents occurred. A band of hooded Klansmen in Virginia Beach abducted Rev. Vincent D. Warren, a Roman Catholic priest who had accompanied a group of black parishioners on an outing, and sped him away in an automobile. The kidnappers trained their pistols on Warren as he prayed with his rosary, interrogated him, and after learning that he had not encouraged whites and blacks to mix for immoral purposes, released him unharmed.[6]

In Whitesburg, Kentucky, near the Virginia border, a four-hundred-person mob composed primarily of Virginians hacked through the jail roof and seized Leonard Woods, a black man accused of murdering a white foreman of a mine. A caravan of over one hundred cars escorted Woods across the border, where the mob placed a chain around his neck, hoisted him into the air, shot him more than six hundred times, and burned his body.[7]

And in two separate incidents in Bristol, masked men thought to be Klansmen reportedly flogged four white women, perhaps prostitutes. The precise nature of the women's offense is unclear, but Bristol was notorious for prostitution; and it would have taken a particularly egregious violation of mores, such as servicing black customers as some white prostitutes in that city did, to trigger such a harsh and public punishment.[8]

Unlike the editors of the other major Virginia newspapers, the *Richmond News-Leader* and the *Richmond Times-Dispatch,* who preferred not to publicize Ku Klux Klan activities, hoping the problem would go away, Jaffe directly and forcefully attacked the Klan.[9] His editorials drew a range of responses from his targets.

Imperial Kleagle Edward Young Clarke, a confident if slightly dull-witted practitioner of the modern "sciences" of public relations and personal salesmanship, took the high road and chatted Jaffe up: "If I could step into your office and have a personal conversation . . . you and I [would] agree on the need and the value of this organization and there [would] be no word of criticism in your heart."[10] The local klavern's communication combined creative punctuation with a basic persuasive appeal: "This-is-just-to-let-you-know-that-there-are-approx.-10,000 men strong in the City of Norfolk. Remember—We know all—See All—hear all—a citizen."[11]

The *Pilot*'s editor deplored the "timidity" and "editorial reticence" that prevented his peers in Virginia's press from attacking the Klan by "dipping their pens in vitriol and cauterizing this infamy from the first day of its public appearance," as he had done.[12]

In addition to attacking the Klan, Jaffe launched a vigorous personal and editorial campaign encouraging Virginia lawmakers to adopt strong anti-lynching legislation.[13] With the assistance of Monroe Nathan Work, a sociological researcher at Tuskegee Institute, he carefully documented each lynching for the purpose of educating the public as to the horrors of lynching and the need to enact legislation that would effectively deal with the crime. In a personal appeal to Virginia's Governor Harry F. Byrd, Jaffe wrote, "I hope you will find a means of forcing a showdown on this outrage—in the name of Virginia and in the name of decency." Byrd suggested that Jaffe outline his ideas regarding his proposed legislation and later presented them to the General Assembly. With few changes, the bill passed through the legislature and was signed by the governor on March 14, 1928. The law, which classified lynching as homicide and made each participant in a lynch mob an accessory to murder, virtually eliminated lynching in Virginia. Byrd later wrote that Jaffe's editorials and personal solicitation, more than any other influence, had encouraged him to introduce the legislation.[14]

Jaffe was awarded the Pulitzer Prize for distinguished editorial writing as typified by "An Unspeakable Act of Savagery," an editorial prompted by the lynching of a black man in Houston, Texas, during the 1928 Democratic National Convention. Jaffe's award was the highest any Virginia newspaper writer had received.[15]

In the mid-twenties, H. L. Mencken, the witty and irreverent editor of the *Baltimore Sun* and critic, shook the complacency of southern writers who had not served in Europe and further inspired the region's war-veteran journalists. His scathing critique of the South, "The Sahara of the Bozart" (a play on the words *beaux arts*), castigated the southern states for their lack of intellectual and artistic achievement. He wrote, "There are single acres in Europe that house more first-rate men than all of the states south of the Potomac."[16]

Although Mencken classified Virginia as the most advanced southern state, he disdainfully dismissed the state's culture and anti-intellectualism: "Elegance, esprit, culture? Virginia has no art, no literature, no philosophy, no mind or aspiration of her own. Her education has sunk to the Baptist seminary level; not a single contribution to human knowledge has come out of her colleges in twenty-five years; she spends less than half upon her common schools, per capita, than any northern state spends. In brief, an intellectual Gobi or Lapland."[17]

Mencken's biting critique reverberated throughout the region and provoked a violent outcry from many who embraced the traditional mores. For years afterward he was furiously assailed. Younger and more sophisticated southerners, however, acknowledged the validity of his charges and responded positively to his criticisms by creating a more intellectual and artistic climate in their vicinities. The revival of southern letters in the 1920s was likely motivated to a great extent by Mencken's criticism.[18]

Louis Jaffe corresponded with Mencken, whose fulminations were greatly appreciated by the *Virginian-Pilot*'s editorial staff. Alonzo Dill told of the staff's admiration for Mencken. "You couldn't help but appreciate someone who was tearing down that sort of iconoclasm. . . . Jaffe admired Mencken; the same was true of Lenoir. . . . We would read the Baltimore papers regularly."[19]

Jaffe had met Mencken under particularly memorable circumstances. Mencken, a confirmed bachelor, astounded his guests during a dinner party by announcing his engagement to Sara Powell Haardt. His friends and colleagues were speechless. Deciding that Mencken was indeed serious, Jaffe, who had been awarded the Pulitzer the previous year, broke the uncomfortable silence by proclaiming, "You are to be congratulated, sir." The awkward quiet ended; and realizing they were not to be the brunts of a joke, Mencken's colleagues rushed forward to compliment him.[20]

It is interesting to speculate regarding the relationship between Jaffe and Mencken. Although Jaffe admired much in Mencken, he must have been troubled by Mencken's highly controversial defense of Germany during World War I and his inclination to underplay the dangers of early Hitlerism. Mencken had an abiding identification with German culture. Jaffe, a Jew by heritage if not by practice, held Germany to be responsible for both world wars and had expressed alarm over the inherent militancy and aggressiveness of the German people during his travels in Europe. The allusions to anti-Semitism and racial prejudice in Mencken's recently released diary suggest another possible source of dissonance.[21]

The Supreme Court's 1954 verdict in *Brown v. Board of Education of Topeka* confronted liberal southern journalists with a fork in the road. Unlike Lenoir Chambers, many of them were unwilling, perhaps unable, to accept the Court's decision; they tenaciously defended the concept of separate but equal. These writers, lobbying for the improvement of the condition of blacks within the confines of Jim Crow, focused primarily on the most egregious offense—lynching—and to a lesser extent on issues such as education, the poll tax, and poverty. To a degree, they were effective in bringing about improvements in the condition of blacks. Their rationale was pragmatic as well as altruistic; they maintained that positive race relations would also benefit white interests. A more moderate racial climate would serve to modernize the region as a whole and help attract outside industry.[22] This argument was likely in part a device to gain support for their humanistic causes.

Virginius Dabney's views on racial relations were illustrative of the unwillingness of many southern liberal journalists to reject separate but equal. Dabney, the son of Richard Heath Dabney, a prominent University of Virginia educator and historian, was one of the South's most renowned liberal newspaper editors.

In 1933 Dabney, who had been significantly influenced by Mencken, was one of two southern journalists to condemn the sentencing of eighteen-year-old Angelo Herndon, a black Communist, to two decades of hard labor for organizing a demonstration of workers to protest the inadequacy of relief programs in Fulton County, Georgia. Three years later, Dabney had argued against the poll tax and the next year had called for vigorous federal anti-lynching legislation.[23]

During World War II the editor had actually written an editorial urging the ending of segregation on Virginia's streetcars and buses. Transportation in the state remained segregated despite the fact that racial activist George Washington Cable had lauded the progressive nature of Virginia's public transportation system nearly sixty years earlier. "In Virginia," Cable wrote, "[blacks] may ride exactly as white people do and in the same cars."[24]

Louis Jaffe had been struck by the seeming contradiction between Dabney's editorials and his continued support for segregation and had written to the *Times-Dispatch*'s editor. Dabney justified his position by asserting that segregation on public transportation was impractical and that its elimination would not lead to further integration.[25]

In 1948 Dabney had received the Pulitzer Prize for editorial writing for his criticism of the poll tax and the South's one-party politics. By the time of *Brown v. Board,* however, the editor was openly referring to himself as a conservative and professing high esteem for archconservative Harry Byrd. Dabney defended segregation, maintaining that it facilitated good racial relations.[26]

During Virginia's massive resistance to public-school desegregation, Dabney, who because of his impressive southern heritage, his status as one of the region's leading spokesmen, and the strategic location of his newspaper in the state's capital, possessed a unique potential for moderating Virginia's racial crisis, would continue to defend segregation. The editor would argue that racial justice could exist under a system of segregation and that supporters of integration were irresponsible extremists. He contended that integration would lead to "racial amalgamation" and advanced the racist arguments of the northern segregationist writer, Carleton Putnam.[27]

In his memoirs, Dabney denied responsibility for the *Times-Dispatch*'s editorials during this period. He claimed that the management of the co-owned *Times-Dispatch* and *News Leader,* publisher D. Tennant Bryan and general managers John D. Wise and Alan S. Donnahoe, had strongly supported resistance to the *Brown* decision and that despite his personal reservations regarding massive resistance, he had recognized management's right to set editorial policy.[28]

This rationalization seems implausible and falls short of relieving Dabney of responsibility for his editorial position. An editor of his stature would have carried considerable influence with management and surely would have exerted it in matters of principle. All else failing in this case, had management held to a stance that conflicted with his convictions on such a far-reaching issue, one would expect Dabney to have proffered his resignation or to have sought another position as Chambers had done in Greensboro.

While Dabney's contortions were undoubtedly painful for him (his failure to take a stand consistent with his earlier stances must have embarrassed him among his peers in the national press), his abrupt about-face and the position he staked out were the rule, not the exception, within the regional press.[29] Southern newspapermen, such as Lenoir Chambers, who supported the *Brown* decision were in a distinct minority. Of fifty-three southern newspapers surveyed by Alfred Hero in the summer of 1954, four accepted the decision, seven took no position but observed that desegregation would result in "traumatic experiences for the South," and the remainder openly attacked the ruling.[30]

The region's journalists should have been aware of the potential dangers of irresponsible reporting. The *Atlanta Evening News*'s reporting and editorials were widely acknowledged to have been a prime cause of Atlanta's tragic race riot of 1906. The paper's editor, John Temple Graves, Sr., had fueled racist hysteria by publishing extra editions with sensational headlines regarding a surge of rapes of white women by black men.[31]

Regardless of this historical precedent, the majority of southern presses behaved irresponsibly. *New York Post* reporter Ted Poston called southern newspaper coverage of civil rights disgraceful and excoriated the region's press: "The majority of southern editors and publishers have been cynically defending a myth that they know to be untrue—white superiority, Negro indolence, and a baseless contention that the region's magnolia-scented values would triumph over the moral and legal might of the federal government."[32]

Hodding Carter considered the *Brown* decision and the ensuing court decisions, administrative orders, and congressional acts the South's greatest opportunity for leadership in this century. "But," he wrote, "most of the press, no less than most of the politicians, responded miserably."[33]

Still there were, in the tradition of Louis Jaffe, courageous southern newspapermen who questioned the region's reactionary racial policies and defiance of the Court. "In Virginia," Carter observed, "whose newspapers generally fell into line behind massive resistance, the *Norfolk Virginian-Pilot* . . . came out in favor of the Supreme Court decision and never wavered. If Kilpatrick's *News Leader* brayed 'This tyranny must be resisted step by step, inch by inch,' the *Virginian-Pilot* hailed the decision as a 'superb appeal to the wisdom, intelligence and leadership of the Southern state.' "[34]

Lenoir Chambers (seated) with unknown team member, Chapel Hill, 1913–14 (Courtesy of Elisabeth C. Burgess, Norfolk)

Lenoir Chambers, World War I (Courtesy of Elisabeth C. Burgess, Norfolk)

Lenoir Chambers with daughter, Elisabeth Lacy Chambers, May or June 1937 (Courtesy of Elisabeth C. Burgess, Norfolk)

Roberta and Lenoir Chambers with Waggles, late 1930s (Courtesy of Elisabeth C. Burgess, Norfolk)

Virginian-Pilot Editor Louis I. Jaffe (left) with Associate Editor Lenoir Chambers, early to mid 1930s (Courtesy of the *Virginian-Pilot*)

7

Chambers as Editor of the Virginian-Pilot

IN 1950 THE CHIMES of black churches in Norfolk tolled Louis Jaffe's death. The editor of the *Virginian-Pilot* was widely respected in the black community for his advocacy of minority rights; and on the day of his funeral, many black businesses on Norfolk's Church Street remained closed until after the services. Jaffe had been ill for some time but had refused to give up his newspaper duties. From his hospital bed, he was directing an editorial campaign to persuade the General Assembly to repeal the state's poll tax (which greatly diminished the size of the black electorate), when he succumbed to a heart attack.[1]

With Jaffe's death, Chambers became editor of the *Pilot*. He found it difficult to move into the editor's office, for he could not help thinking of it as Jaffe's.[2] Chambers had known Jaffe so intimately that he had often joked he knew Jaffe better than he knew his own wife.[3] "I do not have to say to you how much I shall miss this man," Chambers wrote. "I have worked in intimacy with him for fourteen years, and in friendly competition, down the hall, for the past six years; and we have faced together much of what life can bring. In the big issues, personal as well as public, he was a rock to lean on, and in all respects a delight."[4]

Chambers had no intention of trying to imitate Jaffe. To a friend he confided that he could only be himself. He praised his two associate editors, Harold Sugg and William Meacham, noting that they were still Jaffe's men, whom he would have to win over carefully and tactfully. He expressed confidence that in time he could win their allegiance.[5]

Leslie was promoted to the editorship of the *Ledger*, where he would be assisted by George J. Hebert, a capable newsman who had been promoted continually since beginning as an office boy many years before. Chambers's two associate editors at the *Pilot* were William Shands Meacham and the newly promoted Harold Gray Sugg.

Sugg, who was from Greenville, North Carolina, had graduated from Davidson College, studied at the University of North Carolina, and served briefly as the city editor of a small newspaper in Albemarle, North Carolina. He had worked for the *Pilot* as a reporter and as its staff correspondent for political affairs and city government from 1939 to 1948, minus a four-year interruption for military service in the Army during the Second World War.[6] Chambers insisted on having Sugg serve as his associate editor. Although Sugg was comparatively young, he had written editorials for Louis Jaffe and was highly respected for his writing ability.[7] Chambers developed a great fondness for this associate editor, and the two shared a warm professional and personal relationship.[8]

Chambers inherited his other associate editor, Virginia-born William Meacham, whose background included substantial journalistic training and experience and an appointment by Governor Colgate Darden to public service in 1942 as Virginia's first parole commissioner. Meacham had long been interested in penology and had written extensively on the subject.[9] When his appointment was not renewed by Governor Tuck, Meacham accepted a position with the *Virginian-Pilot* as Jaffe's associate editor. Jaffe's relationship with Meacham was tenuous, and Meacham impressed the high command of Norfolk Newspapers, Inc., poorly.[10]

Meacham, who was close to Chambers in age, coveted the editorial position opened by Jaffe's death, and Chambers's transfer to the *Pilot* frustrated him. Consequently their working relationship was at times difficult.[11] Robert Mason, who succeeded Sugg as associate editor, writes of their strained relations: "[Meacham's] vanity was enormous, and although Mr. Chambers took care not to prick it, tension between the two could be discomforting all round."[12]

In many ways Meacham was a paradoxical and comical figure. Although he mentioned his education at a branch of the College of William and Mary, the school had no record of his attendance.[13] And, despite his allusions to teaching at New York University, no evidence existed that he had served on that faculty.[14] Meacham, a large and bulky man with a mustache, was prideful and easily angered over imagined slights. Yet when a colleague stood up to him, he would quickly back away.

Chambers, who abhorred personal conflict, rarely confronted Meacham. "Probably there were confrontations between the two," Sugg reflected, "but I happily arranged not to be around when one seemed to be, or just might have been, aborning."[15]

Mason had similar memories. At some editorial conferences, he recalled, the hostility between the two would be thick. "I would wonder why in the hell they [didn't] get this thing out on the table and settle the differences between them." But, he noted, Chambers would not confront anyone with unpleasantness, and Meacham was in a poor position to do it.[16]

Robert C. Smith, the *Virginian-Pilot*'s young Sunday editor who was promoted to an associate editorship in the final days of Virginia's massive resistance, saw Meacham as no "heavyweight" and as lacking in passion and conviction. Chambers nevertheless deferred gallantly to Meacham because he had been the state parole commissioner. Chambers was careful to assign Meacham topics he could handle. "Meacham wasn't going to tackle Chambers on anything very seriously," said Smith, "and God knows I wasn't. I thought it was my great privilege to be working for him."[17]

Ironically, despite the fact that Meacham wrote many editorials on the massive resistance under Chambers's direction, his colleagues felt he would have been equally comfortable assisting Richmond editor Virginius Dabney (for whom he had worked for six years as an associate editor) or James Kilpatrick, both of whom lent their support to the resistance.[18]

Curiously, Meacham's detailed biography in *Who's Who in the World* contains no mention of his tenure as associate editor at the *Virginian-Pilot*.

In late 1957 Sugg assumed new responsibilities as assistant publisher and embarked on a program of study in Harvard Business School's advanced management program. Chambers and the publisher, Frank Batten, actively recruited Robert H. Mason, the editor and part owner of the *Sanford Daily Herald*, a small newspaper in North Carolina, to replace Sugg as associate editor. Mason was a versatile journalist, whom Chambers held in particularly high regard.

In some respects Mason's background closely resembled Chambers's. Although he had grown up in the small town of Mebane, North Carolina, Mason was a native of Charlotte, as was Chambers, and Mason had graduated from the editor's alma mater, the University of North Carolina. (The University of North Carolina's journalism program was highly rated, and its graduates routinely worked in the Tidewater, Virginia, area.) Mason had served as the city editor of the *Sanford Herald* and the Durham, North Carolina, *Herald* prior to becoming Sunday editor of the *Virginian-Pilot*, where he had worked closely with Louis Jaffe. After military service in the Navy in the Second World War, Mason had invested in the *Sanford Herald* and had returned to Sanford.[19] Chambers was particularly impressed by Mason's knowledge of southern history and by his efforts, as editor of the *Herald*, to improve race relations.[20]

Mason came to Norfolk with the understanding that he would serve as Chambers's associate editor for five years and would succeed the editor upon his retirement. Meacham viewed himself as the most deserving successor to Chambers. Consequently, the relationship between Mason and Meacham was somewhat delicate and uncomfortable.[21]

The editorial staff of the *Pilot* worked from roughly ten o'clock to six, five days a week; during periods of heavy work, the hours were extended. Editorial conferences, convened at approximately eleven o'clock, were thorough and involved.[22]

Reconstructing a typical editorial session, Robert Mason paints a vivid picture of Chambers—athletically trim, minus most of his hair but still in possession of the thin mustache he had acquired as a company commander in France, neatly dressed but not conspicuously fashionable. (He once exacted a pledge from a colleague to strangle any writer who ever described him posthumously as a "natty dresser.")[23] Togged in flannels or tweeds, seersucker in the hot and humid summer, Brooks Brothers shirt buttoned at the collar, striped tie slightly askew, and half glasses, he would pace the floor, flexing his knees, staring out the window occasionally, reading with exaggerated emphasis, and pointing to the individual with whom he was developing a position on a particular event or issue.[24]

Chambers directed the discussion and assigned and outlined the editorials, reserving for himself the topics on which he wished to expound personally. "Writing [editorials]," said Mason, "was a matter of fulfilling what the editor had agreed on and writing what the editor assigned. . . . Chambers was in command. If anything strayed beyond the limits, it would be either rewritten or set aside. Yet there were broad areas in which Chambers would accept the judgment of an associate entirely—Meacham in medical and sociological topics, for instance, and myself in naval and maritime affairs. I found it a pleasant and civilized way to make a living."[25]

In a speech to the Tidewater Builders Association, Chambers described the conferences and the procedure for writing editorials:

> [The editorial staff] may point out this subject or that one, which seems to require or permit analysis, interpretation, or comment. There may be much discussion or little. There may be disagreement, argument, uncertainty; and the conference may adjourn with the realization that we need to know much more than we can find out by any means within reach before we can attempt to say anything. At the end it is agreed what each will do and, broadly speaking, in what manner. For though nobody writes what he does not believe in, everyone writes for a newspaper and not as an individual. Late in the afternoon the fruits come back to the editor's desk, and they are gone over, often with a second conference between the writer and the editor; and there are changes, modifications, or on occasion abandonment of the whole business may follow.[26]

The editorial conferences could at times be tedious. Chambers tolerated more unfocused discussion than Jaffe would have allowed, and the conferences under Chambers's direction tended to last too long.[27] He recognized the problem. "I am afraid we talk too long. I am constantly trying to better our record, but the flesh is weak. We like to talk."[28]

Chambers's desk provided a constant source of amusement at the conferences. It was piled so high with newspapers, reference material, and edi-

torials-in-the-making that the editor had to stand to be seen by his associates. He jokingly maintained that he could produce any material at a moment's notice, as W. C. Fields did in a comedy routine that was popular at
the time.[29] Roberta was justifiably dismayed by his messy office and on occasion would appear with cleaning implements in hand.[30]

Chambers set high standards. He subscribed to the Jaffe editorial formula, which, according to Mason, emphasized first and foremost that "the
subject had to be absorbed."[31] Declaring that editorial writing "must be
informed, with the broadest possible background of personal capacity, education, reading, and experience," Chambers worked hard at his editorial duties and expected the same of his associates.[32]

If he lacked a thorough understanding of a point an associate might
make, he would say, "I'm not sure I take your meaning. Explain it to me
very slowly, just as though I were a child." The editor stressed to his associates the need for complete mastery of editorial topics; and he would press
them, never letting easy answers suffice.[33]

His rigorous expectations likely contributed to the discord with Meacham. Although the associate editor's editorials appeared to be knowledgeable, he had a knack for writing facilely after only cursory research. When
he consulted colleagues on a topic in which they had expertise, he would
quickly become impatient if they furnished more than a superficial background on the subject.[34]

Chambers's temperament and genteel upbringing qualified him poorly
to deal with personal displays of unpleasantness and dissension. He had been
little influenced by the rough surroundings of the newsroom, the overwhelming proportion of his journalistic career having been spent in the rari-
fied environment of the editorial suite.[35]

When he found an associate's editorial wanting, he often preferred to
leave it facedown on his desk exiled in limbo rather than take issue with it.
Editorial disputes that most of his colleagues would have taken in stride
distressed and upset him acutely.[36]

Chambers observed a remarkably consistent code of civility, often in the
face of conduct that did not deserve it. On one occasion a vice president for
public relations, newly hired by the newspaper's publisher, attempted to in-
trude on Chambers's editorial autonomy. Upon hearing some criticism of
the *Pilot* by a cranky retired naval officer, the vice president walked into
Chambers's office and proceeded to tell him how to run his editorial page.
Few editors would have tolerated this kind of interference, but Chambers
heard the man out for an hour. Chambers's manners simply did not permit
peremptory dismissal.[37]

Confronted by rudeness, Chambers would normally give little direct indication of irritation. Instead, he became distant and overly formal and ended the interaction as quickly as he courteously could.[38] Throughout the long massive-resistance ordeal, he maintained his gentility.

When he occasionally received an anonymous harassing phone call at home, his family knew at once from the formal tone of his voice what kind of call it was. Refraining from arguing, he would terminate the conversation politely with "Sir, I can't continue this conversation if you won't identify yourself" or "You have the advantage of knowing my name, and you won't grant me the same courtesy. I'm going to have to hang up."[39]

Chambers had little patience with violations of decorum, even when they were perpetrated by allies in his cause célèbre. A junior member of the NAACP legal team, arriving at the *Pilot* building to pick up a promised copy of the *New York Times,* barged into an editorial meeting and announced excitedly, "Counsel wants the *Times* now!" A staff member quickly located the paper, and the young attorney left, running. The circumstances, as explained to Chambers, did not excuse the breach of etiquette. He pronounced his judgment: "That man has no manners!"[40]

Condescension could provoke momentary departure from his code. Once, while attending a newspaper conference in Bermuda, he stopped at an exclusive men's store and selected a regimental tie. When the British sales-clerk patronizingly suggested that another tie would be better suited for an American, Chambers bristled and demanded, "Are you going to sell me the damned thing or not?"[41]

The Jackson biography distracted Chambers from his editorial duties. In 1947 he had begun his painstakingly researched two-volume work. He would often write well into the night, and his weekends were almost entirely given up to research and writing, the sole respite being a thorough reading of each Sunday's *New York Times.*[42] Church attendance provided no reprieve; though raised in a family of prominent Presbyterians, Chambers, like Jaffe, was not a churchgoer.[43] So assiduously did he apply his time at home to the biography that he would complete both volumes without once taking leave from his editorial position in the twelve years of the biography's production.[44]

He would begin writing immediately after dinner. The evening meal was a special occasion at the Chambers household, observed with considerable formality. Food was presented in silver serving dishes and eaten by candle-light. Roberta, a careful housekeeper and an accomplished cook, specialized in traditional southern fare. Chambers would discuss the day's occur-rences—subjects ranging from world events to office politics—and Roberta would regale the family with cleverly told stories.[45]

The editor was somewhat removed from routine household activities. Roberta delighted in telling of a time she accidentally dropped an egg on the kitchen floor. Hearing her exclaim, Chambers, seated in another room, asked what had happened. Roberta told him she had broken an egg. "The whole egg?" he asked.[46]

Roberta Chambers, attractive and fashionably dressed, was a study in contrasts. The product of a Victorian upbringing, she was intensely private and highly mannered.[47] Sharing her husband's enjoyment of sports, she played golf and became a rabid and knowledgeable baseball fan.[48] She was unusually opinionated for a woman of her era and comfortable in making her views known.

Robert Mason described her as a woman of "some force. You knew what her position was. She didn't mince words."[49] Roberta read widely, and her friends admired her for her intelligence.

By all accounts, however, she was best known for her sense of humor. "Roberta saw something funny in almost everything," said Alonzo Dill, a family friend and a colleague of Chambers, who found her to be witty, keen minded, and delightful company.[50]

Her son, Robert Glenn, elaborated. "Dad loved to laugh at good stories, and Mother could tell [them]. The more ridiculous the human predicament, the merrier. Mother could mimic with a soft touch, not giving offense."[51]

The colorful city of Norfolk provided Roberta with an abundance of humorous material. During World War II, the house next to the Chamberses' became a boarding house for war workers. One Sunday afternoon when Roberta was reading on her front porch, a frustrated roomer unsuccessfully attempted to repair his car. She overheard clanking and cursing, which culminated in the man's throwing a handful of tools into the street and shouting, "I wish this car would go to hell or some other seaport town." For years Roberta, in the words of her son, "dined out" on the story.[52]

The marriage was particularly happy, and the couple remained closely devoted throughout their lives. Roberta's contribution to Chambers's career should not be downplayed. A newspaper editor incurred a plethora of social obligations, and Roberta was an attentive hostess and an engaging conversationalist. The two espoused similar politics, including identical views on racial issues; and despite Roberta's independent nature, she greatly admired her husband's intelligence and respected his opinions. In the turbulent wake of the *Brown* decision, the Chambers household was united in its opposition to massive resistance.[53]

Roberta, like her husband, had limited interaction with blacks. Her daughter, Elisabeth, recalled that when she began her own reporting career many years later, after blacks had begun to occupy positions of elective and appointive office in integrated Norfolk, her mother regarded her as fortunate for having the opportunity to interview and associate with black leaders. "The only black people I have known have been in my kitchen," Roberta remarked to her daughter.[54]

Even with the constraints on his free time, Chambers and Roberta managed to entertain guests regularly. They would invite six to eight couples to dinner, or thirty or so couples for cocktails. Chambers was a particularly attentive host. An admiral's wife confided to Sally Abeles, a friend of the Chambers family, that her somewhat reclusive husband "bloomed" in Chambers's company. (Chambers was much interested in naval history, particularly in the World War I naval engagement of Jutland, and knew the movements of the German and British fleets almost by the hour.)[55] At the conclusion of such an evening, Chambers was careful to walk his guests to their cars and bid them good night.[56]

Elisabeth Burgess believed the "Stonewall years" were lonely for her mother. The family had no television—"I think we were the last human beings on earth to buy one"—so Roberta Chambers spent her evenings chiefly in reading. "Mother used to say about those years that she felt as if she were married to two men—Dad and Stonewall Jackson."[57] Family vacations were often devoted to retracing Jackson's battlefield movements. Roberta would sometimes remain in the car and knit while Chambers paced off military advances and retreats.[58]

Robert Glenn remembered that while traveling, his stepfather would habitually query gas-station attendants and store clerks about a myriad of topics ranging from local politics to crop yields. Chambers often said to his stepson that there were the makings of a book in everyone.[59]

After Robert—"Bob"—married, the remaining members of the Chambers household joined him and his family for vacations on Tybee Island near Savannah, Georgia. There Chambers relaxed as he was unable to do in Norfolk. On the island he unwound thoroughly—so completely that he uncharacteristically let the self-winding Bulova watch that Roberta had given him run down. Normally Chambers, as precise in his punctuality as he was in his dress and manners, would send the watch to the jewelers for adjustment if it was off as much as a minute a month.[60]

The third-floor front bedroom of the Chamberses' old Victorian house served as a study and library. The furnishings were an old bed, a chest of drawers, a file cabinet, a big flat-top desk, a standing lamp, and an erratic typewriter, all dilapidated and in disorderly arrangement.[61] Although the filing cabinet was used, papers and correspondence were stacked high on top of it and weighted down by a book.

Having worked well into the night, Chambers would often arrive at his office later in the morning than other members of the editorial staff, on occasion unaware of late developments in the news. He was too proud to ask his associates for news updates, and this sometimes resulted in longer and less productive conferences.[62] This situation imposed no real burden on the staff and caused no resentment. The biography intruded much more on Chambers's home life and social activity than on his newspaper work.[63]

Despite the occasionally frustrating conferences and Meacham's ego and prickly temperament, Chambers and his associates worked closely, and relations between Chambers and Meacham were often harmonious.[64] Chambers's associates were particularly appreciative of his sense of humor. He found the many colorful characters in the seaport city amusing. "Newspapermen very quickly get on to the eccentrics," said Alonzo Dill, a close family friend and an associate editor under Jaffe. "In fact they make friends with them very readily. [Lenoir] would often talk about this or that encounter or this or that story that he had heard."[65]

Although Chambers was capable of swearing robustly with his associate editors and was distinctly not a prude, his sense of humor did not extend to off-color jokes.[66] A local lawyer, believing that Chambers enjoyed a rough joke, saved stories to repeat to him. Carried away with his own storytelling prowess, the lawyer never perceived the editor's visible deep embarrassment.[67]

Chambers's sense of propriety also excluded him from socializing with the newspaper staff at Freddie Chinchilla's "blind pig," the Jefferson Ward Democratic Club, which operated across the street from the newspaper building in the late 1940s. Despite the fact that liquor by the drink was illegal in Virginia, Freddie, "a minor racketeer," had a full-service bar.

Mason writes, "If Freddie anticipated the newspaper trade, he was not disappointed. . . . Louis Jaffe . . . soon joined us, somewhat to our surprise but also to our delight. Lenoir . . . did not. It's possible that someone asked him to come along, but certainly not I. He ignored the joint."[68]

Chambers, however, was not a teetotaler. The editor enjoyed an occasional drink, usually a bourbon and water before dinner, celebrated with the family toast of "God bless us all."[69] (The toast dated back to World War II when his stepson, Robert, served with the Marines in the Pacific theater. "Mother and Dad would raise their glasses nightly in a 'God Bless Bob' or 'Here's to Bob' toast—with all the unspoken hopes and fears," said Elisabeth Burgess. "Eventually there were no words needed, just a lifting of glasses and a nod to each other. They did this even when out at a friend's house or at a cocktail party.")[70] Chambers also smoked moderately, and would continue to do so until the Surgeon General's Office issued its 1964 report documenting the dangers of the habit.[71]

Chambers sought to publish four editorials a day and preferred that each piece have a different focus, either local, state, national, or international.[72] Of the three original editorial writers, Meacham wrote the largest number, usually three a day. He devoted all of his time to writing. Chambers, with his management responsibilities, wrote one to one and a half a day, most often including the lead editorial. Sugg, who was responsible for letters to the editor, syndicated columns, and the like, wrote one to two editorials.[73]

Although members of the editorial staff developed areas of special expertise, Chambers saw to it that each member of his staff wrote on additional current subjects ranging from local politics to military affairs. This policy applied particularly to massive resistance. Despite the fact that he wrote many of the editorials on the subject and even referred to segregation and integration as "Topic A," both Sugg and Meacham, and later also Mason, "dipped into this problem deeply," according to Chambers.[74] Sugg confirmed that "everybody got into the act on Topic A, [although] Mr. Chambers usually wrote the lead pieces."[75]

By the time Robert Smith joined the editorial staff in early 1959 (to replace Mason, who had become managing editor), Chambers had revised his policy and assumed personal responsibility for all of the editorials on Topic A. Smith believed that despite Chambers's "modesty" and "reserve," he anticipated the fact that his editorials would be nominated for a Pulitzer Prize.[76]

Almost certainly this was the case. Meacham had stymied a Pulitzer nomination that was in progress in 1956 by insisting he share the award with Chambers. Because of Chambers's nightly involvement with the Jackson biography, Meacham wrote the lead editorial—albeit under Chambers's leadership and guidance—more often than would otherwise have been the case. He felt strongly that he should have won or at least shared the award. Gradually, during the period between Sugg's and Mason's departures from the editorial offices, Chambers assumed all responsibility for Topic A editorials.[77]

For Chambers, who set the *Virginian-Pilot*'s editorial policy, massive resistance became much more than a subject for editorials. The editor became intensely involved personally in the impending crisis. Topic A eventually dominated the discussion with his colleagues at lunch as well as at work.[78] Elisabeth Burgess remembered that massive resistance was also discussed with great frequency in the Chambers household: "When Daddy came home at night, my mother would say, 'What's the news on the Topic A front?' "[79]

Harold Sugg, too, became personally involved with this subject. Sugg's wife was active in the Parent-Teacher Association at a Norfolk elementary school. The closing of the schools and the control of the city-wide PTA Council by the Defenders of State Sovereignty and Individual Liberties, the state's most powerful segregationist organization, upset her mightily.[80] But Mason maintained that neither he nor Meacham shared these concerns. "I would write what I thought was the truth," Mason explained, "and what happened next was beyond me. . . . I always had the confidence that the Supreme Court was going to stick to its guns. . . . There was always the satisfaction, when I wrote, of being sure what the war's end was going to be, regardless of who won the immediate battle."[81]

Although Chambers was an accomplished and competent editor, he readily acknowledged that his writing was at times verbose. Said Mason, "He would write too much. He could have been a little sharper. He would have been the first to say that. I had great respect for what he said, but sometimes it could have been improved."[82] "He dismissed his writing frequently in front of us," confirmed Smith. "He was at his best . . . where his own convictions were joined, and they . . . were joined very personally and very strongly on Topic A."[83]

Although Chambers believed strongly that the *Pilot*'s editorials could provide a moral anchor and leadership for the community, he recognized the limitations of their influence. Reflecting on the recalcitrance of the resistance forces and the interminability of his campaign opposing them, he told his staff of a walk with Jaffe, crippled by arthritis, past the paper's loading docks on a stormy day. As the newspapers blew through the parking lot, Jaffe pointed to them and said, "This is what we write for—the wind. The wind. What we wrote yesterday is wasting down this alley, and what we wrote today will follow it tomorrow."[84]

The *Pilot*'s editorial policy had little direct effect on the manner in which news stories were covered or written. The *Virginian-Pilot* had a long tradition of confining its editors' responsibilities and duties solely to the editorial page.[85] Editors and their associates were removed from the activities in the newsroom geographically as well as organizationally. Their three-room suite of offices was located a floor above the newsroom and was isolated from the paper's reporting activities.[86]

Chambers did, however, have an indirect effect on the paper's news staff. He was widely respected, and many reporters admired his stand against massive resistance. "He had an influence on me," acknowledged Luther Carter, then the *Pilot*'s young education reporter, "because I really looked up to him."[87] Robert Smith described the reporting staff as a little in awe of Chambers. "I was before [I joined the editorial staff] and in some ways even more after I saw what he was dealing with."[88]

Despite the fact that he was isolated from many of the paper's daily activities, Chambers conferred regularly with the publisher and the managing editor, who actively sought and took into account his advice on policy matters. His counsel figured importantly in shaping the *Pilot* news staff's coverage of the school closing. The paper practiced judicious restraint in its reportage during the school closing. Warned of the inflammatory effect their stories could have on the community, reporters avoided sensationalism.

The *Pilot* was particularly cautious in its coverage of racial friction. If a black student in a group photograph was holding a hammer, a less provoca-

tive photograph would be chosen. Robert Mason capsulized the paper's policy: "If there was a prospect of confrontation, we sure didn't blow it up. We
didn't hang on it and try to encourage it."[89]

As a result of the reputations of Chambers and Jaffe, the *Virginian-Pilot*
attracted a particularly gifted news and editorial staff. Mason believed that
Chambers never would have left North Carolina except to go to Louis Jaffe,
and Chambers in turn attracted outstanding people. For Mason it was a joy
to work at the *Pilot*. He found the staff to be unusual and exceptionally
stimulating, counting in its membership a number of persons who had written books and otherwise achieved distinction. At one time it included three
lawyers and a minister, and there had been a doctor on the staff. "You
wouldn't have found that in Richmond," said Mason.[90]

The *Pilot*'s news staff took pride in Jaffe's Pulitzer and the editorials
that had earned it and in the campaign Chambers was now masterminding,
which they believed could have a major impact on the South. Many saw the
possibility that the *Virginian-Pilot* could be a great paper, maybe even sur-
passing the Washington and Atlanta presses.[91]

To be a member of the *Pilot*'s editorial staff was to be a member of a
gentlemanly club.[92] The editorial page was generally regarded as the strongest facet of the *Pilot,* and considerable status was accorded editors and their
associates by their newspaper colleagues. Editorial writers at many other
newspapers were bestowed a less laudatory standing. H. L. Mencken had
described the editorial writers in turn-of-the-century Baltimore as

> ancient hulks who were unfit for better duty—copy-readers promoted from
> the city-room to get rid of them, alcoholic writers of local histories and
> forgotten novels, former managing editors who had come to grief on other
> papers, and a miscellany of decayed lawyers, college professors, and clergy-
> men with whispered pasts. . . . If anyone in the city-room had ever spoken
> of an editorial in his own paper as cogent and illuminating he would have
> been set down as a jackass for admiring it and as a kind of traitor to honest
> journalism for reading it at all. No editorial writer was ever applied to for
> a loan, or invited to an office booze party.[93]

Chambers, to the contrary, was heir to an editorial tradition created by
his direct predecessors, Jaffe and former governor William E. Cameron.[94]

The editor of the *Pilot* was also a respected member of Tidewater's social
and professional communities. Editors served as honorary members of the
Norfolk Bar Association and the Norfolk Medical Association and were routinely invited to naval ceremonies and civic gatherings.[95] Chambers moved
in the senior section of Norfolk society, along with the top lawyers and
physicians.[96] He was a member of the prestigious German Club, the Norfolk
Yacht and Country Club (the city's most exclusive country club), and the

venerable Virginia Club, a men's private club with a membership restricted to Norfolk's social elite. He was completely at ease in these surroundings. He could blend "into a clubroom like walnut and leather," Mason observed.[97]

Despite the apparent ease with which Chambers interacted with others, some of his childhood shyness lingered, and he was uncomfortable addressing large groups. He abhorred public speaking and did his best to engage in it as seldom as possible.[98] Nevertheless, he was a prominent public figure and was thrust into the limelight frequently. For a time he regularly broadcast reports from Norfolk's WTAR radio station, and in 1956 he appeared on the national television news program "Meet the Press," where he questioned Mississippi senator James O. Eastland, a hard-line segregationist. Chambers was dissatisfied with his performance: "It ended up with Eastland the complete victor and the rest of us humiliated by our failure to penetrate his thick and oily hide. Amateurs ought not to play with professionals."[99] (Jaffe had also despised public speaking, writing that "there is surely no worse public speaker in the United States than myself.")[100]

Chambers exerted an indirect influence over the *Virginian-Pilot* and *Ledger-Dispatch*'s young publisher, Frank Batten. Batten had been appointed publisher in 1954 by his uncle, "Colonel" Samuel L. Slover, upon the unexpected death of the previous publisher, Henry S. Lewis. Batten, a graduate of Culver Military Academy, the University of Virginia, and Harvard's Graduate School of Business, was only twenty-seven years old at the time of his appointment.[101]

By all accounts Batten was an unusually confident and capable young man. "He had one hell of a lot of nerve," declares Mason. "If he set out on a course, you could be absolutely certain he'd go through with that thing. There wouldn't be any second-guessing, any flinching, anything like that. He was just direct. He was a brave young fellow, as his success indicates. I have all these times, including this moment, thought he had the coolest eye [during stressful times] I ever saw. And he had a great sense of fairness about him."[102]

Batten had great respect for his two editors-in-chief, both much older and more experienced than he—but the young publisher developed a much stronger relationship with Chambers than with Joseph Leslie. "I was much closer to Mr. Chambers," Batten admitted. . . . "He was a man for whom I had enormous personal regard and respect. And I used him often as a sort of elder advisor on a lot of things outside of editorial policy. . . . He was a man whose judgment I respected and whom I trusted implicitly."[103]

Such confidence did Batten place in the judgment of his leading editor that he allowed Chambers the autonomy to set and follow for five years a course that could have resulted in financial disaster for the paper. Some smaller advertisers did cancel their accounts, but established advertisers

stayed with the *Pilot,* probably because its stance on the school issue came
as no surprise in light of the paper's liberal tradition. Readers perhaps stayed
for the same reason or out of curiosity as to what the paper would say next.
The loss of revenue was relatively negligible.[104]

Through example and sharing of insight, Chambers served as a major
influence on Batten during the school crisis, reinforcing the young publisher's disinclination toward massive resistance. Chambers supplied the historical context critical to understanding the closing and helped Batten shape and
articulate his argument for reopening the schools. Batten came to believe,
as Chambers did, that the closing was a scourge on the community and that
the schools must be reopened at any cost.[105]

The publisher's respect for his senior editor was reciprocated. Chambers
held Batten in high regard. The editor's daughter told of the close relationship between the two men and her father's admiration for Batten.[106] In a
letter to his prospective new associate editor in 1957, Chambers described the
publisher as "exceptionally intelligent, well versed in the modern executive
spirit, thoroughly human and capable of constant and healthy growth."[107]

The harmony with which the two men worked—one beginning his career and the other nearing retirement—and their mutual respect enabled
them to provide the *Virginian-Pilot* with a quality of leadership rare among
southern presses. Strong leadership would be required if the *Pilot* was to rise
to the challenge of massive resistance and help preserve Norfolk's public
schools.

8

Norfolk

The Setting for a Conflict

To MANY STUDENTS of politics and history, Virginia would have seemed the southern state least likely to spawn the revolt that was Topic A on Lenoir Chambers's editorial agenda. Although the Old Dominion had contained the capital of the Confederacy, many of the bloodiest battlefields of the Civil War, and Appomattox, the site of Lee's surrender to Grant, by 1949 improvements in the status of blacks had led V. O. Key, in his classic work, *Southern Politics,* to call Virginia's race relations "perhaps the most harmonious in the South."[1] By the time of *Brown v. Board,* additional evidence supported Professor Key's conclusion. Only 22 percent of the state's population was black—considerably less than in the Deep South, where race relations seemed to worsen as the number of blacks approached that of whites. Virginia institutions of higher learning were beginning to integrate their academic programs, and blacks held a number of minor elective and appointive offices.[2] When the rumblings portending the state's campaign of "massive resistance" began, the comparatively sophisticated and liberal city of Norfolk would have seemed a most unlikely place for the crisis to come to a head.

Norfolk in the 1950s was a great port and transportation center. Possessing one of the world's finest natural harbors, the city exported more tonnage than any other Atlantic coast city. Nine major railroads linked Norfolk with the rest of the nation. Consequently, in 1957 the city was one of the ten fastest-growing markets in the country.[3]

Norfolk's strategic location had made its naval base the largest in the world. Most career naval personnel and their families could anticipate serving at least two "tours" of duty in the city; and because the base served as headquarters for the North Atlantic Treaty Organization (NATO), many international visitors were stationed there. The counties and lesser cities surrounding Norfolk were dotted with a wide range of other military facilities, representing all branches of the armed services.[4]

Norfolk's naval base and the Norfolk Navy Yard constituted the area's major industrial enterprises. The federal government employed 60,000 of the city's 162,000 adult males. The civilian labor force alone consisted of 35,000 federal workers, twice the number in Richmond's entire employed population. With a population of 213,513, the city was the state's second largest in 1950 and was growing so rapidly that by the time of the school closing, it would supplant Richmond as Virginia's largest metropolitan area.[5]

Norfolk, however, was a study in contradictions. On the surface the city appeared to be relatively progressive and cosmopolitan. Many of the city's residents had lived elsewhere and had been exposed to differing perspectives on racial issues. Indeed, 13 percent of Norfolkians in 1950 had lived in a different county or abroad during the previous year.[6]

Community leaders claimed that race relations in Norfolk, where 30 percent of the population was black, were better than average. The Norfolk delegation to the state Democratic convention in 1948 had strongly and successfully opposed Governor William M. Tuck's anti-Truman bill, an attempt by the governor to seize control of the Democratic national ballot because of President Truman's appointment of a Civil Rights Commission.

The city's delegates to the Virginia General Assembly also displayed relatively progressive views on racial relations. In the early 1950s Norfolk's representatives supported a bill that would have abolished segregation in public transportation. (The bill, however, was rejected in committee.) Norfolk's representatives supported increased funding for public education, advocated the modification of the poll tax, and generally held stances associated with an advanced view of race relations.[7]

Norfolk's *Journal and Guide* newspaper also served to moderate the city's racial environment. With a readership of sixty-five thousand, the *Journal* was the most widely distributed black newspaper in the South and the fourth in the nation.[8] The newspaper, termed "highly respected and respectable" by Gunnar Myrdal, was also read by a number of liberal whites, including Eleanor Roosevelt.[9]

Its conservative publisher, P. B. Young, Sr., was one of the most influential black men in the United States and was regarded by many whites as an able and safe leader. Some blacks, however, particularly the leadership of the NAACP, were less enamored of the elderly publisher, who could be jealous and prideful and who often preferred using his personal power to working collaboratively with established racial organizations.

Early in his career, Young had been strongly influenced by Booker T. Washington's accommodationist philosophy.[10] Young wrote, "It will not hurt to sacrifice racial heat and temper to gain the greater objective of economic advancement."[11] He exhorted blacks not to migrate to northern cities but to remain in the South and seek the friendship of whites.

Although the publisher felt that the *Journal* could help initiate economic and social progress for blacks, he was leery of directly confronting the white power structure. Young downplayed racial conflict, believing that the *Journal* could help bring blacks and whites together. Throughout much of his career, he displayed a willingness to work toward improvements for blacks within a segregated society.[12] Confident that liberal community leaders such as Louis Jaffe would support him, Young lobbied for improvement of the health conditions in black neighborhoods and for better streets and the like.[13] In many respects he was an effective advocate for the black community.

Certainly some of the credit for the city's comparatively moderate racial climate belonged to the *Virginian-Pilot,* led by Louis Jaffe and later by Lenoir Chambers. In a time when the newspaper was easily the most dominant and influential of the communications media, the *Pilot* championed improved race relations and an enlightened treatment of blacks and racial issues in its reporting and editorials. Jaffe confided to Meacham,

> A sympathetic attitude toward racial perplexity is not enough. There must be a sympathetic understanding of specific things that oppress the Negro Community—remediable things. . . . school overcrowding, lax police attention to Negro crime, grossly discriminatory treatment in the matter of apportioning public improvements, employment hardships, displacement of Negro workers with white workers, etc., etc.
>
> From the publishing viewpoint, I think Southern newspapers over-exploit Negro crime and under-notice Negro achievement. I should like to see the emphasis reversed. Not enough attention is paid on our copy desks to eliminating from our news reports phrases, terms and dialectic crudities that literate Negroes regard as offensive. I do not see the justice of striving for humor or readability at the expense of wounding people in their racial consciousness. I have exactly the same objection to [the] word "nigger" in a news report as I have to the words "wop" or "sheeny."[14]

Under Jaffe, the *Virginian-Pilot* had opposed the Massenburg Bill, which prohibited interracial public assemblages; had attacked National Recovery Administration policies that displaced black workers; and had successfully lobbied for a black beach, black parks, black policemen, and a black college. The *Pilot*'s editor had denounced the Ku Klux Klan, urged the passage of an antimask ordinance, condemned the Scottsboro verdict, and almost single-handedly persuaded Governor Harry F. Byrd, Sr., to introduce the strongest antilynching legislation in the South into Virginia's General Assembly.[15]

Jaffe, who was a regular reader of the *Journal and Guide,* and P. B. Young shared an intimate relationship.[16] The publisher of the *Journal* considered Jaffe to be the southern press's "most outstanding figure" working for the improvement of racial relations.[17] Colonel Slover, the *Pilot*'s publisher, was also friendly with Young, giving him free of charge the mats and plates already used by the *Pilot* and assisting from time to time in fiscal emergencies plaguing the hard-pressed weekly.[18]

Robert Mason credits Jaffe with contributions extending far beyond Norfolk: "He was a national figure in his time. I once mentioned him to Roy Wilkins [Executive Secretary of the National Association for the Advancement of Colored People] and spent the next half hour listening to Wilkins review his associations with Jaffe over the years." Chambers, upon assuming the editorship of the *Pilot* in 1950, continued Jaffe's editorial policies.[19]

Nearly all of the city's black residents appreciated the *Virginian-Pilot*'s efforts to better racial relations. Among domestic workers in Norfolk's black community, working for either the Jaffe or the Chambers household was a particularly sought-after position; status was associated with working for either of these liberal newspapermen.[20]

Sarah Patton Boyle, the wife of a University of Virginia faculty member and one of the few whites who publicly supported the integration of Virginia's schools and colleges, believed there was hope that the majority of the state's citizens would support desegregation and increased rights for blacks. In 1951 Boyle composed a letter to the editor of the *Richmond Times-Dispatch*, urging the "silent south" to speak out against racial discrimination. "There is no just and discerning white man who does not feel shame that fellow Americans in the commonwealth of Mr. Jefferson's birth must fight to obtain human dignity," Boyle wrote.

After Virginius Dabney declined to print the letter, maintaining that it would arouse racial animosity and provoke a flurry of angry letters of protest, Lenoir Chambers ran Boyle's letter in the *Virginian-Pilot*. Boyle was delighted to learn that only five responses opposed her plea.[21]

These major moderating influences—the Navy, the federal government, Norfolk's political leadership, and the city's white and black presses, along with the presence of a black intellectual elite at nearby Hampton Institute and the residency of a large number of well-paid black workers employed in the area's shipyards—helped temper race relations and promote interracial cooperation.[22] The Women's Interracial Council was formed in 1945 and over the next few years rapidly increased in size. The membership of the Norfolk Ministers Association was integrated, as was that of the Norfolk Ministers Fellowship.[23] Joint meetings of black and white school principals had been held for a number of years.[24] Norfolk's Women's Council was interracial and in 1955 successfully sponsored an integrated nursery for the children of its members.[25] That same year, Norfolk Catholic High School was integrated without incident.[26]

Yet, beneath this veneer of racial harmony, Norfolk was strongly influenced by the traditional racial attitudes of the South, in part because much of the city's work force came from the surrounding counties of the state's Black Belt, and partly because the comparatively low educational and income levels of many white residents placed them in competition with blacks.[27]

Norfolk's public schools, opened for white children in 1858 and to blacks in 1863, had been segregated from the beginning except for a period of enforced integration during the federal occupation after the Civil War, when black children were admitted to all four of the city's schools. Churches were also integrated during that time, and black and white soldiers attended services together. When the occupation ended, however, the city's four schools reverted to the education of white students exclusively; and blacks went without education until 1867, when the American Missionary Society began to operate a system of schools.[28] The policy of strict racial segregation remained unbroken after the state established its system of public schools for white and black children in 1870.[29]

Whites and blacks in Norfolk interacted primarily as white employers and black maids or gardeners or janitors, infrequently as equals. The institution of segregation was rarely questioned.[30] To white parents who had interacted with culturally deprived blacks only and had no inkling of blacks' intellectual potential, genuine concern that mixing races in the schools would lower the level of instruction made integration unthinkable. In addition to operating segregated schools, the city maintained separate public restrooms and beaches for blacks and whites.[31]

Even the *Virginian-Pilot* and the *Ledger-Dispatch* under Chambers's editorship, for all their liberality and advocacy of minority betterment, still operated essentially within traditional patterns of segregation. Although these publications were among the most racially progressive newspapers in the South, they were white newspapers, as much a part of the Jim Crow system as was the *Journal and Guide*. Unquestionably, the *Pilot*'s staff was poorly informed about many events in Norfolk's black community. And despite the fact that Chambers regularly read the *Journal and Guide,* he knew little about the daily lives of nearly a third of Norfolk's citizenry. Chambers and the management of Norfolk Newspapers clearly regarded the *Pilot* and the *Ledger* as news and advertising vehicles for a white readership.

Chambers's *Salt Water & Printer's Ink: Norfolk and Its Newspapers* reflects this mindset. Portrayed as a comprehensive treatment of the development of the city's newspapers within a rich historical context, this useful book almost entirely avoids any meaningful discussion of Norfolk's minority population. Astonishingly from today's perspective, Chambers devotes only a single paragraph to his contemporary and peer P. B. Young and the *Norfolk Journal and Guide,* the South's most widely read black press for over fifty years.[32]

These omissions viewed within the context of Chambers's career as a liberal southern journalist are telling. They suggest that although Chambers believed that whites had a responsibility to address remediable wrongs in the black community and to provide a much fairer treatment of minorities, blacks were in other respects frequently invisible to him. In his view the two races, despite their proximity to one another, inhabited separate worlds. This perception in an intellectual of Chambers's liberal leanings bespeaks the degree of entrenchment—indeed the innateness—of segregation in the southern culture of the era.

The social passivity and hopelessness of many blacks led whites to believe that racial relations in Norfolk were advanced.[33] But despite the fact that white leadership portrayed the city as a bastion of racial progressiveness, John Belden of the *Journal and Guide* called the segregation "so thick you could cut it with a knife."[34] Jerry O. Gilliam, former head of the Norfolk NAACP, drew a graphic analogy: "The whites [in Norfolk] deprive the Negro of privileges here like the mythical rat bites. . . . The rat will take a small bite off your toe, and then blow on it so you won't feel it, then take another nibble and blow some more, until the blood starts flowing and you bleed to death in your sleep. That's the way white people lull Negroes to sleep in Norfolk and then bite them till they're bled dry."[35]

Norfolk's black teachers had long been dissatisfied by their low salaries; in the late 1930s, the white janitor at Booker T. Washington High School earned more money than the city's highest paid black principal.[36]

Celestyne Porter, a black social studies teacher at Booker T. Washington High School, a member of the Women's Interracial Council, and later the supervisor of social studies for Norfolk's public schools, recalled that black teachers who advocated salary equalization were openly threatened by the school administration. She told of being summoned by the superintendent, who complained of the "fuss" she was raising and asked what she planned to do when she lost her job. "You're going to hire me to cook for you," she retorted, "because I have a master's degree in history from the University of Pennsylvania. You will never find a cook as well off as I am educationally, and I can cook."[37]

In 1938 Aline Elizabeth Black, a young black teacher at Booker T. Washington High School, with the active encouragement of the National Association for the Advancement of Colored People, petitioned the city's school board for a salary equal to that of her white counterparts. Black's suit, which was directed by the NAACP's Thurgood Marshall, centered on whether her rights under the Fourteenth Amendment were violated by Norfolk's discriminatory salary practices. Virginia Circuit Court Judge Allan R. Hanckel decided for the city, maintaining that the authority to set salaries resided with the school board. Black's contract was not renewed when she appealed the decision, and she subsequently enrolled in a doctoral program at the

University of Pennsylvania. Norfolk's black community vigorously protested her firing; students carried signs comparing the board's behavior to that of Hitler and Mussolini, and twelve hundred pupils signed a petition demanding that she be rehired.[38] The *Virginian-Pilot* editorialized, "The school board's failure to re-employ Aline Elizabeth Black, the Negro high school teacher who has been made the instrumentality of a salary-equalization test case, is an act in which it can take no pride."[39]

Melvin O. Alston, a black teacher at Booker T. Washington and also the president of the Norfolk Teachers Association, agreed with understandable reluctance to serve as the plaintiff after Black's contract was not renewed. Marshall abandoned the Virginia court system and filed suit in federal court. United States District Court Judge Luther B. Way decided against Alston, determining that he had forfeited his constitutional rights when he had entered into a contract with the city. Way's decision, however, was reversed on appeal by a three-judge panel at the United States Circuit Court of Appeals. The case was remanded to the lower courts for settlement.[40]

The city appealed to the Supreme Court, but the case was denied cert on October 28, 1940. Considerable conflict within the black community erupted after P. B. Young of the *Journal and Guide* (perhaps pressured by the city's white leadership) persuaded Alston to reach an out-of-court settlement with the school board. Young believed that black teachers could avoid antagonizing the white establishment by arriving at conciliatory agreements and that he could bargain with the city to provide blacks with a new elementary school. Thurgood Marshall was enraged, feeling that Young and the Norfolk Teachers Association had sold out the decision. Eventually, black teachers agreed to a compromise developed by the NAACP, and salaries were equalized over a three-year period.[41] By January 1, 1943, black and white teachers were receiving equal compensation. Some indication of the toll exacted on Alston is communicated by his physician's request that his patient be given a month's leave for a "complete change and rest needed to improve his physical and nervous condition."[42]

After teachers' salaries were equalized, many black teachers furthered their educations to increase their salaries. At one point, of 129 faculty at Booker T. Washington, 120 had earned advanced degrees.[43]

Reflecting on the significance of Norfolk's salary equalization case, scholar Earl Lewis astutely observes that the importance of Black's case should not be underestimated. By attacking the dual wage scale, the case opened the door for a variety of suits regarding salary inequities.[44]

Norfolk's political elite connected with the Byrd organization conspired to exclude blacks from meaningful participation in municipal affairs. The organization generally opposed racial progress; and blacks, in turn, supported liberal Republican candidates.[45] William L. ("Billy") Prieur, Jr., Byrd's political lieutenant and arguably the most powerful political figure in Norfolk, in his private correspondence to the senator wrote of a committee of blacks who approached him in an attempt to place a black on the school board: "I gave them distinctly to understand they could expect no quarter from us as long as they opposed our candidates."[46]

Blacks, who constituted a racial minority in the city, faced an additional formidable obstacle to bettering their lot through the political process. A state constitutional convention held in 1902 with the openly expressed purpose of disenfranchising blacks had resulted in legislation that drastically reduced the state's black electorate, from 147,000 to 21,000.[47] Under the provisions of the new constitution, voters were subjected to a literacy test until 1904, when a poll tax requirement of three years' payment six months prior to voting went into effect. Exempted from the tax were Civil War veterans of either side, their sons, property owners who had paid taxes in the previous year, and descendants of those who had voted in 1861.[48] Litigation brought by a black resident of Hampton in 1931 nullified most of these requirements, but the poll tax would continue to obstruct black suffrage until 1964, when the Twenty-fourth Amendment to the Constitution would prohibit denial of the right to vote in federal elections because of failure to pay taxes.[49]

Housing for many blacks in Norfolk in the fifties was deplorable. Federal officials classified the city's crowded slums as "the worst in the nation."[50] (During World War II, the city had earned the dubious distinction of being another "worst": the nation's worst center of venereal disease.)[51]

The city's white electorate, basically content with the status quo, was notoriously apathetic, as were most Virginia voters. By 1958, when the city's population had swollen to nearly three hundred thousand, there were only fifty thousand qualified voters, and only one in twelve had voted in recent elections.[52] The city's neglect of its black residents had enabled Communist organizers, such as the charismatic Isaac Alexander Wright, to make inroads into the black community in the 1930s. As a result of his success, military investigators termed Norfolk the most "sensitive" location in the Mid-Atlantic and South-Atlantic regions.[53]

Also belying the appearance of progressive racial relations in Norfolk was, although certainly not as extensive as that of the Deep South, a history of racial violence. In 1865 violence had broken out between occupying Union troops and blacks. Armed soldiers had swarmed into a black neighborhood, terrorized residents, and initiated a full-scale race riot that rapidly spread throughout the city.[54]

Following the Civil War, bands of armed white men attacked blacks participating in a parade celebrating the passage of the Civil Rights Bill. Bricks were thrown at parade-goers, and newly discharged black troops fought back. Gangs of whites randomly attacked and murdered a number of blacks before federal troops could restore order.[55] Over the next several decades, there were a number of reports of lynchings, race riots, and racially motivated murders in Norfolk.[56]

On Independence Day in 1910, after black prizefighter Jack Johnson's victory over his white opponent, Jim Jeffries, two black men walking down Plume Street were heard to exclaim, "Oh, you Johnson!" This sparked a major race riot that one observer likened to a "pogrom."[57] In the wake of the First World War, a celebration planned by the Norfolk City Council for returning black veterans deteriorated into another race riot. Two policemen and five blacks were injured.[58] And in three separate incidents in a ten-month period in the 1920s, Jewish merchants shot three black children to death.[59]

During the Depression white toughs frequently attacked black children walking to school in the Brambleton area of Norfolk, and two black families who attempted to move into "white" apartments elsewhere in the city were beaten by working- and middle-class whites.[60] In the summer months of 1942, rumors that blacks intended to murder whites with icepicks during war blackouts spread throughout the city's white communities.[61]

Much later, in the fall of 1954—the same year as the *Brown* decision— bombings, civil unrest, and cross-burnings occurred when black families moved into two previously all-white middle-class neighborhoods.[62]

These incidents exposed the city's racial tensions in a notorious light that had repercussions considerably afield. Approximately 160 miles away in Charlottesville, Sarah Patton Boyle received an anonymous threat regarding her advocacy of desegregation: "I think we have heard just about enough out of you. If you keep on running your big mouth, you may get something like a big egg planted under your house like they are getting in Norfolk. WATCH YOUR STEP SISTER."[63]

And so Norfolk, with its contradictions—especially in its racial relations—was, as *Virginian-Pilot* reporter Luther Carter wrote, "a complex city . . . provincial and cosmopolitan . . . Southern, modified by the presence of the non-Southerner."[64]

9

The Issue of the Century

BY CALLING FOR an end to segregated public schools in its *Brown v. Board of Education* ruling, the Warren Court propelled the South into a belligerent campaign to openly subvert the "law of the land" in order to preserve a way of life predicated on racial hierarchy. The Court had consolidated four legal cases in four states, including Virginia, and a fifth case in the District of Columbia to test the constitutionality of state laws that mandated the maintenance of segregated educational facilities. The defendants, citing the precedent of the Court's decision in *Plessy v. Ferguson* in 1896, argued that "separate but equal" school systems were constitutional.[1] The plaintiffs, led by future Supreme Court justice Thurgood Marshall, asserted that segregation deprived black students of equal protection under the laws, as guaranteed by the Fourteenth Amendment.

Chief Justice Earl Warren, writing the opinion for a unanimous court, concluded that "in the field of public education the doctrine of separate but equal has no place. Separate educational facilities are inherently unequal."[2] Importantly, the Court maintained that even if segregated school systems possessed equity of resources—a condition few could meet—the "effect of segregation itself" deprived the minority of equal educational opportunities.

Resistance to the *Brown* decision—"massive resistance"—became what historian J. Harvie Wilkinson III termed Virginia's issue of the century.[3] Virginia's resistance would in many ways define that of the South, and the collapse of the state's system of segregated schools would foreshadow the dismantling of the entire Jim Crow system.

Virginia's official response to *Brown v. Board* was immediate and at first surprisingly moderate. Within two hours Governor Thomas B. Stanley called for "cool heads, calm, steady and sound judgment."[4] The governor hinted that it would be possible to devise a policy response that would both abide by the Supreme Court's decision and be acceptable to Virginia's citizenry. Stanley also indicated that he would establish a commission to recommend a response to *Brown*. Attorney General Lindsay Almond's reaction to the decision was also restrained: "Virginia will approach the question realistically and endeavor to work out some rational adjustment."[5]

Across the state, in Virginia's counties and metropolitan areas, informal reactions to *Brown* varied widely. In the Black Belt—thirty-one contiguous, mainly agricultural counties in Southside and eastern Virginia, where the black population often exceeded the white and racial stereotypes prevailed—whites had perpetuated a rigid caste system. White citizens in this belt predictably were incensed.[6] Elsewhere in the state, reactions ranged from somewhat less extreme to fairly progressive.

The *Norfolk Ledger-Dispatch*'s initial editorial response to *Brown v. Board* was calm and relatively supportive. In a lead editorial, "The Segregation Decision," the paper acknowledged that although the Court had infringed on the rights of the states, there was a perception among Virginians that "many former attitudes on racial questions [were] out of step with the times."[7]

The *Ledger* maintained that desegregation would not traumatize Virginia—most specifically, Norfolk—to the degree it would much of the South. The ratio of blacks to whites in Virginia was considerably lower than in many southern states, and it was likely that most of Norfolk's black schoolchildren would continue to attend the black schools that had been constructed near their homes.

Subsequent editorials written on this topic praised Governor Stanley's moderate reaction to *Brown,* in particular his call for the establishment of a commission charged with formulating a policy response to the Supreme Court's decision. The commission's recommendations should be based on a deliberate, thoughtful, and unemotional discussion of the issues, the *Ledger* counseled; and the body should include blacks among its membership. The paper's editorials deplored the efforts of the NAACP to force hasty implementation of desegregation.[8]

The *Virginian-Pilot* editorials on the *Brown* decision were similar in substance to those of the *Ledger*. In a lead editorial, "The Decision on Segregation," the *Pilot* acknowledged that the effects of the Supreme Court's decision would be "vast and far-reaching." Virginia, however, would not be as severely affected by the decision as would many other southern states. The Court was lauded for deliberating the issue thoroughly and not pressing the South for immediate compliance. The editorial concluded with a call for responsible leadership: "This is a time for statesmanship, and the South will rise or decline as it produces it."[9]

In additional editorials on this subject, Chambers wrote that there were many Souths. Some southern communities, such as Norfolk, the *Pilot* pointed out, were capable of prompt compliance with the Court's decree. Other areas, such as Virginia's Black Belt, faced a more problematic desegregation and would need more time to accommodate the Court's decision.

The *Pilot* urged southerners to adjust to integration with "good will, determination, and an earnest effort to adjust old folkways with newly defined constitutional law."[10] Rash action and emotionalism must be avoided.

Southerners should approach racial problems soberly and responsibly, with the "best thought" they could produce, not on how to overturn the Court's ruling, which they could not do, "but on how to adjust . . . to the philosophy and requirements of the decision," which they must do.[11]

Immediately following the Court's decision, Governor Stanley set about developing a stratagem to subvert the intent of *Brown*. On May 24, 1954, he summoned to the state capital five black leaders including Oliver W. Hill, chairman of the Virginia legal staff of the National Association for the Advancement of Colored People; Dr. R. P. Daniel, president of Virginia State College; and P. B. Young, Sr., the publisher of the *Norfolk Journal and Guide*. He urged these leaders to influence Virginia's blacks to accept segregation voluntarily. They refused.[12] And in June, Stanley met in Richmond with nine of his peers from southern and border states to discuss state responses to *Brown*. It was the consensus among the governors that their states would not willingly comply with the decision.[13]

Chambers had editorialized against such a meeting, maintaining that it would accomplish little of benefit and that there was a danger that governors from the more moderate Upper South would be swayed by their reactionary peers from the Deep South. "The positive danger is that such a conference, called at a time when some Southern emotionalism is running hot, will produce its own special brand of emotionalism and thus affect unhappily those states—of which we think Virginia is one—which are striving with some success to maintain an even balance and to deal with difficult issues with a maximum of wisdom and a minimum of prejudice."[14]

From within the state, especially from the Southside, the governor was pressured to adopt a more militant response to desegregation. On June 19 twenty state legislators met in a Petersburg fire station and expressed their opposition to the mandate of *Brown*. State senator Garland Gray was elected chairman of the group. Across the state other groups of segregationists, granted a hiatus while the Court pondered how best to implement its decision, began to organize.[15]

Most significantly, the governor was under duress by Senator Harry Byrd to harden his position. A decade later Stanley's successor, J. Lindsay Almond, referring to Byrd, would confide that after the governor's mild response, "I heard . . . that the top blew off of the U.S. Capitol."[16] A later Virginia governor, Mills E. Godwin, supported Almond's perception that the senator influenced the governor.[17]

Gradually a policy of resistance to the federal government began to emerge. Virginia, with its prestige among the other southern states, would provide leadership in the battles to come.

On June 25 Stanley yielded to pressure and, reversing his previous position, vowed to "use every legal means at my command to proclaim resistance to the court order."[18] He also urged that consideration be given to the repeal of Section 129 of the state constitution, which mandated that the state maintain free public schools.[19]

On August 30 the governor appointed a thirty-two-member legislative committee to examine the effects of *Brown* and "make such recommendations as [might] be deemed proper."[20] Although the committee was bipartisan, it was all white and heavily skewed with representatives and senators from the Southside.[21]

At the first meeting, state senator Garland Gray was appointed chairman. In addition to being a militant segregationist, "Peck" Gray was an intimate of Byrd and an ambitious politician who harbored a strong desire to succeed Stanley as governor.[22]

Two months after the establishment of the "Gray Commission," another organization that would have a profound effect on the emerging crisis took form. The Defenders of State Sovereignty and Individual Liberties, though never exceeding a membership of fifteen thousand, would exercise tremendous leverage over the state legislature. This organization objected to *Brown* primarily on the grounds that the decision usurped rights constitutionally reserved for the states and that integration would lead to intermarriage—"mongrelization of the races."[23]

The Defenders claimed as members a number of prominent Virginians, including Byrd-organization insiders former governor William Munford ("Bill") Tuck and Congressman Watkins M. Abbitt. Other notable public figures such as former governor John Stewart Battle and future governors Mills E. Godwin, Jr., and Albertis S. Harrison, Jr., regularly attended Defenders' functions. James Jackson ("Jack") Kilpatrick, Jr., the young and energetic editor of the *Richmond News Leader,* also attended many of these events.[24]

The National Association for the Advancement of Colored People mounted a vigorous campaign opposing the Defenders. Virginia's NAACP was exceptionally well organized, by 1958 claiming an impressive membership of twenty-seven thousand.[25]

The association quickly found litigation more effective than political organizing. Local NAACP attorneys, who had the primary responsibility for initiating lawsuits to challenge segregation, were assisted by the national NAACP Legal Defense and Educational Fund. The Legal Defense and Educational Fund was blessed with a talented legal staff of attorneys such as Robert L. Carter, Spottswood ("Spot") Robinson, Thurgood Marshall, Jack Greenberg, Louis T. Redding, James Nabrit, and George E. C. Hayes.[26] The phenomenon of these solicitors, most of whom were black, competing with their white counterparts and prevailing was both a repudiation of the folkways of the South and a powerful refutation of the myth of black inferiority.

The NAACP actively sought, under adverse circumstances, to ensure that the South complied with the Supreme Court's mandate. The organization was the sole means by which blacks could gain admission to segregated schools. Blacks would apply for entry to white schools, be denied, and pursue remission in the courts. The NAACP provided the only legal expertise available to these black plaintiffs. Desegregation litigation was initiated and carried out not by any agency of the government but by the NAACP alone.[27]

Within the white community the role of opposing the Defenders fell upon the Virginia Council on Human Relations. This organization, which was affiliated with the Southern Regional Council, was founded in February 1955, with the goal of readying the state for the peaceful implementation of *Brown*. Its biracial leadership included academicians, clergy, and social workers. Established political leaders were conspicuously absent. The council attempted to influence Virginians through educational activities rather than political action.[28] Leaders of some religious denominations such as the Methodists, Presbyterians, and Baptists also expressed opposition to the states's rapidly hardening segregationist sentiment.[29]

Sarah Patton Boyle of Charlottesville continued her personal campaign against racial prejudice and segregation. By the fall of 1954, she had published sixty articles in black newspapers and over seventy articles, book reviews, and letters to the editor in white newspapers, chiefly the *Virginian-Pilot* and the *Richmond Times-Dispatch*.[30]

On January 19, 1955, the Gray Commission issued a preliminary statement. Citing findings based largely on a single public hearing that had been held some months earlier, chairman Garland Gray announced the commission's conclusion that the overwhelming majority of Virginians were opposed to racial integration of the public schools and convinced that it would virtually destroy or seriously impair the public system in many sections of the state.[31] Gray advised the governor that the commission would work to develop a program to prevent such integration.

In the late spring of that same year, the Supreme Court issued its long-awaited decision concerning the implementation of *Brown*. Often referred to as *Brown II*, the decision mandated that integration of public schools should proceed with "all deliberate speed."[32] The Court reasoned that the lower courts, because of their proximity to their communities, could best enforce compliance with *Brown*.

By this delegation of responsibility to the lower courts and by the ambiguity of the phrase "all deliberate speed," the Court, albeit unintentionally, helped create an environment in which obstructionist maneuvering and legal delaying tactics could flourish. In retrospect, one wonders if an immediate abolition of segregation might have forestalled the organized resistance that the Court's decree encountered. In metropolitan areas such as Norfolk, with experienced law enforcement agencies and with relatively sophisticated citizenries, immediate desegregation would likely have met with only token resistance.[33]

Norfolk's two leading newspapers still espoused quite similar views. Leslie praised the moderation of *Brown II,* asserting that the decision took into account the difficulties involved in integration and that the implementation of the decree would not force schools to desegregate too precipitately.[34] He argued that maintaining a system of public education was an essential responsibility of the state and opposed any efforts to repeal Section 129 of the Virginia State Constitution, which mandated a free system of public schools.[35]

Chambers, too, extolled the insight of the justices. In a lead editorial he called the decision "a wise attempt to adjust constitutional principles and practical problems."[36] He warned, however, that it was unlikely either proponents of immediate integration or intransigents on the issue of segregation would be satisfied by the decision. "Somewhere in the South," the editorial ended, "a state will rise to leadership in this probably long and difficult duty. We hope it will be Virginia."[37]

During the next several days, the *Pilot* continued to call for responsible leadership which, unlike the Gray Commission, would be representative of a diversity of viewpoints pertaining to integration, and for depoliticization of the issue: "The state needs the advice of men and women of all races who are above political pressures."[38] The editorial staff also urged good-faith compliance with the Court's order and cautioned against delaying tactics and resistance.

In a lead editorial, "The Opportunities of the Decision," Chambers wrote that attempts to subvert the Court's mandate would prove ineffective. "The Supreme Court has reached a decision and has handed down a supplemental opinion, and it expects its judgement to prevail in the United States."[39]

The Defenders of State Sovereignty and Individual Liberties responded to *Brown II* almost immediately by issuing "A Plan for Virginia." The organization called for the amendment of state legislation providing for free public schools and prohibiting expenditure of state monies for private education. Also recommended were the removal from the state constitution of any mention of compulsory education and the enactment of legislation that would prohibit the state from expending even a single dollar for integrated public schools. The Defenders' recommendations constituted the first organized demand for total state resistance to the Court's decree.[40]

Although the Defenders' recommendations were intended to subvert the Supreme Court's mandate, some public officials in Norfolk indicated their inclination to behave in keeping with the spirit of the decision. Norfolk's school board, chaired by industrialist Paul T. Schweitzer, responded to *Brown* by issuing a statement on July 1, 1955, that the board would support public education and "without reservation" obey the law.[41] However, the board maintained that overseeing compliance with *Brown* was not within its powers, and it looked to the State Department of Education and the legislature to supply leadership to that end.

Less than a week later, Walter E. ("Beef") Hoffman, former football official, former Republican candidate for attorney general, and newly appointed United States District Court judge, rendered a decision requiring that the management of nearby Seashore State Park rescind its policy of refusing to admit blacks. But rather than alter its policy, the state's Department of Conservation and Development closed the facility for nearly eight years. Hoffman's decision outraged many. "When you get the volume of mail you get after one of those decisions, you wonder if you are going to live another day," he wrote.[42]

The judge was an especially outspoken opponent of the Byrd organization and had earned its enmity well before his appointment to the bench. Clerk of Courts Billy Prieur, Byrd's ranking lieutenant in Norfolk and the city's political boss, was critical of Hoffman. Prieur reminded Senator Byrd that Hoffman "took occasion to castigate you in the recent [gubernatorial election] outside and beyond the record."[43]

Perhaps motivated by the Defenders' proposals, Attorney General J. Lindsay Almond initiated a friendly suit to assess the constitutionality of expenditure of state monies for private schooling. Section 141 of the Virginia Constitution prohibited such expenditure. To test the legality of this prohibition, Almond filed a petition with the Supreme Court of Appeals of Virginia for a writ of mandamus ordering the State Comptroller to authorize payments for the children of deceased and disabled war veterans under Item 210 of the Virginia Appropriation Act of 1954. On November 7, 1955, in an opinion written by Chief Justice John W. Eggleston, it was determined that Item 210 was unconstitutional in light of Section 141.[44]

10

Legislative Ploys

THE LONG-AWAITED Public Education Report of the Commission to the Governor of Virginia, the "Gray Report," exposed the fundamental differences in the views of the editors of Norfolk's leading newspapers toward the implementation of the *Brown* decision and set the editorial policies of the papers on diametric courses. In the report, issued on November 11, 1955, the commission proposed legislation under which authority for pupil assignment would reside with local school boards, not with the state. School boards would take into account factors such as "availability of facilities, health, aptitude of the child, and the availability of transportation" in deciding where to assign children.[1] The commission also proposed legislation ensuring that compulsory attendance laws would not force children to attend integrated schools. Parents who objected to their children's enrollment in integrated schools would be eligible to receive tuition grants to support private-school education.

The *Norfolk Ledger-Dispatch* enthusiastically embraced the commission's recommendations of local option and tuition support for private education. In a lead editorial written a few days after the report was issued, Joseph Leslie stated that the recommendations were well conceived and well considered and that they provided effective solutions to the problems Virginia would face. The recommendations were flexible enough to accommodate the diverse range of racial situations in Virginia and would help to preserve public education.[2]

The *Ledger* supported the Gray Report's call for a limited constitutional convention for the purpose of amending Section 141 to provide state funding for private education. The paper urged legislators to enact the recommendations as rapidly as possible, to ensure that defenses against integration would be in place by the beginning of the next school year.[3]

It was over this issue of public support for private education that the editorials of the *Ledger-Dispatch* and the *Virginian-Pilot* began to diverge emphatically. While Lenoir Chambers and his associates agreed that the Gray Report in many ways represented an "earnest effort to find practical and legal solutions for difficult problems," they cautioned that time was needed to deliberate the outcomes of the report's recommendations.[4] Chambers noted that the commission—which had operated in virtual secrecy, without input from many concerned interest groups—had taken a year to prepare its report. To expect Virginia's citizenry to support the convening of the convention without the opportunity for thoughtful evaluation of its consequences was unreasonable.

The *Pilot* found the recommendations pertaining to private schools particularly unclear, and the paper asked a number of obvious but difficult questions. With what facilities would these private schools operate? How would the schools be staffed? What standards would govern their existence? How would they be funded? Would their operation be constitutional?[5]

Chambers also expressed concern over the divestment of the electorate in the decisions that would be reached by a constitutional convention. Although the referendum proposed by the Gray Commission would provide voters with the opportunity to declare their support or opposition to the convention, their participation would be limited to that declaration.[6] Chambers summarized his reservations in a lead editorial: "It is difficult now—in our opinion, impossible—to learn from available information the extent, the costs, the effects, the administrative practicality, and the constitutional soundness of a tuition payment plan. . . . The legislators who represent the people don't know the answers. The people whom they represent don't know."[7]

Although the Gray Commission included many members of the Byrd organization, the senator distanced himself from its findings. While on a congressional trip to Europe, he was sent a copy of the "Gray Plan." "This won't do," he is quoted as having said.[8] Byrd issued a statement in which, although he endorsed tuition grants, he avoided supporting local option.[9]

Many political observers felt that he was embarrassed by the recommendations of the commission. In addition to controlling nearly every facet of Virginia's politics, Byrd, as chairman of the Senate Finance Committee and the senior member of Virginia's congressional delegation, was a formidable national leader. The senator's southern colleagues had expected Virginia to play a leadership role in impeding the implementation of *Brown,* and the policies of the commission seemed to imply a strategy of compromise rather than confrontation.[10]

Byrd hurriedly worked to develop a regional response to *Brown:* "Ten other states are confronted with the same acute problem. These states are all seeking a way to preserve their schools, and it is possible that some form of action can be accepted as a pattern for all."[11]

On November 30, 1955, the General Assembly met in a special session to consider the Gray Commission's recommendation that Section 141 be amended to allow for tuition grants. The section stated that "no appropriation of public funds [should] be made to any school or institution of learning not owned or exclusively controlled by the state or some political subdivision thereof."[12] The delegates, with only six objections, voted to support the amendment. A statewide referendum to ratify the revision of Section 141 was scheduled for January 9, 1956.[13]

The State Referendum Information Center was established in Richmond on December 9, 1955, for the purpose of creating public awareness of the need to vote in favor of tuition grants. The efforts of the center were supported by most of Virginia's political elite, including the entire Byrd organization, by the Defenders of State Sovereignty and Individual Liberties, and by nearly all of the state's white presses.[14]

Privately, within the normally unified Byrd organization, the issue of local option was fractious. Some moderate organization members, such as former governors John Stewart Battle and Colgate W. Darden, Jr., preferred that public schools continue to operate, even at the risk of integration. Hardliners such as Byrd, Stanley, and Congressmen Bill Tuck, Watkins Abbitt, and Howard W. Smith vehemently supported segregation regardless of the costs.[15] The Referendum Center officers who had issued the statement that local option would be upheld would later be chagrined over their proclamation.[16]

As the January 9, 1956, date for the referendum grew nearer, the disparity between the *Virginian-Pilot*'s and the *Ledger-Dispatch*'s editorial views widened. The *Ledger* dismissed the *Pilot*'s charges that the constitutional convention was undemocratic. Leslie insisted that the mechanism by which Section 141 would be amended ensured maximum input from the citizenry. Voters would have the opportunity to elect delegates to the limited constitutional convention; and the General Assembly, which consisted of elected representatives accountable to the electorate, would formulate the actual tuition legislation.[17]

The *Ledger* also argued that providing public assistance for private schooling was in the best interest of the state's black schoolchildren. Should Section 141 not be amended, it was probable that public schools would close in many communities. These closings were especially likely in the twenty-two Virginia counties in which black students formed majorities of the school populations. By voting for the convention, voters would make certain that a strong and viable public school system continued to operate.[18] Leslie and his staff assured readers that voting for the convention would in no way affect Section 129 of the constitution, which mandated that the state maintain a free system of public schools.[19]

On the evening of the referendum, the *Ledger* warned that not voting for the convention would fuel extremism: "If the constitutional amendment is rejected, there can be no question that the attitude of those who accept the Gray plan as a middle-of-the-road course between the two extremes on the segregation issue will be changed."[20]

The *Virginian-Pilot,* with growing concern, continued to oppose the recommendations contained in the Gray Report: "The Gray Commission idea . . . is vague as a whole and unidentified in its most important aspects, and would involve the disestablishment, or dismantling, of the public school system as we know it today."[21]

Chambers and his associate editors saw merit in a plan advanced by two members of the faculty of the University of Virginia. With the purpose of depoliticizing the desegregation issue, these academicians suggested establishment of a new advisory commission. This biracial commission, to be appointed by the presidents of Virginia's state-supported colleges and the University of Virginia, would consist of elected officials and representatives from academia, professional educational organizations, and parent-teacher groups. Similar groups would be formed at a local level. The *Pilot* agreed that advisory groups such as these would more accurately reflect the sentiments of Virginia's citizens and would devise more innovative solutions to racial problems than the Gray Commission had provided.[22]

The Gray Plan was seen by the *Pilot* as an overreaction to the racial problems of a single community, the Southside's Prince Edward County. Limited integration could likely occur without undue difficulty in most of Virginia's school districts. If the state, on the whole, demonstrated good-faith compliance with the Supreme Court decision, the Court would be understanding of the difficulties faced in integrating schools in areas with entrenched racial attitudes. In these communities even the most minor steps toward desegregation would constitute compliance.[23]

Chambers accused Virginia's leaders of intentionally creating an emotional climate to reap political benefits: "The advocates of the Gray Commission program seek to gain political advantage by conjuring up the nightmare of 'enforced mixing.' "[24] The paper also questioned the constitutionality of the use of tax dollars for private education. Chambers anticipated that the Supreme Court might well declare tuition support illegal.[25]

The *Pilot* concluded its unsuccessful campaign to persuade readers to vote against the constitutional convention with an editorial entitled "The Voter's Choice Tomorrow." In it, the Gray Plan was dismissed somewhat contemptuously as "an idea, not a plan."[26]

Also opposing tuition support was the Virginia Society for Preservation of Public Education (VSPPE). The VSPPE argued that state support for private schooling would destroy public education. The NAACP, the Virginia Council of Human Relations, some religious leaders, a handful of political representatives, and what vestiges of organized labor existed in Virginia supported the society's efforts. The *Virginian-Pilot* and the *Ledger-Dispatch*, alone among the state's white presses, sided with the VSPPE.

The referendum to amend Section 141 to permit appropriation of state and local government funds for nonsectarian private as well as public schooling took place January 9, 1956. The results demonstrated conclusively that Virginians strongly supported the provision of tuition assistance for private education. Regional percentages of voters supporting the amendment varied predictably, ranging from 84.3 in the Black Belt to 56.4 in the White Belt.[27] In Norfolk, perhaps as a result of the *Virginian-Pilot*'s editorials, the results were nearly even.[28]

The overwhelming public support for amending Section 141 helped reinforce the perception among Virginia's political leadership that incendiary segregationist posturing and rhetoric would be strongly supported. This impression, along with the efforts of organization hard-line segregationists, had the effect of escalating resistance to *Brown*.

Seeking to broaden public approval of the segregationist stance, Jack Kilpatrick of the *Richmond News Leader* helped disinter the forgotten doctrine of "interposition"—the invocation of state sovereignty to negate attempts by the federal government to usurp rights the states believed were justly afforded them by the Constitution.[29] Developed in the late eighteenth century by Thomas Jefferson and James Madison and later employed by John C. Calhoun, doctrines of nullification and interposition were seen by many massive resisters as potentially effective roadblocks to desegregation.[30]

Kilpatrick, a respected advisor to Senator Byrd, quickly became a widely influential publicist on the related topics of interposition, states' rights, and white supremacy. At the peak of the debate surrounding interposition, Kilpatrick launched an editorial campaign, lasting from November 21, 1955, to February 2, 1956, in which he touted the virtues of the doctrine.[31]

Many members of the Byrd organization, the senator included, naively saw interposition as a legal means of circumventing the Supreme Court's order.[32] Others, such as Kilpatrick and Almond, viewed this stratagem as a symbolic protest and realized from the outset that the courts would ultimately reject the doctrine and its manifestations. Kilpatrick, acutely aware of the importance of public relations, believed that interposition would shift the focus of the debate over desegregation from racism to the higher ground of states' rights.[33]

In addition to his editorial duties, Kilpatrick served as the publications director of the Virginia Commission on Constitutional Government. The commission, funded by the state, attempted to counter the unfavorable press coverage Virginia's resistance policies had generated across the nation.[34]

The adoption of an "Interposition Resolution" by the General Assembly on February 1, 1956, signified the increasingly blatant resistance to the *Brown* decision. Strongly influenced by the *Richmond News Leader*'s two-month editorial campaign, the legislature decried the infringements of the federal government, pledged the assembly's intent to resist by every means available the federal government's encroachment upon Virginia's sovereign powers, and urged its sister states to do likewise.[35] The assembly also scheduled a special summer session to enact more segregationist legislation.[36]

The *Norfolk Ledger-Dispatch* responded ambivalently to the assembly's adoption of the interposition resolution. While the paper saw some merit in the resolution as a symbolic protest against the federal government's infringement of rights constitutionally delegated to the states, it conceded that interposition would do nothing to nullify the Court's decision.[37]

Chambers and his staff vehemently voiced their opposition to the resolution, calling interposition "an exercise in fantasy."[38] They wrote that "in the calm, cool second thinking" that would come later, the futility of the resolution as a solution to the school problem and as a likely influence on federal legislative and judicial action would be apparent, as would the murkiness of the resolution's language and the circumstances of its adoption.[39]

The "Interposition Resolution" was a symbolic gesture and little more. Anti-organization Democrat Robert Whitehead called interposition "nullification nonsense" and colorfully dismissed the overblown emotionalism surrounding the resolution: "The lightning flashed, the thunder struck, and a chigger died!"[40] Seeking clarification as to exactly what the resolution meant, Whitehead wrote to Attorney General Almond. Almond admitted that the resolution did not constitute a defense against *Brown* but touted the resolution as "an unequivocal epitome of Virginia's unyielding devotion and loyalty to the perpetuation of that constitutional system of government which, more than any other state, she molded and launched in the formation of the Union."[41]

With opposition to integration at a fever pitch, on February 24, 1956, Senator Byrd called for "massive resistance" to integration, predicting that if the southern states organized to resist the *Brown* mandate, the rest of the country would realize that racial integration would not be accepted in the South.[42] The senator appears to have been the first congressional representative to use the term "massive resistance."[43]

Byrd has been classified by political scientist Francis M. Wilhoit as massive resistance's foremost "tutelary genius," the person most responsible for determining the structure of the movement. Supporting this conclusion, author Nunman Bartley states that Byrd was the South's prime mover in its opposition to the Supreme Court's decision in *Brown v. Board of Education*.[44] However, his role in the shaping of the resistance was carefully concealed from the public. According to Robert Mason, the senator remained in the background, where he was an elusive target, throughout the campaign. "But," says Mason, "it became pretty apparent who was pulling the strings and who was answering to whom."[45]

Many historians and journalists ascribe Byrd's advocacy of massive resistance more to political survival than to racial prejudice, although white supremacy certainly motivated many organization insiders such as Abbitt and Tuck.[46] For the first time there were indications that the omnipotent organization led by the aging senator was in decline. The 1954 gubernatorial election had been hotly contested, and only with Byrd's personal intervention did Stanley survive the challenge of Theodore Roosevelt ("Ted") Dalton, the popular delegate from Radford.

Its superiority threatened, the organization sought and became increasingly dependent on support from whites living in the Black Belt. Byrd used the issue of integration to rally the support of these voters. "This will keep us in power another twenty-five years," an anonymous leader in the organization is quoted as having said.[47]

The senator correctly perceived that massive resistance had great popular appeal in regions other than the Southside. White Virginians elsewhere, nearly all of whom wished to maintain their tradition of segregated schools, differed from their counterparts in the Black Belt only in regard to the sacrifices they were willing to endure to stave off integration.

Byrd's reasons for embracing massive resistance were political and personal. As one of the primary architects of the "Southern Manifesto," which was being developed in the U.S. Senate during this time, Byrd felt it only appropriate that Virginia provide leadership for the rest of the South in maintaining segregated schools.

Representatives assembled in Richmond on March 5, 1956, to hold the limited state constitutional convention mandated by the January 9 referendum. The forty delegates voted unanimously to amend Section 141 to provide public funding for private schools.[48]

The Declaration of Constitutional Principles—the "Southern Manifesto"—was issued on March 12, 1956. The document was introduced by Senator Walter George of Georgia in the Senate and Representative Howard W. Smith, a key figure in the Byrd organization, in the U.S. House of Representatives. Byrd and Senator Strom Thurmond of South Carolina had been the foremost architects of the manifesto. One hundred one southern congressmen, the vast majority of the region's federal legislators, including both of Virginia's senators and all ten of its representatives, signed the document.[49]

The authors of the Southern Manifesto called the *Brown* decision "a clear abuse of judicial power."[50] They pledged "to use all lawful means to bring about a reversal of this decision which is contrary to the constitution and to prevent the use of force in its implementation."[51] Byrd called the document part of the "plan of massive resistance we've been working on."[52]

Heartened by the early victories of massive resistance—the tuition referendum, interposition, and the Southern Manifesto—Senator Byrd assembled his upper echelon of leaders for a secret conclave in the nation's capital on July 2, 1956. With Stanley, Gray, Tuck, and Abbitt in attendance, Byrd reached the decision to escalate further the resistance to integration by prohibiting state funding for desegregated schools. The local option feature of the Gray Plan was rejected out of hand.[53]

Speaking from his Berryville apple orchard in late August, the senator drew a line in the sand. "Virginia stands as one of the foremost states. Let Virginia surrender to this illegal demand [the desegregation order] . . . and you'll find the ranks of other southern states broken. . . . It's no secret that the NAACP intends first to press Virginia. . . . If Virginia surrenders, if Virginia's line is broken, the rest of the South will go down, too."[54]

In an atmosphere of extremism, the governor convened a special session of the General Assembly on August 27, 1956. The same Governor Stanley who had responded to *Brown* in such a moderate fashion and had supported local option now advocated massive resistance. Gray and the majority of the members of his commission performed a similar about-face. The obstructionist legislative scheme they proposed became known as the "Stanley Plan."

The plan consisted of three principal redoubts to integration. First, local school boards would be divested of pupil-placement responsibilities. A three-member Pupil Placement Board, to be appointed by the governor, would assign the state's public-school students to specific schools. Ostensibly this board would assign students objectively; in reality it would exist solely to rebuff integration.[55]

Should black students bridge this obstacle—and it was anticipated that with the federal courts' assistance some would—they would confront a second and more formidable barrier. Schools that were integrated, either voluntarily or as a result of students' appealing decisions of the Pupil Placement Board, would be closed by the governor. The state would provide funding for the private education of students and for the salaries of teachers and principals locked out of the closed schools.

Finally, although the city councils of the closed systems could petition the governor to reopen their schools, the state would deny funding to these bodies if they chose to do so. Most localities would find it very difficult, if not impossible, to continue to operate schools without assistance from Richmond.

Joseph Leslie and his staff tentatively supported the Stanley Plan. The

Ledger conceded that the provisions of Governor Stanley's plan would likely close schools in some areas, but argued that the integration resulting from local option would almost certainly result in school closings in large areas throughout the state. The editor also warned that local option would lead to mass integration.[56]

In response to the governor's assurance that schools would remain open unless members of one race attempted to enroll in schools designated for students of the other race, the *Ledger* stated that "Stanley lean[ed] upon a fragile reed."[57] There was no reason to believe that the threat of school closings would dissuade the NAACP from continuing its efforts to desegregate schools. The *Ledger* predicted that whether local option or the Stanley Plan was adopted, there was a very real risk that schools would be closed.[58]

The *Virginian-Pilot* also saw no merit in the Stanley Plan and vehemently denounced the provisions that would eliminate state funding for integrated schools. In a lead editorial, "How Many Schools Are Expendable?" Chambers and his staff expressed their astonishment that the General Assembly would consider adopting legislation that would inevitably result in the closing of the schools in the five Virginia communities (Norfolk included) soon to be under court order to desegregate their schools.[59]

In "A Primary Concern of the State," the editorial staff contended that much educational progress in Virginia would be undone by the Stanley Plan. Localities would no longer be required by law to provide students with school terms of a nine-month duration, fixed state appropriations for local schools would become tentative, and school superintendents would be divested of important responsibilities. "The threat Governor Stanley's program poses to the public schools," the *Pilot* declared, "is an appalling reality. Once the standards are gone, the work of a generation may be destroyed."[60]

Chambers urged the General Assembly to reject the Stanley Plan and, instead, adopt a local-option plan similar to that recommended by the Gray Commission. The *Pilot* maintained that the Stanley Plan would be ruled illegal by the courts.[61]

Chambers argued that local option would stand a far better chance of satisfying the courts and at the same time would discourage massive integration. The *Pilot* conceded that local option would not be the choice of most Virginians, who would prefer to retain the existing school structure. If local option was "operated deceitfully to try to block any change anywhere," the *Pilot* warned, that choice would be rejected by the courts as a subterfuge. If, however, it was implemented honestly in accordance with the law and the requirement to maintain public education, it would significantly reduce the impact of the change resulting from the *Brown* decision.[62]

The legislation that constituted the Stanley Plan did not receive unanimous support. Moderates, including embarrassed members of the Referendum Information Center such as University of Virginia president Colgate W. Darden, Jr., as well as many members of the State Board of Education, objected to the plan's fund-withholding provisions. Two faculty members in the University of Virginia's Department of Education resigned in protest. Darden, a former governor, declared, "If I were a non-Virginian, I don't think I'd want to come in here for the next ten or fifteen years."[63]

In the end, however, Black Belt legislators and the Byrd organization won an unusually close vote: 59 to 39 in the House of Delegates and 21 to 17 in the Senate.[64] Virginius Dabney would conclude that "the racial attitudes of most whites in Virginia's Black Belt, constituting only a small fraction of the state's population, had been imposed on the entire Commonwealth."[65]

In addition to the legislation that made up the Stanley Plan, a number of other bills intended to ward off integration were approved. Organizations that promoted or opposed race-related legislation would now have to furnish the State Corporation Commission with the names of donors and members. NAACP members feared that if their affiliation became known, they would face retaliation ranging from loss of jobs to denial of credit. The new laws were formidable impediments to those working for integration.[66] As one segregationist said, "As long as we can legislate, we can segregate."[67]

The fears of the NAACP were justified. After their affiliation was revealed, a number of leaders and members received obscene or threatening telephone calls. Crosses were burned near some members' homes. And while the president of Norfolk's NAACP was away from home, a hearse arrived at his house to collect his body.[68]

After the passage of Virginia's legislation, five other southern states followed suit by ordering the NAACP to release lists of contributors and members.[69]

Also that autumn Lindsay J. Almond, bucking the Byrd Machine, independently declared for the governorship. As attorney general he had positioned himself as a contender and earned a reputation as a highly capable opponent of integration. Although Almond was not a Byrd favorite because of his past deviation from organization orthodoxy, pragmatism prevailed, and Byrd endorsed Almond because of his popularity.[70]

Almond announced his candidacy in the midst of participating in the argument of a major court case in Norfolk.[71] Two suits, *Adkins v. School Board of the City of Newport News* and *Beckett v. School Board of the City of Norfolk,* had been brought by black plaintiffs to test the constitutionality of Virginia's pupil-placement laws.[72] Judge Hoffman had consolidated the cases because of their similarities. (Although whites would later play important roles in initiating legal action to reopen Norfolk's schools after the closing, it is noteworthy that both the *Adkins* and the *Beckett* suits were brought by black plaintiffs and directed by NAACP attorneys.)

Hoffman found the pupil-placement act to be unconstitutional on its face, in view of the fact that it considered the race of students in determining school assignments. While he acknowledged the conundrum of local officials who were caught between conflicting state and federal statutes, he pointed to the primacy of federal laws and chided the General Assembly for its lack of effort "to in good faith implement the governing constitutional principles."[73] He deplored the ambiguity of *Brown II*'s "with all deliberate speed"—which he interpreted as meaning there must be some effective steps toward compliance.[74]

Hoffman concluded his decision by enjoining the defendants to abolish their practice of assigning students to particular schools solely on the basis of race. The decree was to become effective August 15, 1957.

Judge Hoffman's ruling in *Beckett v. Norfolk* was anticipated by both newspapers. At the *Ledger,* Leslie downplayed the significance of the decision, calling it "only one skirmish in the school segregation battle," and noted the certainty of appeal: "The state is committed to full-scale resistance to integration and this includes all possible delaying action."[75]

Chambers and his staff expressed the hope that the General Assembly and local officials would take note of the decision and the emphasis Hoffman placed on good-faith implementation of the Supreme Court's desegregation order.[76] The *Pilot* praised the moderation of the judge's decision, in which he called for gradual rather than immediate integration. Hoffman's order mandated integration in only the first grades of the city's elementary, junior high, and high schools and encouraged the redrawing of school districts to minimize further the impact of desegregation.[77]

Hoffman's judgment and the events surrounding it provide insight into the impending crisis and the emerging power struggle. In his decision the judge made some complimentary references to Norfolk school officials, an indication that he probably was attempting to forge an alliance with the city's educational leadership.[78]

Byrd, too, sought to influence the school board, and in his correspondence with Kilpatrick, expressed gratification in his apparently successful attempts to persuade the board to defy the federal courts. "I am very much pleased to hear from private sources that Norfolk is going to stand by us and the school board has made this decision. That Jackass, Hoffman, was attempting to make a deal with them by agreeing that there would be modified integration over a long term of years."[79]

The disaffection between the senator and the judge bordered at times on open hostility. While Hoffman was trying *Beckett* and *Adkins,* Billy Prieur informed Byrd that the judge had directed some extrajudicial barbs at the organization.[80] Byrd reacted to Hoffman's decision and the reported attacks by accusing the judge of having determined the case without having heard evidence and of having let the NAACP ghostwrite his decision. "I don't know how he got all that information," Hoffman marvels; "but of course, if I did all of that, I ought to have been impeached. I'd be the first to admit it."[81]

Chambers puzzled over Byrd's charges and telephoned Hoffman in an attempt to obtain transcripts to determine the accuracy of the accusations. The judge recalls the editor's inquiry: "It doesn't make any sense to me that you would write an opinion without having anything in the files." Hoffman responded, "Well, Lenoir, if they're not going to look in the clerk's office where the files are kept, there's nothing I can do about it." After reading the voluminous transcript, Chambers wrote an editorial entitled "In Fairness to Judge Hoffman," which refuted Byrd's accusations. Additionally, the editor confronted Byrd during a telephone conversation: "I've got the record down here—five hundred and some pages. I'll send it to you. . . . You owe Judge Hoffman an apology." "Well, I'll keep owing it to him," Byrd retorted.[82]

The United States Court of Appeals, Fourth Circuit, upheld Hoffman's decision. The circuit court's decision was appealed to the Supreme Court, which denied certiorari on October 21, 1957. The August 15, 1957, deadline for Hoffman's injunction having passed, the desegregation of Norfolk's public schools was set for the beginning of the 1958–1959 school year.

Billy Prieur, who regularly reported to Byrd on Chambers's editorials, wrote to the senator: "I have read Chambers's [editorial] and, in my opinion, it is so much eyewash. He, as well as the other editors of the *Pilot,* are more critical of the position taken in Virginia with reference to integration and I am inclined to doubt the sincerity of his statements in private conversation."[83]

Chambers corresponded with the senator in an effort to elucidate the *Virginian-Pilot*'s views on massive resistance.

> We have never urged swift or sweeping mixture of the races in the public schools. We do feel certain that mixing in varying degrees is inevitable in a future that is difficult to measure in time; and we think strongly that government and citizenship, and all leadership, have the duty to try to appraise these problems, calmly, carefully, with good spirit, and with justice.
>
> Much that has been done in the South reflects, I am afraid, a different spirit. We conceive it our duty in these circumstances to do what we can to encourage a climate in which the best minds and spirits of Virginia (and other states), and not only the most extreme or the best organized, can make their wisdom and intelligence count in dealing with these grave and complicated problems.[84]

Chambers reminded Byrd of his "statesmanship" in sponsoring Virginia's anti-lynching legislation and urged the senator to include blacks in the search for a solution to the state's racial problems.

Byrd responded by expressing his concern that moderate integration would lead to massive integration. The senator asserted that if Virginia adopted a policy of local option, the NAACP would initiate on a local level a large number of lawsuits that would result in widespread integration. "Modified integration," Byrd wrote, "is not going to satisfy the NAACP and others who favor the real integration of our public school system."[85]

Prieur disapproved of Byrd's entreaties to the *Pilot*'s editor. The clerk of courts wrote to Byrd, "I feel you are wasting your time in writing to him on the subject [of massive resistance]. He is, in my opinion, a most charming person personally, but a rabid integrationist in his news columns. . . . This paper and its editorial columns are not for the Organization."[86]

Prieur's scrutiny of Chambers continued over the years, and his opinion of the editor remained constant: "I am enclosing an editorial which appeared in the *Virginian-Pilot*. I do this for the reason that this paper seldom, if ever, has anything nice to say about you."[87]

Although Chambers believed that the senator was ultimately responsible for the state's worsening racial relations, he refrained from personally attacking Byrd.[88] Given the adversarial nature of today's press and of some of Chambers's contemporaries in the Deep South, this policy is puzzling. The most obvious rationale—that the *Virginian-Pilot*'s editor and management were afraid of incurring the wrath of the powerful senator and his supporters—is incorrect. Chambers's associates recall scant fear of retribution. A more accurate explanation is the gentility with which journalists from the Upper South, particularly Virginia journalists, practiced their craft during the Chambers era. Virginia editors were expected to conduct themselves as gentlemen; and they, particularly Chambers, would have considered it bad manners to impugn the motives and character of the state's senior senator. But even to Robert Mason, who had practiced journalism in neighboring North Carolina for many years before returning to the *Pilot* as an associate editor, the policy seemed odd.[89]

A probable second reason Chambers refused to personalize the struggle was that he did not consider Byrd a militant racist, as he did some organization insiders. The editor attributed the senator's development of massive resistance to his states' rights philosophy and his suspicion of federal government.

Chambers was uncertain as to the extent political pragmatism figured in Byrd's policies. He wrote to William Wing, a young Norfolk man who had left the *Virginian-Pilot* for the *New York Herald Tribune*, "There are in

Virginia many politicians who know very well that trumpeting the hard seg-regation point of view is good for another election. . . . They would not hesi-tate to exploit that issue to the utmost. . . . How much Senator Byrd has been influenced, consciously or unconsciously, by the political expediency of the segregationist point of view, I do not know."[90]

Chambers was harshly critical of President Dwight D. Eisenhower's lack of leadership throughout the desegregation crisis. Until violence in Arkansas forced him to act in the autumn of 1957, Eisenhower had practiced a policy of neutrality that many southern leaders had interpreted as tacit support of segregation. The editor wrote that the president should have begun to speak and act immediately upon the issuance of the initial *Brown v. Board* decision. "That was the time," Chambers editorialized, "for the President to begin exerting the leadership of the presidency to the end that citizens and states understand, appreciate, and prepare wisely for the immensely complicated tasks of adapting constitutional principles to the life of the Southern States. How much might have been done in intelligent leadership is impossible to estimate now. But what happened was nothing—nothing in genuine na-tional leadership."[91]

In the 1957 Virginia gubernatorial race, Chambers aligned himself with Ted Dalton, who again faced an uphill struggle in his representation of the anti-Byrd electorate. The *Pilot* was the state's only major white newspaper to back Dalton.[92]

Almond, capitalizing on the fanning of segregationist passion by Presi-dent Eisenhower's dispatchment of federal troops to Little Rock that Sep-tember, depicted Dalton as an integrationist, which he was not.[93] In his most inflammatory and popular campaign speech, Almond vowed that he would lose his right arm before a single black child enrolled in a white school in Virginia.[94] He defeated Dalton by a wide margin.[95]

Byrd pressured Almond to use his inaugural address to denounce the usurpation of states' rights by the federal government.[96] The governor ac-quiesced, and much of his address on January 11 was devoted to "the sover-eignty of the states, the security of a nation—with particular reference to the problems of our public schools," and "the challenge that awaits our en-tire system of education in light of the Russians' ominous moon [the U.S.S.R. satellite Sputnik]."[97]

Almond's inaugural speech drew a glowing endorsement from the *Ledger-Dispatch*. Leslie wrote that at no time had "the case for continued racial segregation been presented with more force and logic" than in the address and that Almond "went deep into the truth of the whole integration issue" when he maintained that forcing parents to send their children to integrated schools would result in chaos.[98] The paper urged that the General Assembly immediately enact the legislation Almond recommended in his address, authorizing the governor to close schools that were policed by federal troops.[99]

Chambers and his staff viewed the inaugural address with concern. Almond had insulted the Supreme Court by drawing a comparison between it and Sputnik, categorizing both as "revolving bodies." The *Pilot* remarked that "these [were] strange words from a governor who lived his professional life in the law."[100] The paper also expressed displeasure at the singular focus of the address. Almond's defiant speech might have earned him additional support from hard-line segregationists, but this was no substitute for providing the state with legitimate and much-needed leadership.[101]

The momentum behind Lindsay Almond's campaign and rousing victory over Dalton fueled massive resistance in Virginia.[102] In January the legislature met in regular session and enacted still more resistance laws.[103] Chapter 642 of the 1958 session of the General Assembly limited the expenditure of state funding to "efficient schools." Efficient schools were defined as schools that were not integrated.[104] Chapters 41 and 319, known as the "Little Rock Bills," ordered the closing of schools whose operation was policed by federal military forces.[105] Also illustrative of the tenor of the session was the enactment of legislation that further obstructed black suffrage by increasing the literacy requirements for voter registration.[106]

The federal courts continued to dismantle massive-resistance legislation. That same month a three-judge panel sitting in Richmond ruled that state statutes intended to curtail the legal activities of the NAACP and force the organization to release its membership lists were unconstitutional.[107]

Surprisingly, this panel's decision would be overturned by the Supreme Court, with Chief Justice Earl Warren and Justices William O. Douglas and William Brennan dissenting. The Court felt that the panel should have delayed its ruling until the state courts had been given the opportunity to interpret the state statutes.[108]

11

The Resistance in Norfolk

WITH THE APPROACH of the new school year, the people of Norfolk braced themselves for the long-delayed enforcement of the *Brown* decision and the possible closing of the city's public schools. Chambers and his staff monitored with apprehension the eleventh-hour mobilization of the resistance.

On June 7, 1958, Hoffman announced from the bench that the city must, with reasonable promptness and without regard to race, act upon the transfers of black students who were requesting assignment to white schools.[1] Prieur responded by making preparations to evoke the state's massive-resistance laws. "As you have no doubt read in the papers," he wrote to Byrd, "Norfolk will be on the front line when the schools open. Our definite plans are to close the schools if the Negroes attempt enrollment. All of this, of course, within the new laws of Virginia."[2]

On June 27 the State Corporation Commission of Virginia issued a certificate of incorporation to the Tidewater Educational Foundation, the segregationist private-school organization connected with the Defenders of State Sovereignty and Individual Liberties.[3] Among the five directors of the organization were James G. Martin IV, a local attorney, and W. I. McKendree, a vendor of duplicating equipment and the past president of the city Parent-Teacher Association Council. Martin, with his strong social standing, afforded the foundation an air of gentility, whereas the zealous McKendree, a charter member of the Defenders with roots in the working class, represented the constituency most likely to feel threatened by desegregation.[4]

Besides objecting to integration on the grounds that it usurped state sovereignty, that it was not in the best interest of blacks, and that it would lead to "mongrelization" of the races, these principal members of the foundation professed the belief that integration was a communist plot intended to sow dissent and enervate the nation's youth.[5]

Later, during the making of a Columbia Broadcasting System television documentary on the closing, Martin would state the nature of his objections to public-school integration. "As a device in implementation of this scheme of subversion of American institutions, the Soviet has adopted this technique called integration . . . with the dual purpose, first since time means little to these master scientists—over the long haul, to so amalgamate the races in America that there will ensue a mongrel race so debilitated and so diffused that it has little or no principle left with which to withstand the avalanche of Communism, which then plans to take over."[6]

McKendree also appeared in the documentary: "Hitler first federalized the police force, gaining under him the power to coerce the people throughout the land. And secondly, he federalized the school system to capture the minds of all the children. And thus having done this, he set himself up as a tyrant that would dictate to all of the people of that land. Many of the states, throughout the Union, are now familiar with the crushing hand, the iron glove of this unit known as the Supreme Court of the United States of America. My friends, we teeter on the brink of total dictatorship. Let it not happen here."[7]

The Tidewater Educational Foundation began work to establish an alternative school system. McKendree and his associates energetically began to lay the groundwork for obtaining substitute school facilities and a teaching staff.[8] Of the five directors of the TEF, only one, a history teacher at a local high school, had any professional experience as an educator.

On July 17, 1958, Norfolk's school board issued a resolution that enumerated the criteria for assessing the suitability of students attempting to transfer between previously all-black and previously all-white schools. The standards purported to take the would-be transfer students' health, academic backgrounds, physical and moral fitness, mental ability, social adaptability, and cultural backgrounds into account, as well as the health, safety, and cultural backgrounds of the pupils already enrolled in the requested schools. The resolution charged superintendent John J. Brewbaker with responsibility for overseeing the administration of a battery of tests and personal interviews that would be used to evaluate the students.[9]

The board promised to base the assignments on all pertinent facts, "without regard to race or color."[10] It had earlier stated that in the event of a conflict between state and federal laws, it would regard the latter as paramount. NAACP attorney Oliver Hill praised the board for its excellent attitude.[11]

On August 18, 1958, the State Supreme Court of Appeals issued an injunction restraining the school board from "performing any act of enrollment or placement of pupils in the public schools of the City of Norfolk." The court asserted that responsibility for assigning students rested with the state Pupil Placement Board. This restraining order, which would remain effective well into the school year, was issued after the Circuit Court of the City of Norfolk had refused the request of the board for an injunction prohibiting the assignment of the black students.[12]

That same day, the school board denied all of the 151 applications by black students for transfer to previously all-white schools. Sixty-one students had declined to take the prescribed California Achievement Test, one had withdrawn his application, one had refused to submit to the personal interviews conducted by the five-member panel of educators and psychologists, and sixty students had failed to meet the minimum scholastic requirements. Of the remaining twenty-eight applicants, twenty-four had requested transfer to schools in the racially tense Norview area, where, the board maintained, their assignment would incite racial conflict. The board determined that the final four students would be so isolated in white schools that they would suffer psychological harm.[13]

The next day thirty of the would-be transfer students petitioned Hoffman to overrule the board's decision.[14] The judge, who knew most of the seven board members personally, met with them on August 25. He clarified the mandate of the Supreme Court, examined the rationale advanced by the board for refusing admission, and expressed his willingness to meet with school officials to furnish them with additional clarification. In precise language he informed them that racial tension, the threat of schools being closed, and the isolation of black students were not valid reasons for refusing to approve transfers. The results of achievement tests and personal interviews could, he said, be used as grounds for denial, provided these criteria were fairly administered. Hoffman concluded his instruction by ordering the board to reconsider the transfer requests and to report the results of its activities on August 29.[15]

Taking a highly unpopular position in a lead editorial, "The School Board and the Law," Chambers supported Hoffman's remarks, calling them "warm," "human," and "reflective at all stages of the perplexities that are inherent in the segregation-integration issues." Chambers continued, "The remarks do one thing that seems to us of great importance: they bear down heavily on the law and the requirements of law. In asking the school board to think again, Judge Hoffman seems to us to have acted wisely. The legal thinness of the board's cited reasons for denials in some instances were not difficult for laymen to see."[16]

Hoffman experienced considerable stress as the date set for the opening of schools, September 8, neared. He received hate mail and threatening telephone calls from rabid segregationists, and a cross was set on fire in front of his home.[17] "He did not show it," recalls Farley Powers, his law clerk during that period, "[but] he was under stress, I know."[18] The crisis affected Hoffman on a personal level as well as a professional one. Many of his friends ostracized him. A popular joke at the time—one that had some basis in reality—concerned the inability of the judge, an avid golfer, to find three partners with whom to play golf.[19] Unlike many southern judges, whose children received private educations, he would choose to continue to send his children to public schools.[20]

Nevertheless, Judge Hoffman continued to attack segregation. On August 29, in a relatively minor case that foreshadowed events to come, he granted a preliminary injunction barring municipal officials in the neighboring city of Portsmouth from operating a golf course that refused to admit blacks.[21]

Two days after Hoffman ordered reconsideration of the students' transfer requests, the Pupil Placement Board telegraphed the school board to request that applications be sent to the Placement Board. "[We] cannot see," the executive secretary cabled, "how the furnishing of such information could possibly be construed as contempt of any court."[22]

On August 29 Chairman Schweitzer reported to Judge Hoffman that the school board had reluctantly assigned seventeen black students to six of the city's formerly all-white schools. Three junior and three senior highs were named as the schools to be integrated.[23] The six had a combined enrollment of nearly ten thousand students.

The board then, on the same day, delayed the opening of schools until September 22, appealed Hoffman's decision to the Court of Appeals for the Fourth Circuit, and filed a motion to postpone the desegregation order until September of 1959. Three days later Hoffman denied the motion.[24]

In a lead editorial entitled "The School Board and the State," Chambers applauded the board's decision to admit the black children, while questioning its judgment in refusing admission to the other 134 students. As the date of the impending school closing drew closer, the *Pilot*'s editor admonished state officials: "There is no moral justification for the harsh punishment of the state's largest city by locking up its junior and senior high schools because its school board, pursuant to law and the direction of a court, will assign this handful of Negro pupils to schools where other pupils are white. Surely there is greater wisdom in Virginia than this would imply."[25]

Despite its obvious recalcitrance and grudging compliance with the district court's order, the school board, none of whose members favored integration, found itself castigated by hard-line segregationists.[26] At a meeting held in Richmond on September 1, the Defenders of State Sovereignty and Individual Liberties called on the governor to overrule the Norfolk board's action. The Defenders argued that the Pupil Placement Board was vested with the sole power to assign students.[27]

Governor Almond responded the next day by informing reporters that the state's Pupil Placement Act could not legally be interposed to postpone desegregation in Norfolk.[28] Nevertheless, on September 4, 1958, the governor advised the superintendents of school divisions under federal order to desegregate that they had been divested of their responsibility to assign students. Almond warned these local officials that if they did not abide by his order, they would be held in violation of the state laws and risk the "disfavor" of the General Assembly.[29]

Eight days later, the Tidewater Educational Foundation announced that it had secured sufficient facilities to educate forty-five hundred pupils.[30] The directors of the TEF had made arrangements with a number of churches and businesses to provide substitute classrooms should the public schools be closed.[31] McKendree and several colleagues approached Superintendent J. J. Brewbaker in an attempt to recruit faculty, and according to McKendree, Brewbaker seriously considered assigning teaching staff to the foundation.[32]

The governor and Davis Y. Paschall, Virginia's superintendent of public instruction, were also attempting to devise a plan to educate the ten thousand students. According to their plan, schools would be reopened with the exception of the specific grades to be integrated at the schools to which black students had been assigned. White students in those grades would be transferred to schools in neighboring cities and counties.[33] This scheme was abandoned, however, when it was not supported by Norfolk's school board.[34] The board likely realized Judge Hoffman would not have allowed such a blatantly obstructionist maneuver to circumvent the spirit of the Supreme Court's decision.

On September 12 the school board asked Hoffman to dissolve the Virginia State Supreme Court's injunction barring the board from making pupil assignments.[35]

The following day, Almond directed Attorney General Albertis S. Harrison, Jr., to institute a test case in the Virginia State Supreme Court of Appeals to assess the legality of tuition-grant payments, a critical component of Virginia's massive-resistance laws. The validity of tuition payments hinged on whether Virginia's constitution was violated by statutes that mandated the closing of integrated schools and the reallocation of state funding for tuition grants. The governor and the attorney general believed that a test of resistance legislation would ultimately occur and that a more favorable judgment would be provided by the state courts than by the federal courts.[36]

Virginia's first school closing took place September 15, 1958, in tiny Warren County in Northern Virginia. Twenty-two black students had been assigned to Warren County High School in the county seat of Front Royal after federal district judge John Paul had issued an injunction prohibiting the school board from barring their admission. Black students had been attending schools in neighboring counties because Warren County had no high school facilities for blacks. Even though this practice placed the county in flagrant violation of the law, the closing was unexpected. Attorney General

Harrison had thought it likely that legal maneuvering could postpone integration for another year.[37]

In "First School Closing," Chambers chastised the legislature for implementing the massive-resistance legislation that made the closings inevitable. And the *Pilot*'s editor warned that history would not judge the closing well: "The public schools of the state have been placed in an indefensible position by the *incoherence* of the 'massive resistance' laws. Those laws placed this state, which has been called the fountain and source of constitutional law, on the wrong side of a legal contest over constitutionality within its own borders. The historic fact will not be forgotten."[38]

On September 18 Hoffman issued an injunction to prevent the state courts from denying the right of Norfolk's school board to assign pupils.[39] The next day, the board delayed the opening of the city's six white and three black secondary schools until September 29. That same day, after a similar set of postponements, Charlottesville became the second Virginia community to experience a school closure. A high school and an elementary school were closed, displacing seventeen hundred students.[40]

On September 23 the United States Court of Appeals for the Fourth Circuit denied the request of Norfolk's school board for a stay of Hoffman's desegregation order. The court had refused similar requests from officials in both Warren County and Charlottesville.[41]

Four days later Almond ordered Norfolk's white secondary schools closed. Earlier that day, the court of appeals had upheld Hoffman's order admitting the seventeen black students to the city's all-white junior and senior high schools. A certified copy of the order was transmitted to the district court in Norfolk.

Upon hearing that its appeal had been denied, the school board approved the transfer of the students and notified the governor of its action.[42] Chairman Schweitzer, understanding that the assignment would close the desegregated schools, requested that Almond use the "best efforts of [his] office to effect the reopening of [the] schools at the earliest possible time."[43]

That same day, Almond removed the six desegregated schools from Norfolk's system. The governor assumed complete jurisdiction over the closed schools: "All authority, power, and control over such schools, principals, teachers, and other employees and all pupils now enrolled or ordered to be enrolled, will thereupon be vested in the Commonwealth of Virginia, to be exercised by the Governor."[44] The order became effective September 29.

In a lead editorial, "The Schools Must Be Opened," Chambers encouraged local citizens, municipal officials, and teachers' groups to take responsibility for "reversing this unjust and cruel policy." Chambers called the closing "an injustice against which Norfolk people are already showing that they will protest in the full conviction that the state has no moral right—and probably no legal right—to punish them thus."[45]

Although Warren County and Charlottesville were able to develop alternative school arrangements for nearly all of the 2,779 students of their three closed schools, Norfolk was deplorably unprepared. Forty-four hundred of the 9,950 dispossessed students would receive educations in informal tutoring groups. Twenty-seven hundred students would be unaccounted for, presumably having dropped out of school or for other reasons receiving no education at all.[46]

If massive resistance was Virginia's issue of the century, certainly the school closing was one of Norfolk's most significant historical events of the century. Veterans of the crisis find it difficult to convey the emotionalism of the time. The subject eclipsed all others, and people talked of little but integration, the resistance, and the closure, often in rabidly partisan terms and tone. "I'm not sure that people who didn't go through that can understand how high the emotions were," says Frank Batten. "[It was] a very tense time."[47]

For a brief period after the closing of Norfolk's white secondary schools on September 27, 1958, passions subsided as Norfolkians disbelievingly contemplated what had occurred. Although the Supreme Court's decision and the Byrd organization's confrontational stance had made such an outcome almost inevitable, to most people the closing of public schools was inconceivable.

Two days after the closing, the city's two black junior high schools and its only black high school were opened. One white junior high school and all of the city's elementary schools, black and white, would also operate throughout the remainder of the closure. No integration had been ordered at these schools.

The next day the city council petitioned Governor Almond to invoke the emergency powers granted him under Chapter 69 of the General Assembly's extra session of 1956 and reopen the closed schools.[48]

Throughout the closing the school board pressured the council to encourage the governor to reopen the schools, pointing out in a resolution to the council, "It is now apparent that under the decisions of the United States Supreme Court, such public education cannot be had without some measure of integration."[49] The same school board that had actively sought to obstruct the integration of Norfolk's public schools now became a prime force working to reopen them.

The city council's petition to the governor provided it with a convenient excuse for its inactivity in attempting to reopen the schools. Pressed by pro-school forces, the council could easily disclaim responsibility, blaming the governor for the impasse.[50]

Mayor Fred Duckworth refused to endorse a plan for city-operated schools until a city-wide referendum could be held.[51] Only fifty thousand of Norfolk's three hundred thousand residents were qualified voters, and only one in twelve had voted in recent elections. Many observers of Norfolk politics saw the results of such a referendum as a foregone conclusion. Results of past elections in the city suggested that two-thirds of the electorate would support Byrd-organization candidates.[52]

Chambers viewed the referendum as a transparent attempt by city council to abdicate responsibility for dealing with a difficult problem. In "Leadership, Not an Opinion Poll," he wrote, "All the councilmen know very well the toll that 10,000 Norfolk children are having to pay for the loss of their classrooms . . . They need not lean on the confusion, the bitterness, the desperation, and the politics that Virginia's officials have sown on the people . . . Let the City Council act."[53]

Duckworth placed much of the blame for the school closing on the National Association for the Advancement of Colored People. He accused the organization of attacking the southern city that had done the most for its black population.[54] If the seventeen black students would simply withdraw their applications, he said, the closed white schools could reopen immediately.

Almond was not keen to become the scapegoat for the state's crisis and did not acknowledge receipt of council's petition. This necessitated a personal letter from Duckworth advising Almond that if the closed schools were reopened in a segregated condition and operated by the state, the courts would allow them to remain open while the litigation proceeded.[55] The governor responded in writing to the mayor's letter the next day and arranged a meeting with representatives of the council and Attorney General Albertis Harrison. The governor, however, declined to act hastily, insisting the matter required careful reflection and deliberation.[56]

In reality the governor was stalling for time. He had never imagined that the schools would actually be closed, and he had little idea as to how the state should respond. Massive resistance was becoming more and more expensive; Norfolk's closed public schools were costing the state $172,000 a month.[57]

Senator Byrd provided little assistance to the governor throughout the closing. The two had not spoken during the summer leading up to the closure; and the senator and Blackie Moore, speaker of the House of Delegates, were vacationing in Alaska throughout much of September.[58]

Even after the senator's return to Virginia, he made himself inaccessible to the governor. Almond, with growing concern, sought Byrd's counsel: "After the [Byrd's senatorial] election, I hope we can get together for a talk on this terrible crisis."[59] "I have been away for a couple of weeks," Byrd breezily wrote, "and therefore, have not written to you."[60] The governor replied with increasing frustration, "I hope in the near future you and I can sit down for a long talk relative to our problems."[61] Governor Almond was learning that unlike legislators, who cast their votes within a congregation of other voters, governors bore the solitary responsibility for the maintenance of order within their states.[62]

Chambers, impatient with flimsy delaying arguments, succinctly debunked a trio of them in a lead editorial entitled, "The Voices for the Schools." "The cliche that states' rights must be won now or lost forever is not the truth. The shibboleth that the Supreme Court's order may be legally ignored is not the truth. The myth that Virginia is in contest with alien forces is not the truth."

"The truth is that Virginia can open all its schools, and cannot with justice and good sense keep any of them closed. Virginia and its children need their schools."[63]

As resisters and pro-school forces battled for the support of Norfolk's citizens, the clear and consistent voice of the *Virginian-Pilot*'s editorial staff rang out, encouraging reason, moderation, and lawfulness. The *Virginian-Pilot*'s editorials would be widely read by the public and closely monitored by the state's political elite and other key actors in the closing. In what Byrd called a "war of propaganda," these editorials would do much to influence the peaceful outcome of the crisis.[64]

12

Advocacy for Reopening the Schools

THE ACTIVITIES OF the Virginia NAACP provided the governor and other hard-line segregationists with little solace. The chapter held its annual convention in Norfolk's neighboring city of Hampton October 10–12, 1958. A goal was set to increase the state membership, already the largest in any southern state, from 27,000 to 50,000 by the end of 1959. NAACP leaders also revealed that of 422,663 blacks of voting age in Virginia, only 131,626 were registered to vote.[1]

The NAACP worked hard to raise consciousness among Norfolk's blacks. Many black residents, who had lived their lives oppressed by Jim Crow, were apathetic and saw little chance that the city's schools could ever be integrated. Black teachers, who enjoyed an elite status in the black community, worried that they would lose their teaching positions. Black educators could not imagine that white parents would ever allow blacks to teach white children. (Throughout the South, many black principals and teachers would indeed lose their jobs as a result of school integration.) NAACP attorneys and staff frequently addressed the members of black churches, fraternal organizations, business groups, and professional associations to build backing for school desegregation. Their efforts were effective, and a groundswell of support arose in the black community.[2]

During the summer preceding the school closing, the Norfolk branch of the NAACP had sought to prepare the seventeen black students for the problems they would face when they eventually entered the white schools. Hortense Wells, a black Norfolk school supervisor, recommended to NAACP attorneys J. Hugo Madison and Victor Ashe that classes for the seventeen students be held at historic Bute Street First Baptist Church, one of Norfolk's most prestigious black churches. Wells also procured supplies and developed a curriculum.[3] Instruction for the displaced black students continued at First Baptist throughout the school closure.

For a week a substitute schoolteacher, Katherine Quarles Allen, taught all of the students. After Allen returned to substitute teaching, the Norfolk NAACP asked Vivian Carter Mason, a Norfolk resident and graduate of the University of Chicago, to oversee the preparation of the students. Mason's background qualified her impressively for this responsibility. A former presi-

dent of the National Association of Negro Women and onetime special delegate to the United Nations Commission on the Status of Women, she also
had served during the early 1940s as New York City's director of social services.[4]

In an effort to prepare the students psychologically for integration,
Mason arranged for speakers who had experienced desegregation in other
areas of the country (such as Louisville, where desegregation had taken place
peacefully despite the fact that blacks made up 27 percent of the city's school
population) to visit Norfolk to share their observations.[5] In their discussions,
Mason and the invited speakers leveled with the students regarding the ob-
stacles they would face.

> We told them one morning that they have left their childhood behind
> them—it's finished for all of them. That is because they have been trained
> and taught to see and hear nothing that is aimed at them in a detrimental
> and provocative manner. They are not to take cognizance of unfriendly or
> hostile actions on the part of their fellow students. They are to apply them-
> selves with great vigor to the job of mastering the academic work required
> of them. Lastly, they are not to withhold warmth and friendliness from
> those who extend it to them. They have accepted the role of pioneers.[6]

To prepare the students academically, Mason established a school consisting of five grades and twelve subjects. To staff the school she secured the
services of an interracial faculty of eight teachers. Teachers received small
stipends from the NAACP and the Seafarers' Union. Gertrude Perry, a retired Norfolk schoolteacher with forty years of service, supervised their activities.[7]

First Baptist Church provided a nurturing and supportive environment
and served as a social center for the displaced black students. The students
would later recall that the church provided a place to cry, talk, and give vent
to their feelings and strengthened them for the weeks to come.[8]

Events such as these in the black community received little comment on
the *Virginian-Pilot*'s editorial page. Chambers enjoyed a mutually respectful
relationship with P. B. Young and wrote to the editor, "The *Journal and
Guide*'s analyses and comments, under very difficult circumstances, have
been thoughtful and stimulating to us here." However, Chambers was isolated from the black community and lacked personal contact with black leadership.[9] Had he possessed the acute sensitivity his predecessor displayed toward racial injustice and Jaffe's easy intimacy with black leaders, the *Pilot*'s
editorials might have argued more directly and forcefully for social justice
for blacks.

Certainly, Chambers was pragmatic in not aligning the paper's editorial
page with the NAACP. Simply by arguing for adherence to the "law of the

land" and for preservation of public education, he aroused the ire of Virginia's political leadership and much of Norfolk's electorate. To have openly embraced the NAACP would have significantly diminished his credibility and influence and the effect of his editorials on Norfolk's white citizens.

The *Virginian-Pilot*'s news staff, too, lacked far-ranging contact with Norfolk's black community. Luther Carter admits that although he was amenable to seeking out blacks and reporting on the crisis from their perspective, he consulted white sources far more often than black.[10] Unquestionably, the addition of black reporters and editors to the *Pilot*'s all-white news staff would have improved the quality of coverage of the school closing and of Norfolk's large black population.

The activism of the NAACP contrasted strongly with the unwillingness of the majority of Norfolk's white population to take action to reopen the schools. A "Rally for Open Schools," held in the Norfolk Arena on October 13, attracted only a thousand participants.[11]

Of the white organizations working to reopen Norfolk's schools, none was more active than the Norfolk Committee for Public Schools (NCPS), a miscellaneous coalition of white citizens. Although this group portrayed itself as pro-public schools, not pro-integration, and declined to accept blacks lest their inclusion reduce the committee's effectiveness, its members encountered hostility.[12] The *Virginian-Pilot* identified six members of the executive board but did not name the seventh, who preferred anonymity.[13] Many of the prominent businessmen and politicians whom the committee actively lobbied sympathized with its goals, but none joined, for fear of repercussion. Nevertheless, the NCPS became the most visible and influential white organization working to reopen the city's schools.[14]

Norfolk's ministers and many members of its religious community also worked toward this goal. Sixty-six members of the biracial, Protestant Norfolk Ministers Association, which represented seventy-four congregations, wrote a statement urging political leaders to take immediate steps to reopen the schools.[15] Chambers editorialized, "The church has acted with great speed, commendable boldness, and heartening unanimity. . . . It was the response of educated men unaffected by politics. It was the response of the institution to which much of Norfolk entrusts its conscience. . . . It was a response to evil and peril that this city and this state cannot ignore."[16]

A number of other local religious organizations and individual congregations issued statements disapproving of the closing, but the outcry from the religious community seemed to have no effect on state policy. Governor Almond informed a delegation of five representatives from the Ministers Association that although the schools would not remain closed permanently, he had little idea when or how they would be reopened.[17]

Jane Reif, in her pamphlet *Crisis in Norfolk,* notes that the association's members who spoke out against the closing did so as individuals, not as representatives of their congregations.[18] The clergymen's parishioners were deeply divided over the closing. James Martin, a leader in the Tidewater Educational Foundation, reportedly disapproved so strongly of his minister's pro-school sermons that he sat in the front pew and read a magazine during church services to show his disrespect.[19]

Although many Jews supported the reopening of the schools, they acted as individuals, not as congregations. Their leadership felt that Jews themselves could easily become targets of racism if their opposition to the closing became too visible.[20] Despite the fact that white citizens' organizations did not officially sanction anti-Semitism, some individuals practiced it, and two southern temples were dynamited in 1958.[21] In Norfolk, racist hate literature circulated widely throughout the crisis, but anti-Semitism did not feature prominently in the closing. Rufus Tonelson, the young Jewish principal of a Norfolk high school, received anonymous telephone calls vilifying him as a nigger lover, a communist, a red, and threatening to burn a cross on his lawn; but not once did a caller allude to his Jewish heritage.[22]

A number of women's organizations such as the American Association of University Women, the League of Women Voters, and the Women's Interracial Council also opposed the closing. In general, women's groups appeared to value the public schools more than did organizations dominated by men.[23]

Late in October 1958, Frank Batten began to organize Norfolk's business community to urge the reopening of the schools.[24] Batten, one of the city's youngest business leaders, and Pretlow Darden, former mayor of Norfolk and the brother of former governor Colgate Darden, would become the two primary organizers of the business community's long-delayed protest. Conversations between the two men took place over a period of months as they explored ways to mobilize their fellow businessmen for a role in ending the crisis.[25]

Some of the delay in the business community's response likely came from fundamental differences between Batten and Darden regarding integration. Batten supported the Supreme Court's decision, although he believed that integration should proceed gradually and cautiously to avoid possible repercussions.[26] During regular luncheon conversations on "Topic A" with members of the *Pilot* editorial staff, he left no doubt that his concerns about the closing matched those of Chambers.[27] Despite Batten's personal feelings, however, he greatly respected Darden's political acumen and sense of timing.[28]

Darden had much less respect than Batten for the Supreme Court's decision.[29] He thought it was wrong, and he refused to act until the Virginia

Supreme Court ruled on the legality of the closing. Not until the state court so directed did he intend to assist in carrying out the *Brown* mandate.[30]

Batten faced a formidable task in organizing the business community to protest the closing. Business leaders did not like to challenge the Byrd organization, which stood for low taxes and anti-union legislation as much as for white supremacy. In *Southern Politics,* V. O. Key observed that the organization enjoyed "the enthusiastic and almost undivided support of the business community and the well-to-do generally, a goodly number of whom [were] fugitives from the New York State income tax."[31]

What ultimately would motivate the city's lethargic business community to organize was the fear that the closing would have a negative impact on the area's economy—in particular, that the Navy would close its large base, a wellspring of the city's prosperity. Chambers stimulated the fears of the city's business community by reprinting an article, "What Massive Resistance Costs," that had been published earlier in *Business Week* magazine.[32] "This article," Chambers wrote to *Business Week*'s editor, "seems to us to summarize very well indeed some important ideas and possibilities. We have been trying to impress these on the business community here."[33] "A gnawing fear among businessmen," the article read, "is that Navy patience will wear thin, that uncertainty among naval personnel about the opportunity for educating their children will provoke a shifting of operations to other Atlantic ports."[34] "If the Navy left," an observer later claimed, "Norfolk would sink."[35]

In "To Norfolk Businessmen," Chambers commended the reprint to readers and warned the business establishment of the economic consequences of continued inactivity on their part. "The struggle that began as a racial effort for equal opportunity, and became a legal war, and grew into a political movement, and is an educational and human tragedy, is also an economic problem of visible effects and serious potentialities. . . . The problems before Norfolk are not insoluble. They are difficult . . . They demand intelligence, wise action, and determination from Norfolk's business community."[36]

Publicly, the Navy dissociated itself from the crisis. Sailors and officers were instructed not to make their association with the Navy known if they participated in political activities linked to the crisis. Still, the closing affected many Navy children, and Navy families worried. One Navy wife wrote to Schweitzer, "You may wonder why Navy personnel have not been heard from in more numbers. Many people do not know that we have been ordered not to make our connection with the Navy known when we speak out against the crisis. But make no mistake about it, we Navy people are deeply concerned. . . . Something will be done and Norfolk may well be hurt permanently by what is done about the Navy in Norfolk." [37]

Navy personnel were somewhat removed from local politics. Many did not pay state taxes and therefore could not vote in state and local elections.[38] Although a number of Navy parents worked for the Norfolk Committee for Public Schools, they obeyed the order concerning disclosure of their affiliation.[39]

Behind the scenes, the Navy exerted pressure on Mayor Duckworth and the city council to take steps to reopen the schools. Rear Admiral F. Massie Hughes, Commandant of the Fifth Naval District, the popular "Navy mayor" of Norfolk, made known to the city administration the Navy's displeasure with the closing. Although the Navy and the city had not always cooperated, in recent years relations had improved significantly. During a meeting of the Hampton Roads Sales Executives Club, the admiral reminded his audience that four out of ten children in the Norfolk area had parents who worked for the federal government. "I hope and pray to God," he said, "[the school crisis] will soon clear up."[40] The military employed 44 percent of the area's work force, and this audience of business leaders listened closely to Hughes's message.

Noting the significance of Hughes's talk, Chambers directed his readers' attention to the admiral's telling remarks in a lead editorial, "Bite the Hand that Feeds Us?" The *Pilot* asserted that the city council's increasingly reactionary policies were backing the Navy into a corner. The editorial was accompanied by a detailed chart that illustrated the Navy's vital contribution to the region's economic health.[41]

Duckworth and Hughes were friends, and the mayor would have received the commandant's criticism of the closing. However, Hughes's attempts to influence Duckworth went unheeded. As the crisis grew, Duckworth's politics became increasingly reactionary; and as Roy Martin, Duckworth's successor, observed, "there was no working with Duckworth."[42]

Norfolk's public-school teachers played a major role in subverting militant segregationists' plans to establish an extensive private-school system for whites. On October 2, 1958, the Norfolk Education Association, a professional teachers' organization for the city's 1,100 white teachers, voted 487 to 89 in favor of a resolution requesting that city council petition Governor Almond to allow Norfolk to operate the public schools on an integrated basis if the governor could not reopen them in a segregated condition.[43] The president of the NEA warned that many teachers were considering changing careers and that the city would find it hard to rebuild an efficient teaching corps.[44]

Chambers praised the teachers' action. In "No Secession of Mind in NEA," he wrote, "The Norfolk School Teachers have spoken with the voice of an intelligence that has not seceded from the difficulties of the closed school situation. The voice is one of a courage that has shown no recession in the presence of a closed school dilemma charged with emotionalism and confusion. It is good to have teachers speak with a voice like this."[45]

Some observers had viewed the NEA as a passive and politically unassertive professional organization until the closing.[46] However, when members saw their jobs and careers threatened, they closed ranks and urged the reopening of the schools.[47]

Duckworth arranged for James Martin, a director of the Tidewater Educational Foundation, to recruit teachers at a meeting of the NEA. Only one teacher elected to join the foundation's faculty. Most Norfolk teachers declined to work for the private organization so as not to undermine the public schools and restricted their assistance in order to stop the tutoring groups.[48]

Many teachers feared that parents would perceive the tutoring groups as substitutes for public schools. On October 18 Rufus Tonelson advised teachers to cease their participation in these groups by the beginning of the new year.[49]

In "The Teacher War on Complacency," Chambers supported the controversial decision to discontinue assisting the tutoring groups. "[Teachers] are not willing to be for an indefinite time parties to makeshift schooling and a mockery of federal law . . . Public schools cannot be conveniently converted to non-public schools as an escape from desegregation. A large portion of teachers, and the most professional among them, simply will not accept the terms of the transformation."[50]

Chambers did not escape the harassment that was directed at the other principals in the struggle to implement the *Brown* mandate—the NAACP, the black children seeking to attend white schools, and Judge Hoffman. He received threatening letters and phone calls throughout the closing, and he met with the Federal Bureau of Investigation to determine the best strategy to protect himself and his family. Once the *Pilot* received a bomb threat, likely in reaction to Chambers's editorials, and the newspaper building was evacuated and cordoned off.[51]

In addition to the threats, which he took seriously, Chambers encountered some snubs and cold stares. Incidents such as these did not intimidate him; on the contrary, they often amused him, and he laughed about them with his associates.[52]

13

A City Divided and Beleaguered

A S THE SCHOOL CRISIS grew more heated and neared a boiling point,
Chambers's voice could be heard consistently attacking massive resistance and urging a peaceful and lawful resolution. The editor's normally
restrained tone, however, on occasion became harsher and more satiric, suggesting that his patience with the resistance was wearing thin.

The rancor and divisiveness displayed at the Virginia Congress of Parent-
Teacher Associations held in Richmond on October 20–22, 1958, symbolized
the degree to which Virginians were divided over the school closing and
foreshadowed the struggle that lay ahead in Norfolk. On the opening day,
Governor Almond addressed the convention with a strongly segregationist
speech. His fifteen-minute address was interrupted eleven times with cheers
and applause. Nevertheless, moderates defeated an attempt by William I.
McKendree, the president of the Norfolk PTA Council and a leader in the
Defenders of State Sovereignty and Individual Liberties, to take over the
state PTA.[1]

By a tie vote of 557 to 557, the parent-teacher congress rejected a resolution expressing support for massive resistance. Later in the convention,
moderates managed to pass by the narrowest of margins—515 to 513—a resolution supporting local option as the best means of solving Virginia's school
crisis.[2]

Chambers found the PTA's narrow support of local option heartening,
editorializing:

> The State P-TA is saying to Governor Almond that "massive resistance" is
> a weapon that has been turned against the public schools. It has already
> struck them with great damage, but has left the Supreme Court and other
> federal courts, against which it was presumably aimed, unscathed. Their
> orders are in force and will remain in force until they are obeyed.
>
> The state P-TA is saying to Governor Almond that closed Virginia
> schools are no defense and that "massive resistance" is a state policy of
> self-destruction in public education.[3]

Although McKendree failed to persuade the state Parent-Teacher Association to adopt a pro-massive-resistance stand, he succeeded easily in controlling the Norfolk City Council of PTAs. The council operated under rules

that allowed the appointed chairpersons of its many committees to vote in its proceedings. This enabled McKendree, his officers, and the appointed chairs to outvote the local school representatives.[4]

Earlier the city council of Parent-Teacher Associations had issued a statement opposing the desegregation of Norfolk's schools. The statement read, "We believe desegregation to be unnecessary and impractical and that it will create for all children a hitherto unknown standard of inferiority. . . . We urge our Norfolk City School Board and Superintendent of Schools to take all possible and necessary action to retain the present equal opportunities now afforded all children."[5]

Probably other Defenders of State Sovereignty and Individual Liberties members besides McKendree served on the PTA council.[6] The previous year, the leadership of the Defenders had urged its membership to join PTAs and encourage others of like mind to join.[7]

Efforts by Rufus Tonelson to influence the PTA council to adopt a pro-school resolution encountered a stone wall. "I learned that it's possible to take over an organization in a legitimate fashion," said Tonelson. "I think Hitler did this. . . . Anything that came up that would favor opening the schools was always voted down. . . . Everything we would propose and every challenge we would make, [the PTA parliamentarian] would always say, 'You're out of order.' "[8]

William McKendree strongly opposed the efforts of the PTAs of the closed schools to continue to meet, fearing they would challenge the pro-resistance stand of the city-wide council. McKendree consulted with the national leadership of the organization to support his pronouncement that the chapters in the closed schools were defunct and should not be recognized.[9] Despite his efforts, nearly all of the statements issued by Norfolk's individual PTAs favored reopening the schools and passed by large majorities.[10] The one notable exception was Norview High School's chapter, whose resolution to reopen the school barely passed, 65 to 64.[11]

Across the state, individual PTAs issued position statements in attempts to influence state leaders. Lindsay Almond's gubernatorial papers contain many examples of these petitions, with predominantly pro-resistance statements from schools in the Southside and pro-school petitions from the northern and western parts of the state.

On October 22 a delegation from the Norfolk Committee for Public Schools presented Almond with a petition signed by 6,190 white citizens of Norfolk, urging the reopening of the schools.[12] The delegation warned the governor that the closing was having a profoundly negative impact on the city's economy and that the Navy was disturbed by the effects of the crisis on military families. Committee members assured Almond that the majority of Norfolk's citizens would accept minimal integration "in a spirit of calmness and cooperation."[13] The governor informed the delegation that Norfolk's schools would reopen only when the federal courts declared the closing to be illegal.[14]

Five days later, the Norfolk Committee for Public Schools brought suit against Governor Almond in federal district court on behalf of twenty-six white students displaced by the closing. This suit, to become known as *James v. Almond,* was named after one of the plaintiffs, Ruth Pendleton James.[15] James was a student at Maury High School and the daughter of Ellis James, a member of the NCPS's executive committee. Dr. C. Lydon Harrell, Sr., a member of the committee's executive board, also brought suit on behalf of his two grandchildren, both students scheduled to attend Blair Junior High School. (As president of the Medical College of Virginia, Harrell had lobbied hard to desegregate the state's medical society.) Several days later Victor J. Ashe, a local NAACP attorney, instituted a third suit on behalf of the seventeen black students.[16]

All of the suits challenged the constitutionality of the state's massive-resistance laws and charged that the school closing violated guarantees of equal protection as stated in the Fourteenth Amendment. All three suits named Almond as a party.[17] A three-judge panel consisting of chief judge Simon E. Soboloff of the Fourth Circuit Court of Appeals, circuit judge Clement F. Haynsworth, Jr., and district judge Walter E. Hoffman would hear the suit.

Prior to *James v. Almond,* all suits for integration had been brought by black plaintiffs. The NCPS had reasoned, however, that a court order for integration would more likely be obeyed in a suit filed by white litigants than in a case initiated by the NAACP. Dr. Forrest P. White, the treasurer and a later president of the NCPS, wrote, "The reaction against another NAACP suit might have tipped the balance toward further defiance.[18]

The committee encountered great difficulty in obtaining an attorney to argue its case. A number of prominent Norfolk lawyers, unwilling to risk incurring the wrath of the Byrd organization, refused to become involved.[19] Eventually Edmund D. Campbell of Arlington, Virginia, agreed to represent the plaintiffs. A Norfolk counsel, Archie L. Boswell, would assist Campbell. The defendants were represented by a formidable defense team consisting of three Norfolk attorneys; state attorney general Albertis Harrison; and Harrison's assistant, Walter E. Rogers.

Harrison v. Day, a test case of massive-resistance legislation, was being heard in the Virginia State Supreme Court of Appeals at the same time.[20] Almond's initiation of this "friendly" suit angered Senator Byrd. However, the governor believed that a judicial test of the constitutionality of resistance legislation was inevitable, and he saw an advantage in being able to "frame the issues."[21] Almond later explained that both he and his attorney general felt it would be better to get an interpretation from the Virginia courts.[22]

The editorial responses of the *Ledger-Dispatch* and the *Virginian-Pilot* to the initiation of *James v. Almond* were limited in their number. The *Ledger* was critical of the Norfolk Committee for Public Schools' action in bringing the suit. In "This Might Increase Confusion," Joseph Leslie held that concurrent tests of the constitutionality of massive-resistance legislation at both the state and federal levels would likely confound matters. The editor wrote, "The federal case so closely parallels the action previously instituted before the state court, that its value as a means of clearing up the situation created by the closed schools is open to question. It might add to, rather than reduce, the confusion in which the school issue is involved."[23]

In a lead editorial, "Is School Closing Constitutional?" Lenoir Chambers and his staff declared that the institution of *James v. Almond* underlined the determination of white parents to reopen the schools and evinced the parents' belief that federal courts would provide the most responsible forum for facilitating an end to the school crisis. "It is apparent," Chambers wrote, "that the plaintiffs in these suits hoped the guidance would come from elsewhere, by through [*sic*] the action of others. They waited. It has not come. . . . Leadership from those who ordinarily would be expected to provide it has not appeared."[24]

As the third week of October approached, members of the Norfolk Education Association voted to end their participation in the tutoring groups. Lieutenant Governor A. E. S. Stephens responded tersely to the association's refusal to support massive resistance: "When you pick up the paper and see that a large party of teachers have voted not to participate in the private school movement, you ask yourself: where is their loyalty?"[25]

On October 30 the Virginia Education Association, the statewide white teachers' and administrators' organization, passed a resolution expressing strong disapproval of the closing and advising Governor Almond to take immediate action to reopen the schools.[26] With near unanimity, the organization's board of directors declared its opposition to the state's inflexible massive-resistance legislation and expressed a growing militancy: "We reaffirm that we will exert all possible effort toward the preservation and improvement of a system of free public schools in Virginia."[27]

The Virginia Teachers Association, the black teachers' professional organization, adopted a similar resolution urging the state to obey the Supreme Court's mandate. One hundred delegates meeting in Richmond passed the resolution unanimously. Meeting in Hampton, the Virginia Congress of Colored Parents and Teachers also enjoined the legislature to comply with *Brown* and urged the governor to include blacks in efforts to resolve the school crisis.[28]

In the November 4, 1958, senatorial election, Byrd handily defeated his competition, which amounted only to a symbolic protest against massive resistance. Dr. Louise O. Wensel, a Fishersville physician, ran as an independent, and Clarke T. Robb as a Social Democrat. Byrd was so confident of his victory that he declined to mount a campaign.[29]

Wensel was a native of North Dakota and had moved to Virginia only five years before the election. Her disrespect for Virginia's senior statesman infuriated organization supporters; she described Byrd as "an old man who proposes to destroy the very foundation of our democracy—our public schools."[30]

The *Virginian-Pilot*'s editorial page grudgingly endorsed Byrd. While Chambers viewed Wensel's protest campaign as a "bold individual effort that represents honest conviction," he conceded that she had absolutely no experience in politics and government and was poorly suited to represent Virginia at the national level, which Byrd as chairman of the Senate Finance Committee and as ranking Democrat on the Armed Services Committee was uniquely qualified to do. In "The Election is for a Senator," Chambers attempted to explain to readers how the *Pilot* could both oppose massive resistance and support its architect: "The *Virginian-Pilot* regards the massive resistance legislation as rear-guard action of dubious constitutionality and of obvious and demonstrated impracticality and injustice. When massive resistance was the central issue in the campaign for the governorship between J. Lindsay Almond and State Senator Ted Dalton, the *Virginian-Pilot* urged the support of Senator Dalton. But the major issue now is the choice of a senator to represent Virginia in the United States Senate."

In the same breath, Chambers uncharacteristically chided Byrd: "It would have been better if Senator Byrd had spoken freely and frankly to Virginia voters about many subjects of public importance instead of treating them with silence and publicly ignoring the election itself. In such a time he should give an account of his stewardship."[31]

Although Byrd received 317,221 votes to Wensel's 120,224 (Robb's showing was negligible), the anti-Byrd vote in Norfolk increased significantly from that of 1952, from 29 to 40 percent. Clearly, there was in the city a growing level of dissatisfaction with the senator's intransigence.[32]

Organization loyalists' celebratory mood over the senator's reelection changed to one of concern a week later when Jack Kilpatrick spoke to the Richmond Rotary Club. Although the *News Leader*'s editor had been one of the primary architects of massive resistance, he had come to see that its end was in sight. His speech was the first major indication of disharmony regarding the resistance in the normally unified Byrd organization. He told his audience, "I believe the time has come for new weapons and new tactics. I believe the laws we now have on the books have outlived their usefulness, and I believe that new laws must be devised—speedily devised— if educational opportunities are to be preserved and social calamity is to be avoided."[33]

Kilpatrick, Virginius Dabney, and the management of the co-owned *Richmond Times-Dispatch* and *News Leader* had driven to Byrd's home in Berryville to inform him that they intended to end their support for massive resistance. The senator was cordial to his guests but informed them that he had no intention of abandoning his resistance to desegregation.[34] Kilpatrick believed that the courts would declare the state's massive-resistance legislation illegal. The editor now saw local option and tuition grants as the best means of combating public-school integration.[35]

Congressmen Watkins M. Abbitt and William M. Tuck categorically rejected Kilpatrick's "Johnny-come-lately" moderation. Abbitt urged localities to close their black schools if white schools were shut down as a result of litigation. Tuck blustered, "We cannot allow Arlington or Norfolk to integrate. If they won't stand with us, I say make them stand."[36]

Billy Prieur bristled at Tuck's remarks. Although he supported massive resistance and was every bit as loyal an organization man as the congressman, he resented Tuck's intrusion into the clerk of court's territory. Prieur told Tuck to mind his own business and called his statement "arrogant and presumptuous."[37] Tuck shot back, "As a Virginian who loves every foot of her soil I think I have the right to voice my views."[38] Chambers, downplaying the disagreement between these two Byrd lieutenants as a relatively minor family spat, wrote, "No one should infer from the Tuck-Prieur debate that the cogs in the Byrd machine have suddenly begun to slip."[39]

The most critical response to Kilpatrick's Rotary Club speech came from Byrd. The taciturn senator issued a rare public statement: "I have supported the strong anti-integration school policy of Governor Almond and his firm stand against the usurpation of power by the Warren Supreme Court. I shall continue to support this policy which I believe to be in the best interest of the people of Virginia."[40]

Nevertheless, there were some indications—albeit minor ones—that Governor Almond was considering a change in his hard-line policy. The day after Kilpatrick's speech, he acknowledged that the Virginia General Assembly's barriers to integration might be declared unconstitutional by the courts. "If [our laws] are stricken down, it is my present purpose to appoint a representative commission composed of members of the General Assembly for the purpose of advice and to receive the suggestions which I shall make at that time," he said. Still, Almond pledged to comply with the statutes of Virginia as long as they remained vital.[41]

On November 11, circuit court judge Clyde H. Jacob and state supreme court chief justice John Eggleston, of Norfolk, refused to issue an injunction prohibiting Norfolk's city council from holding an informative referendum to determine whether voters wished council to petition the governor to return control of the schools to the city for operation on an integrated basis.

A group of citizens had sought to enjoin the city from holding the referendum, in the belief that council should display leadership to reopen the schools immediately rather than use the predictable results of the election as an excuse for continued inactivity. The election was set for November 18.[42]

The wording of the referendum's ballot was very controversial. The form included a section entitled "For Information Only," warning voters that "in the Event the Closed Schools are returned to the City of Norfolk, and are reopened Integrated by the City, It will be necessary, because of the loss of State Funds, for every family having a child or children in Public Schools from which State Funds are withheld, to pay to the City a substantial Tuition for each child in or entering such Public School."[43]

The referendum's opponents protested that the inclusion of such a section was an intentional attempt by council to influence citizens to vote against petitioning the governor. The Defenders, campaigning against petitioning Almond, declared that support of city-operated schools was equivalent to surrendering "to various pressure groups and professional race mixers."[44] The Defenders of State Sovereignty and Individual Liberty also said that parents would be forced to bear the brunt of the expense incurred by local operation of schools. The Norfolk Committee for Public Schools and the Norfolk Education Association warned of the dire effects on the public school system and the local economy if schools were not reopened shortly.[45]

The *Ledger-Dispatch* and the *Virginian-Pilot* took antipodal positions on the November 18 referendum. Leslie and his staff defended the holding of the "special informative election." The *Ledger* insisted that Norfolk's city council was well within its rights in determining the sentiments of the city's voters before deciding whether to petition the governor.[46] Although the results of the referendum would not be binding, the editor stated, they would enable the council to respond more confidently to the crisis.[47] The evening before the election, the *Ledger* fueled the emotional atmosphere surrounding the closing by declaring that a vote for petitioning the governor was tantamount to supporting the mixing of races in the city's public schools.[48]

Chambers and his staff strongly opposed the referendum. The *Pilot* adopted an unusually caustic and cynical tone for its criticism, writing that "the expected usefulness of the ballot is as uncertain as the arrangement of capital letters in its text. Sifting through the ambiguities, the perplexities, and the senselessness of the ballot and a note appended, in which voters are informed that a reopening of the schools would entail 'substantial Tuition [*sic*]' for each child enrolled, is a dispiriting experience."[49]

The *Pilot* disputed the *Ledger*'s claim that a vote for petitioning the governor was a vote for mixing the races in schools. In an attempt to defuse the crisis, the *Pilot*'s editor reasoned that the issue was not integration, but whether the schools should be reopened.[50]

In a lead editorial, "The Best Choice: Vote 'For,' " Chambers enumerated his concerns over the referendum. He called on the city council to display leadership in reopening the schools, rather than wait for the results of a poorly conceived and ambiguous referendum. Voters were likely to be especially confused by the referendum's inflammatorily worded ballot, which suggested that an uncontrolled wave of integration would result from reopening the schools. In reality only the seventeen black students would enter the white schools.

Chambers also criticized the portion of the ballot claiming that should the city operate the schools, it would have to charge parents a substantial tuition for their children's education. The editor maintained that there were many ways the city could fund schools aside from charging tuition.[51]

Their severe reservations concerning the referendum and its ballot notwithstanding, Chambers and his staff advised voters not to boycott the election but to vote for petitioning the governor. Chambers wrote that the referendum presented Norfolk's electorate with an important opportunity to display its support for public schools.[52]

Despite the efforts of the *Virginian-Pilot* and the Norfolk Committee for Public Schools, which had also lobbied hard to return control of the schools to the city, Norfolk's "special informative election" on November 18, 1958, resulted in victory for Mayor W. Fred Duckworth and other massive resisters. (The NCPS had gone so far as to print a guide ballot for the referendum that omitted any mention of the "substantial tuition" that parents allegedly would have to pay if control of the schools returned to the city.)[53] The city's electorate voted 12,340 to 8,712 (three to two, as predicted) to keep the schools closed. Only 21,052 in a city of well over 300,000 residents voted. George Kelley, the *Virginian-Pilot*'s political reporter and a Byrd-organization stalwart, wrote that "massive resistance to school integration won a new direct endorsement from Norfolk's qualified voters." In fact, however, the referendum demonstrated little, aside from the continued notorious apathy of the majority of the city's electorate.[54]

Leslie called the outcome of the referendum "a positive and direct declaration by the voters of their will to resist school integration even at the cost of closed schools."[55] The editor observed that the proportion of white voters opposing petitioning the governor was much higher than three to two. If the thirty-five hundred votes cast by blacks—nearly all in support of the petition—were deducted from the referendum totals, the results indicated that white voters overwhelmingly opposed the petition, two and a half to one.[56]

Duckworth proclaimed that the people had spoken.[57] The referendum hardened the resistance of the municipal government.[58] City council assumed total control over all of the city's public-school funding on November

25 and began to allocate funding for the city's schools on a month-by-month basis, effective December 25, 1958. The ordinance stated, "The appropriation herein made for said public schools is made on a tentative basis, and no part of the funds so appropriated shall, in any event, be available to the School Board of the City of Norfolk except as the Council may, from time to time, by resolution authorize."[59] This ordinance placed council in a position to close the city's black schools by eliminating the funding for these schools.[60]

Billy Prieur collaborated closely with Duckworth in orchestrating the escalation of the school crisis. "I am enclosing," he reported to the senator's son, Harry F. Byrd, Jr., "headlines in the Norfolk newspapers which indicate further steps we are contemplating taking. I believe that we have the City's budget in such a state that we can cut off the Negro schools as of January 1, 1959."[61]

After the referendum, Duckworth adopted an antagonistic stance toward the city's teachers. In a confrontation with the mayor, school superintendent James Brewbaker defended his teaching staff, calling them good teachers. "With what some of them have done, along with others in your system," the mayor replied, "I would have to disagree with you."[62] Rufus Tonelson tells of a similar incident: "Duckworth had called in Mr. Brewbaker and told him that if [the principals of the closed schools] didn't change [their] philosophy about keeping the schools open, he wanted us fired. And Mr. Brewbaker said, 'Well, you can fire me, too.' "[63]

The mayor achieved widespread notoriety as a result of his increasingly militant position, as Robert Mason discovered during a trip he took throughout the South during the closing: "Everybody knew Duckworth. His name had become [almost as well known as that of Governor Orval Faubus, the segregationist governor of Arkansas]. . . . That got to him. . . . Everybody was congratulating [him], including the senior senator of [his] state."[64]

Duckworth grew closer to Senator Byrd as the crisis escalated. After the reopening of the schools, Prieur would write to Byrd that the mayor "is one of your strongest admirers."[65] Duckworth's strong support of the organization's stand on school integration placed him firmly in the organization's inner circle. "The more I see of Fred Duckworth," Byrd wrote to Prieur, "the abler I think he is, and the finer."[66]

If Byrd admired Duckworth's leadership qualities, moderates working to defuse Norfolk's school crisis did not. The mayor's militant position worried Dr. Forrest P. White, a principal member of the Norfolk Committee for Public Schools. White warned Duckworth that his policies could lead to violence: "One stick of dynamite under each of a certain two Negro houses would open Granby and Maury tomorrow. Is this what you want? I don't believe it is. But if it happens can you disclaim all responsibility?"[67]

White also wrote to Almond to suggest that he develop "scape-goats" for the crisis. By suggesting to Virginians that Communists and northern industrialists were the only two constituencies benefiting from the crisis, White believed Almond could justify the reopening of the schools and suffer minimal political damage. "If you can find any better scape-goats than the Yankee industrialists and the Communists to aid the swing from massive resistance, you'll be doing well," the pediatrician wrote. "I personally regret the necessity of straining the bounds of logic to find emotionally appealing reasons for logical acts—but I do believe it is necessary."[68]

On the national level, although President Eisenhower continued to display a lack of leadership in resolving the school crisis, some members of his administration did speak out.[69] On December 1, Secretary Arthur S. Flemming of the Department of Health, Education, and Welfare called the school closings in Arkansas and Virginia indefensible and warned that children kept out of school would suffer serious consequences.[70] During the crisis, Attorney General William Rogers made several speeches to the effect that political leaders were misleading southerners to believe that the Supreme Court's mandate could be legally ignored.[71]

In November and December 1958, Stuart Saunders, the president of Norfolk & Western Railroad, informally organized a group of Virginia's leading businessmen and industrialists to address his perception that Virginia was not as effective as other southern states in attracting out-of-state industries.[72] North Carolina, which had never closed its schools, had enjoyed an exceptional business expansion throughout Virginia's school crisis.[73]

Saunders's concern likely originated from University of Virginia economist Dr. Lorin A. Thompson's report, "Virginia Education Crisis and Its Economic Aspects," which had circulated throughout the state before its publication in *New South*.[74] Thompson placed the blame on the school closing for the state's reported failure to attract new businesses. He contended that new businesses were unable to persuade highly skilled workers to move to Virginia due to the unstable condition of the state's public schools. He further claimed that some of Virginia's skilled work force had already relocated to other states because of the school problem.[75] Thompson's views could hardly have been considered objective in light of his active involvement in Charlottesville's pro-public-schools movement.

At Saunders's behest, the twenty-nine businessmen and industrialists met in Richmond in November or early December to discuss ways to promote economic development. Frank Batten attended, as did future Supreme Court justice Lewis Powell, then a Richmond attorney. The assemblage generally agreed that Virginia would face continued difficulty in attracting businesses until the resolution of the school crisis. The group decided to try to persuade Governor Almond to adopt a more moderate position on school integration.[76]

In late December, at a secret dinner meeting at the Rotunda Club in Richmond, the twenty-nine business leaders met with Almond, Lieutenant Governor A. E. S. Stephens, and Attorney General Albertis Harrison.[77] Batten reported that the governor adamantly resisted the group's appeal: "We just got hit by this barrage from the governor of the same kind of things he'd been saying in his speeches for months, in which he talked about the evils of integration and everything else."[78] Almond expressed particular contempt for Chambers's editorials on massive resistance. "In the midst of this speech, he spent about ten minutes blasting the editorial policy of the *Virginian-Pilot*," Batten recalled.[79]

Although Almond later conceded that the business leaders' entreaties had a profound effect on him, the school closing was only one factor—likely a minor one—that out-of-state businesses would have considered before deciding whether to locate their plants in Virginia.[80] In retrospect, the fears of the state's business leaders appear to have been unrealistic.[81] Shortly after the reopening, Almond wrote to Senator Byrd, "I have not been able to find any documented evidence that any industry has declined to locate in Virginia because of the pending school problem. Throughout the struggle, our industries in Virginia have continued to expand and from 1950 to date, there has been a steady and substantial acquisition of new and stable industries not only in Virginia, but throughout the South."[82]

On December 22 Judge Hoffman announced that his three-judge panel had completed its decision in the *James v. Almond* case. Hoffman stated that the decision would be made public "within a reasonable number of days."[83]

The judge had good reason for delaying the release of the opinion. Earlier, while playing golf at a nearby country club, Hoffman coincidentally had met state supreme court chief justice John W. Eggleston, whose court was deciding the crucial *Harrison v. Day* case. Eggleston persuaded Hoffman to postpone the release of the *James v. Almond* decision until the state court could act: "I just think it would be better for the people of Virginia if we spoke first." Hoffman immediately called Simon Sobeloff: "I told him about Eggleston; and he said, 'Walter, for God's sake, hold that opinion. He's absolutely right.' "[84]

Almond was an astute enough lawyer to predict what the courts' opinions would be. He had managed to secure a conference in Washington, D.C., with the elusive Senator Byrd. At the meeting, the governor described the precarious condition of massive resistance. Should the courts decide as anticipated, Almond told Byrd, the only means by which total segregation could continue would be to shut down all of the state's public schools.

The senator, however, remained unalterably opposed even to token integration and expressed concern over what his southern senatorial colleagues would think if Virginia's resisters capitulated to the federal courts. Powerful organization insiders present at the secret meeting, among them Representatives William M. Tuck and Watkins M. Abbitt, echoed Byrd's stand and vehemently supported continued massive resistance. Tuck even advanced the notion that Almond should go to jail before he allowed black students to enter white schools. The governor rejected this ploy on the grounds that it would do nothing to stop integration and that it would constitute a public relations catastrophe for the Byrd organization. The meeting ended without arrival at a satisfactory solution.[85]

On December 30 Norfolk's city council allocated another month's funding for the city's schools. Council prohibited the use of any of these resources to operate the city's closed schools.[86]

On January 13 the council, in an action that exceeded the severity of the state's massive-resistance laws, voted six to one to cease funding all of the city's schools beyond the sixth grade. This would have had the effect of adding another five thousand black students and nineteen hundred white students to the ten thousand pupils already locked out of Norfolk's schools. Because blacks would be affected by this resolution to a much larger extent than whites, hard-line segregationists hoped the measure would persuade the seventeen black students applying for admission to the city's white schools to withdraw their transfer applications.[87]

Vivian Mason had addressed the council and in an impromptu and impassioned speech implored the councilmen to consider the way in which Norfolk would be viewed by the world if all of the city's secondary schools were closed. Mason's speech had little effect.[88]

Roy Martin, Jr., the only city council member to oppose Duckworth, had differed with the mayor throughout the closing, but never publicly. He had tried to convert other members of the council to his position, but had found them unalterably committed to the resistance.[89] So as to portray an image of a unified council to the public, Duckworth confined such disagreement to unofficial Monday-morning council meetings that were closed to the public.[90]

On January 14, in "The Council's Lock-Out," Chambers harshly criticized Duckworth's and the council's action, calling it "incredible" and "impossible to justify." "The cruelest blow of all to the Norfolk public schools came not from the state's massive resistance program but from the Norfolk City Council. The resolution passed by the Norfolk City Council yesterday was an act of retaliation against Negro pupils that inflicts senseless punishment upon the city's schools."[91]

Duckworth's attempt to close the city's black schools proved too extreme for even some massive resisters. Almond, sounding increasingly moderate, expressed disapproval of the council's action: "I have opposed any retaliatory moves against the Negro children in Virginia. It has been my purpose and will continue to be my policy to see to it that as far as I am able that all of Virginia's children receive the educations to which they are entitled."[92]

On January 19, 1959, Robert E. Lee's birthday and a legal holiday in the state, the Virginia Supreme Court of Appeals and the three-judge federal district court released their decisions in *Harrison v. Day* and *James v. Almond*. The decisions delivered a one-two knockout punch to massive resistance.

The federal court, which was sitting in Norfolk, unanimously determined that the state of Virginia, by operating some schools and closing others, was in violation of constitutional guarantees of equal protection and due process. Although the decision was per curiam, Judge Hoffman had written the opinion.[93] Hoffman wrote, "We do not suggest . . . the state must maintain a public school system. That is a matter for state determination. We merely point out that the closing of a public school, or a grade therein, . . . violates the right of a citizen to equal protection of the laws."[94]

Hoffman and the other judges dismissed out of hand the value of interposition as a defense against integration, emphasizing the supremacy of federal over state law: "It is our duty to apply constitutional principles in accordance with the decisions of the United States Supreme Court and when state legislation conflicts with those constitutional principles, state legislation must yield."[95]

The state supreme court decision was as devastating to massive resistance as was that of the federal court. In a decision written by Chief Justice John W. Eggleston of Norfolk, the court determined that "the state must support such public free schools in the state as are necessary to an efficient system, including those in which the pupils of both races are compelled to be enrolled and taught together, however unfortunate that situation may be."[96] Ironically, Almond and his wife, Josephine, had hosted a dinner for the justices in the governor's executive mansion the previous evening.[97]

Two justices, Willis D. Miller and Harold F. Snead, dissented. During the previous summer, these same two justices had attempted to issue an injunction restraining Norfolk's school board from assigning black students to the city's white schools.

The court attempted to soften the blow by sympathizing with the motivations of resisters: "We deplore the lack of judicial restraint evinced by [the Supreme Court] in trespassing on the sovereign rights of this Commonwealth reserved to it in the Constitution of the United States. It was an understandable effort to diminish the evils expected from the decision in the *Brown* case that prompted the enactment of the statutes under review."[98]

Although Almond privately conceded that massive resistance was doomed, on January 20 he made a last defiant speech. "We have just begun to fight," he vowed. "I call upon the people of Virginia to stand firmly with me in this struggle. Be not dismayed by recent judicial deliverances."[99] Expressions of approval and support poured in to the governor from resisters across the state.

Later, however, Almond regretted this speech: "I don't know why I made that damn speech. If I had listened to my wife, I wouldn't have. . . . I saw the whole thing crumbling." He had been tired and distraught, he said. "I agonized and gave vent to my feelings, which never should have been done. My underlying thought and motivation was to show the people that we had done everything we could do."[100]

Despite the fact that Byrd applauded Almond's inflammatory speech, the senator carefully maintained a generous distance between himself and the governor. Almond's many telephone calls to the senator went unanswered.[101]

Time also appeared to be running out for Duckworth and the Norfolk city council, who seemed to be on the verge of being left to twist slowly in the wind. At an open city council meeting on January 20, Duckworth lost control of the proceedings and was jeered by a pro-school crowd.

The evening after the governor's speech, "The Lost Class of '59," a television documentary examining Norfolk's school closing, aired nationally at prime time on the Columbia Broadcasting System television network. The program was produced by the nationally acclaimed journalists Edward R. Murrow and Fred W. Friendly. Although "The Lost Class" featured many prominent actors in the crisis, Mayor Duckworth did not appear. Duckworth had made it known that he wished the producers of the documentary would "get the hell out of town."[102] Jane Reif wrote, "Murrow's telecast helped crystallize half-formed opinions. Its national top television time, and the reputation of Murrow, impressed many Norfolkians who could no longer deny the facts."[103]

The same day CBS aired "The Lost Class of '59," Norfolk received additional national exposure during a presidential press conference. Eisenhower, although still refusing to exert his personal influence to press for southern compliance with the *Brown* decision, expressed his concern for the children of Norfolk's federal workers and hinted that his patience with Virginia's policies was running out.[104]

For Leslie, who had appeared prominently in the Murrow documentary, the combined blows from the federal district court and the state supreme court were too much. Leslie acknowledged that the battle—if not the war—was over. In a lead editorial, "Massive Resistance Breaks Down," Leslie wrote on January 20, 1959, "The [*Ledger-Dispatch*], which has fought for school segregation with every persuasive means at its command, reluctantly concludes that massive resistance as we have known it has come to an end, and it becomes necessary now for those who believe in segregation to seek some other field from which to carry on the fight."[105]

Although the *Ledger* conceded that Virginia's resistance laws no longer offered a defense against school segregation, the editor, as Judge Eggleston had done, held that massive resistance had been an understandable response and had served a worthwhile purpose in communicating to the nation the degree to which Virginians were opposed to the Supreme Court's decision in *Brown v. Board*. Leslie decried the *Brown* decision, calling it a "tragic mistake," and warned that the court and the country would be haunted by the decision in years to come.[106]

Leslie also defended his paper's role in the crisis, writing that the *Ledger* had provided a voice for the citizens of Hampton Roads, the vast majority of whom supported massive resistance. "We have placed the North," Leslie wrote, "and the NAACP, and some of our own people who did not realize the intensity of the opposition to racial integration, and the dangers inherent in it, on notice as to what these dangers are."[107]

The next day Leslie suggested that Virginia adopt a policy of containment to replace that of massive resistance. The editor recommended the development of pupil-screening procedures that would minimize the number of blacks allowed to enter white schools. He also encouraged the state to begin to provide private-school students with tuition support.

The day after the courts' opinions were made public, Chambers and his staff emphasized the importance of the two decisions by devoting all three of their major editorials to the courts' findings. The *Virginian-Pilot* urged citizens to abide by the decisions. Chambers wrote that the state supreme court was Virginia's court and that its decisions therefore should be respected. The federal court's opinion was portrayed as restrained and logical, and the *Pilot* wrote that it too was worthy of Virginians' respect. "A historic opportunity now opens for Virginians," Chambers wrote. "The great of heart and mind will rise to it."[108]

Unlike Eggleston and Leslie, Chambers could discern no positive results from the state's policy of massive resistance. The editor's writing was uncharacteristically harsh:

> The massive resistance legislation was always considered by those who viewed it dispassionately to rest on most dubious constitutional pillars. It remained only for the courts to take a long, hard look at the monstrosities of the Stanley and Almond programs. This they have done, and the results are devastating. It remains now for the people of Virginia, including their elected officials, to ask themselves whether this distinguished commonwealth means to go on with the tragedy of legislative pretense that in practice has been legislative injustice and cruelty and perhaps permanent impairment to thousands of Virginia children.[109]

In an editorial later that week, Chambers denounced attempts by hard-line massive resisters to block the nomination of Justice Lawrence W. I'Anson of Portsmouth to the state supreme court. I'Anson, who had been temporarily appointed to the court to replace a deceased justice, had sided with the majority in *Harrison v. Day*. Chambers also aired his concerns about the recent denial of Thomas C. Boushall, a moderate on the subject of massive resistance, to reappointment to the State Board of Education. Boushall had been replaced in this position by South Norfolk's superintendent of schools William J. Story, Jr., a militant segregationist and an avowed white supremacist. (Story, later a candidate for Virginia's governorship, was providing schooling for nearly a thousand of Norfolk's white schoolchildren in the public schools of the city of South Norfolk.) The *Pilot* feared that Story's appointment and the opposition to I'Anson's confirmation signaled that public officials who had opposed the school closings would be punished. Chambers urged legislators to protect the court's "right to think independently."[110]

In "A Decree That Is a Landmark," Chambers emphasized that the federal decision in *James v. Almond* was "controlling" and that it prohibited the state, as well as the localities, from engaging in any evasive schemes designed to circumvent public-school integration. The *Pilot* warned that any plans designed to maintain total segregation would likely be declared illegal by the courts.[111]

After his defiant speech of January 20, 1959, Almond broke with the Byrd organization and began to display independent leadership. He called for the General Assembly to meet in special session January 28, urged the legislature to establish a commission of legislators to study the state's school problems, and recommended the adoption of a law designed to stop bomb threats. The governor also advised the legislators to repeal the state's compulsory-attendance law and consider the adoption of a tuition-assistance plan for private-school students.[112] The Defenders of State Sovereignty and Individual Liberties felt strongly betrayed by the governor's about-face and began to refer to him as "Benedict Almond."[113]

14

The Turning of the Tide

O N JANUARY 26, 1959, 141 days after the school closing and a week after the courts had rejected massive resistance, Norfolk's business community finally acted to reopen the schools. One hundred of the city's business leaders placed a statement in the *Virginian-Pilot,* urging city council to take steps to end the closure. The petition read,

> While we would strongly prefer to have segregated schools, it is evident from the recent court decisions that our public schools must either be integrated to the extent legally required or must be abandoned. The abandonment of our public school system is, in our opinion, unthinkable, as it would mean the denial of an adequate education to a majority of our children. Moreover, the consequences would be most damaging to our community. We, therefore, urge the Norfolk City Council to do everything within its power to open all public schools as promptly as possible.[1]

Although some of the signers of the petition would encounter animosity for their actions, each of the businessmen who signed the petition received a rose from Grandy the Florist.[2]

In "A New Clear Voice Speaks in Norfolk," Chambers noted the "striking and welcome change" in Norfolk's long-silent business community. The *Pilot* underscored the prestigious membership of the committee, which included two former mayors; the principal officers of the Chamber of Commerce, the Hampton Roads Maritime Association, and the Norfolk Port Authority; nine former "First Citizens"; and much of the city's business and professional leadership. Chambers counseled that the petition receive "thoughtful consideration from one end of Virginia to the other."[3]

Persuading the city's business leaders to sign the petition had been problematic for Frank Batten and Pretlow Darden, the former mayor of Norfolk. Approximately a week before the courts issued their rulings, Darden determined that the time was finally right for action. With the assistance of several other prominent businessmen, Batten and Darden developed the wording of the statement, and then the two organizers contacted business leaders throughout the city. "We had to modify the wording of the petition to get a number of people to sign it," Batten recalled. "We ended up with what we wanted, but we had to qualify . . . it."[4]

The petition infuriated Duckworth, who felt betrayed by the signers, many of whom were supporters and close friends. Pretlow Darden broke the news to the mayor: "I called Fred and I said, 'Now Fred, we are going to run an ad in tomorrow's newspaper saying that the schools ought to be open.' He said, 'Hell, why didn't you tell me?' I said, 'We didn't want to embarrass you. We know what your position is and how come you supported massive resistance.' 'Well,' he said, 'you have just stabbed me in the back.' I said, 'Would you like to see it?' 'Hell no, I don't want to see it if I can't do anything about it.' "[5]

Three years later, when Roy B. Martin, Jr., succeeded Duckworth as mayor, he found the framed petition hanging on the back of a closet door in the mayor's office. "Any time that door was opened [he saw it]. He really felt very . . . betrayed by a lot of his friends."[6] Sam Barfield, a signer of the petition, who later was elected to city council on a reform ticket, recounted a story that Duckworth used the petition as a dart board: "They tell me the dart hit my name the most. You can imagine how I felt when I got elected. . . . I didn't have an ally."[7]

An overriding concern for the well-being of Norfolk's schoolchildren probably was not the predominant motivation for many who signed the petition. Certainly economics figured prominently in their decision. Simply put, the business community had come to believe that the school closing was bad for business.[8]

The same day the businessmen's petition appeared in the *Virginian-Pilot*, Duckworth appeared in Judge Hoffman's court to attempt to defend his plans to close all of the city's junior and senior high schools.[9] The following day Hoffman issued his decision in *James v. Duckworth*.[10] The judge enjoined city council and the city treasurer from enforcing council's resolutions of November 25 and December 30, 1958, and prohibited Norfolk's city council from engaging in any "evasive schemes" designed to subvert the will of the court.[11]

The city's political leaders acquiesced to the court's verdict and grudgingly began to make plans to reopen the six closed schools. Interestingly, one of the many plaintiffs in *James v. Duckworth* was Chambers's godson, Louis I. Jaffe, Jr., the son of the former editor of the *Virginian-Pilot*.[12]

On January 28, 1959, Virginia's General Assembly met in special session. The governor's opening address began with vintage Almond and gave no indication that he was about to abandon massive resistance: "Encompassed by the iron will of arrogated power, buffeted upon the storms of an uneven contest, pierced with the daggers of political expediency and battered by the unholy alliance of a conspiracy to destroy the Constitution, Virginia, true to the faith of the founding fathers and refusing to desecrate her heritage, must never recede in this struggle to preserve her rights nor suffer her voice to be stifled in the councils of nations."[13]

Partway through the speech, however, Almond changed course, revealing that he was distancing himself from the inflexible racial policies of Senator Harry Byrd: "I report as a fact, and not in a spirit of criticism, that the laws enacted to prevent the mixing of the races in our public schools . . . have been stricken down by a Federal Court, and by the Supreme Court of Appeals of Virginia. The imminence of the peril to our people of the crisis thus engendered challenges the loyalty and dedication of our hearts and minds, and the prompt application of our talents and efforts, to the very best we can give in the service of Virginia."[14]

Importantly, the governor conceded that the powers of the federal government superseded those of the state: "I have repeatedly stated that I did not possess the power and knew of none that could be evolved that would enable Virginia to overthrow or negate the overriding power of the Federal government."[15] Almond continued by making clear that he had no intention of forcing the federal courts to send him to jail as some hard-line resisters had suggested. That strategy, he maintained, would contribute to "nothing but the ridiculous."[16]

Almond concluded his speech by proposing repeal of Virginia's massive-resistance legislation, abolishment of compulsory-attendance laws, provision of $250 tuition stipends to parents objecting to their children's attendance of integrated schools, and appointment of a forty-member legislative commission to examine future responses.[17]

The General Assembly passed these proposals by large majorities. The assembly immediately named forty of its members to the recommended study commission—the "Perrow Commission," after state senator Mosby Perrow of Lynchburg.

The *Virginian-Pilot* protested the legislation that repealed the state's compulsory attendance law and provided for private-school tuition.[18] Chambers also criticized the composition of the assembly's study commission. He viewed it as too large to function effectively, and he objected to the exclusion of blacks and women from its membership.[19]

Still, he praised Governor Almond's conversion to moderation and reason. Chambers wrote, "It must be said that in a critical moment Governor Almond stood up for realism and practicality—and he won. In consequence Virginia has at least more hope of reasonable action ahead than at any time since Governor Stanley surrendered in 1954 to the massive resistance movement."[20]

Almond's pragmatism angered resisters and displeased some pro-school forces. Three hundred residents of the Southside met in Kenbridge on February 8, 1958, and unanimously adopted resolutions denouncing the actions of the governor and the General Assembly. "Virginia has . . . suffered at the hands of her own officials a most severe defeat," they declared.[21] The Defenders of State Sovereignty and Individual Liberties, in various meetings throughout the state, accused Almond of integrating the schools. A petition calling for the governor's impeachment was widely circulated throughout the state. It was later determined that Lincoln Rockwell, president of the American Nazi Party, had printed the petitions.[22]

On the other side of the issue, the Virginia Council on Human Relations, opposing the provision of tuition grants and the repeal of the compulsory-attendance laws, called the actions "hasty, unnecessary, and ill-advised."[23]

The day following the governor's controversial address, Norfolk's city council directed Superintendent J. J. Brewbaker to reopen the six closed schools on February 2, 1959.[24] The city's black community and pro-school forces celebrated council's action. Blacks packed the city hall and cheered the vote to reopen the schools.[25]

On February 2, 1959, the day the General Assembly recessed, Norfolk's schools were reopened. Although city officials carefully downplayed the possibility of violence, they had prepared for every conceivable contingency. Plainclothes police and FBI agents inconspicuously positioned themselves near the schools scheduled to be integrated, and guards kept watch over the homes of the seventeen black students. The situation in Norfolk was closely monitored by Attorney General William P. Rogers's staff, and U.S. marshals were placed on alert.[26]

Reporters, photographers, and film crews from more than fifty different newspapers, wire services, and television stations gathered at the schools—many at Norview High School, where there seemed the greatest likelihood of racial violence. A few years before, when nearby white communities had been integrated, a number of racial incidents had occurred in the Norview section.[27]

Frank Batten specifically directed that reporters from the *Virginian-Pilot* and the *Ledger-Dispatch,* as well as staff from WTAR-TV Services (also owned by Norfolk Newspapers, Inc.), behave responsibly. To avoid fueling hysteria, reporters were instructed to retain as low a profile as possible, and television cameras were told to keep away from school doors.[28]

Nevertheless, the reopening of the city's schools took place uneventfully. Vivian Mason, recently returned from a trip to Africa, put one of her arms around a black student and one around principal Charles "Bolo" Perdue and strode up the steps of Norview High School.[29] Although some name-calling occurred, a cross was burned near a school, and racist literature was mailed from an unidentified source within the city, black and white students attended school together without incident. At worst, the black students suffered the isolation and loneliness for which Mason had prepared them so well.[30] Forrest White wrote that the press covering the reopening "had a rather dull day. The students arrived, went to school, went home again and that was that."[31]

Of the ten thousand students displaced by the school closing, only sixty-four hundred returned. Nearly two thousand had received no schooling since the closure.[32]

The integration of the state's previously all-white schools was a watershed in Virginia history. Luther Carter later wrote, "The desegregation of schools in Norfolk and Arlington, coming the day the assembly was recessed, cut away an important psychological underpinning of the resistance program. Once the barrier was broken by even a handful of Negro children, all talk of Virginia as a fortress of segregation sounded hollow."[33]

Leslie and his editorial staff wrote that the reopening of the schools should not signify a surrender to the NAACP and substantial integration. Leslie recommended that strategies of containment, which would limit the number of black students attending school with white students to an insignificant few, replace massive resistance. "This state's initial 'massive resistance' line has been breached, but 'massive integration' doesn't automatically follow."[34] The *Ledger* advocated the development of "legal, carefully planned procedures" to prevent the "appalling destruction of the school system which integration itself, unless checked, would surely bring about in a matter of months or years, depending on how aggressively the NAACP pursues its drive."[35] Leslie defended Virginia's massive resistance to school desegregation, calling it an effective "bulwark" that had postponed integration for three years.[36]

Although Leslie continued to oppose integration vigorously, he encouraged readers to abide by the laws, despite the "displeasure and bitterness which are bound to be the by-products of the years of conflict provoked by the Supreme Court's ill-timed and ill-advised pressure for race mixing in the schools."[37]

Lenoir Chambers also urged readers to abide by the law and reminded them that the country's attention was focused on the city. He wrote, "Norfolk's citizens all have obligations to the principles by which Americans live—principles of fairness, of justice, of opportunity, of obedience to law, and of good citizenship. In such respects this old city, with its good name for understanding, can add greatly to its own stature this week, and can set a fine example for the nation—indeed the world—that watches."[38]

Frank Batten would shortly end his policy of affording his editors complete autonomy. He had decided that Norfolk Newspapers would begin to speak with a unified voice on the resistance. "It was a combination of my conscience and my concern for the community," he said. "I just couldn't condone something I was absolutely convinced was wrong." The young publisher had made his views on the school closing clear to Leslie for several months and finally instructed him to end his defense of segregation. Leslie conceded defeat but asked that Batten, who claimed little talent for writing, write the editorial announcing the change in policy. "It was the worst editorial that has ever been in the paper," declared Batten.[39]

Remarkably, the high regard in which Chambers and Leslie had held each other at the outset of the long debate withstood their fervent exposition of opposite positions on the school closing.[40] Several months after the reopening of Norfolk's schools, Chambers wrote to a friend, "I am forever poking my head into Joe Leslie's office to see how my friend is—to catch a little more of the twinkle of his eye and feel again the strength of his virtues."[41] Leslie, sharing this affection, wrote, "Your friendship has been one of the possessions which I shall always prize most highly."[42]

Among the accolades Chambers received upon the publication of his Stonewall Jackson biography later that year came praise from a surprising source, arch-adversary Harry Flood Byrd, Sr. Byrd felt a Virginian's near-reverential respect for the memory of the general, some of whose historic campaigns had been waged near the senator's Winchester home. Byrd wrote that he was enjoying the biography of his hero immensely but could not resist mentioning that Jackson had served as a role model as he (Byrd) strove "to defend the Right of the States" in the massive-resistance struggle.[43]

Johnnie Rouse, Carol Wellington, Olivia Driver, and Alveraz Gonsouland (left to right), February 2, 1959, leave school grounds at Norview Senior High School after schools are reopened. (Courtesy of the *Virginian-Pilot*)

Chambers (center) in his office with Managing Editor Robert Mason (left) and Publisher Frank Batten (right) after Chambers learned he had won the Pulitzer Prize for Editorial Writing, 1960. (Courtesy of the *Virginian-Pilot*)

Virginian-Pilot Editor Lenoir Chambers, c. 1950s (Courtesy of Elisabeth C. Burgess, Norfolk)

15

The Influence of Lenoir Chambers

MANY KEY FIGURES and interest groups contributed to the resolution of the massive-resistance crisis in Norfolk and the integration of the city's public schools. Among the factors were the landmark decisions issued by the federal and state courts, the refusal of the city's teachers to align themselves with the private-school movement, and the energetic campaign conducted by the Norfolk Committee for Public Schools. The NAACP relentlessly sought school integration; and black leaders, with *Journal and Guide* publisher P. B. Young, Sr., in the vanguard, used their influence to defuse the school crisis.

Well-meaning but less-influential groups, such as the Norfolk Ministers Association, the American Association of University Women, the League of Women Voters, and the Women's Interracial Council, supported the pro-school position. The Navy's Rear Admiral Massie Hughes, commandant of the largest naval base in the world, lobbied for a resolution to the closure. Finally, Norfolk's business community issued a long-delayed statement urging that the schools be reopened.

Yet without the example set by the *Virginian-Pilot* and the moderating influence of its thoughtful and persuasive editorials, this coalition would have operated less effectively.

Robert Mason concluded,

> The union of [the pro-school] elements was loose. But as each stood up, it had a rallying point. It had a veteran of the conflict to follow. It had the clear, unwavering, unafraid example set and maintained by The *Virginian-Pilot* throughout the difficult months.
>
> For all during the school crisis, and particularly during the year of its nadir—1959—Lenoir Chambers said and said again in his editorial columns what the law was, and what justice was, and what reality was. He never wavered. He wasted no time on the fiction of what might have been or might be.
>
> It is not too much to say, I am persuaded, that Lenoir Chambers has done more, and under conditions more vexing and longer sustained, to give logic and direction to Virginia, and to the whole South, in the school problem than any other editor.[1]

In 1960 Chambers was awarded the Pulitzer Prize for distinguished editorial writing—the nation's highest award for journalism. The citation read that Chambers received the prize "for [his] series of editorials on the school segregation problem in Virginia, as exemplified by 'The Year the Schools Closed,' published January 1, 1959, and 'The Year the Schools Opened,' published December 31, 1959."[2] (Although the editor's two-volume *Stonewall Jackson* was nominated for the Pulitzer in biography that same year, Samuel Eliot Morison received the award for his study of John Paul Jones. Some knowledgeable observers believe Chambers's biography would have received the prize had he not been awarded the Pulitzer for his editorials.)[3]

Chambers had been nominated for the honor four years earlier for his editorials on massive resistance. However, that application was complicated by associate editor William Meacham's insistence that he should receive or share the award. Harold Sugg believed that "these efforts . . . confused the situation and delayed Chambers's Pulitzer by at least two years. If Bob Mason had not picked up the effort . . . and given it one more try, Chambers could have missed out altogether."[4]

Chambers was gracious in his acceptance and acknowledged the important contributions of his associate editors, writing that "*Virginian-Pilot* editorials are written after conference and consultation in which many persons may play a part. I am especially indebted to the associate editors, William S. Meacham and Robert C. Smith; to earlier associate editors, Harold Sugg and Robert Mason; to members of the news staff and to others familiar with school problems; and to *The Virginian Pilot*'s publisher, Frank Batten, and its president, Paul S. Huber, Jr., for their constant encouragement." [5]

Chambers spent much of his $1,000 prize on the addition of a bathroom for his home. The remainder was used to replace his space-skipping typewriter. As soon as he received notice of the award, he called a local store. "I've won the Pulitzer Prize," he told the owner, "and I'm coming down there to buy a new typewriter."[6]

For Alice Jaffe, Louis Jaffe's widow, Chambers's prize-winning editorial campaign had been a continuation of her husband's work. She wrote to Chambers, "I feel happy not only about the well-deserved honor, but because of the special series of editorials singled out, in which the subject of human and racial justice followed the precedent of Louis' earlier prize. This series did much to influence current thought and action also, as did his. Yours was one of the very few voices raised in public utterance for schools, for law, for moderation, for intelligence—the voice never wavered through dark days and (I'm sure) abuse, and the words were as measured and firm as the voice itself."[7]

The announcement of Chambers's prize also brought Jaffe to mind for Stringfellow Barr, a Princeton University faculty member who had written editorials for Jaffe. "I wish Jaffe could have been alive to see you win it. But given the kind of guy Louis was, he probably does know."[8]

The national press believed Chambers's award was well deserved. The *New York Times* termed the *Pilot*'s editorial page a "voice of reason on a political battlefield that was a testing ground in the South. Mr. Chambers warned against the danger to the fabric of government that was inherent in resistance to a Supreme Court decision. His was a leading voice and a persuasive voice and it was heard beyond the bounds of his own state in the Southern region. The Pulitzer Prize in this instance crowned a long career that has been dedicated to the defense of civil liberty and public morality."[9]

C. A. ("Pete") McKnight, the former editor of *Southern School News* and editor of the *Charlotte Observer,* one of the nation's most knowledgeable journalists on the subject of massive resistance, wrote to Chambers: "I have followed your thoughtful and persuasive editorials with great interest and am quite sure that Norfolk's limited integration program went off so quietly because of the influence of your fine newspaper."[10] McKnight later wrote, "I have told many people that I thought your editorial writing on the desegregation problem was the most distinguished I had seen anywhere."[11]

Chambers's peers had long applauded his injection of reason and moderation into the emotional debate over integration. R. H. Estabrook, the editorial page editor of the *Washington Post,* wrote, "I cannot resist writing to commend your courage and common sense in your editorial[s]. It is a great deal more difficult for you to say these things than for us across the polluted waters of the Potomac. I think you are abundantly right, and it gives me great heart to know this sort of comment is continuing in our super-heated atmosphere."[12]

The editor and publisher of the *Journal and Guide,* one of the nation's most widely circulated and influential black presses, were highly appreciative of Chambers's role in defusing racial tensions. Thomas W. Young, editor of the *Journal and Guide,* had chastised Henry R. Luce, *Time* magazine's editor, for neglecting to mention the *Virginian-Pilot* in a *Time* article on southern newspapers challenging segregation. In a letter to Luce, Thomas Young called the *Pilot*'s editorial page "a beacon in the South where the lights of reason and statesmanship are going out all over the land. I should imagine that Editor Lenoir Chambers and his associates, William S. Meacham and Harold Sugg, are high on the list of enemies claimed by the White Citizens Councils and other invisible Southern state governments, both hooded and unhooded."[13]

P. B. Young, the editor's father, wrote to Chambers, "Your contributions to the proper understanding of the elements which go to create racial tensions have been wonderful. I am sure your paper has the gratitude of all patriotic citizens who read it, and who are influenced by it."[14] Thomas Young would later congratulate Chambers for receiving the Pulitzer, writing, "Those of us who believe the editorial pages of our newspapers still exert a powerful influence on public opinion can certainly find a relationship between the courageous and convincing editorial voice of the *Virginian-Pilot* throughout the months of Norfolk's dilemma and the easy restraint and ultimate containment of massive resistance forces in our community."[15]

Although the national press's acknowledgment of Lenoir Chambers's role as an advocate for racial understanding and moderation is a significant indicator of the editor's influence, it is the testimony of on-the-scene participants and witnesses that establishes his most important contribution to the outcome of the crisis: the role he played in influencing key actors in the drama. School board chairman Paul Schweitzer, who despite personal reservations regarding public-school integration ultimately adopted a moderate position and helped to persuade members of the board and Superintendent J. J. Brewbaker to adopt conciliatory positions, was deeply inspired by Chambers's editorials. The chairman wrote, "This community is indebted to you for the calm, dignified stand you maintained throughout the period of our recent controversy. Your reasonable approach, sound reasoning, and ability to clearly express your logic was a tremendous factor in resolving the problem we faced. You were, and remain, an inspiration to me personally in the humble part I had in this ordeal. All our civic problems are not yet resolved but with your continued leadership through the editorial pages of the *Virginian-Pilot*, Norfolk can look to the future with confidence."[16]

In two major developments in the breakdown of the resistance—one leading to and one following the opening of the schools—Chambers clearly served as a catalyst. Frank Batten attested to the editor's influence on him, which helped solidify his opposition to the city's stance on the school issue. Batten took the first steps toward organizing Norfolk's business leaders, and he remained a prime force in their intervention in the crisis. Although the young publisher initiated this intercession independently and solely of his own volition, Chambers figured significantly in the conviction that led to Batten's action. Chambers thus indirectly helped set in motion the business community's crucial support, which accelerated and moderated the opening.

Chambers likewise counted indirectly in the publisher's decision to terminate the *Ledger-Dispatch*'s editorial alliance with the resistance movement. The end of that paper's endorsement damped the segregationist fire in the area by removing an important source of doctrine and encouragement, and hence facilitated the transition taking place in the schools. Additionally, some of Leslie's faithful readers likely tempered their objection to the mixing, and some probably came around to his new editorial position.

Judge Walter E. Hoffman read the editorials of the *Virginian-Pilot* and the *Ledger-Dispatch* closely during Norfolk's school crisis. Although the judge's actions were based on his interpretation of the law, not on media influence, he felt that Chambers practiced exceedingly responsible journalism and played an important role in defusing the crisis. Hoffman recalled that the *Pilot*'s editorials were "being written by people who were responsible to get the true facts." The judge had less respect for the *Ledger-Dispatch:* "[Joe Leslie] blasted the devil out of me, and I knew Joe very well. . . . Not that I respected his opinion, because I'd read through it; and from the facts' standpoint, he had nothing to go on."[17]

Other pro-school forces and figures were rallied by Chambers's editorials. Shortly after the schools reopened, the Norfolk Education Association, which had played a critical role in the closing by refusing to support the activities of the Tidewater Educational Foundation, commended the editor for his "editorial policy on the troubled public school situation."[18] Edie White, a key figure in several pro-school organizations, later praised the *Pilot*'s role: "Our morning newspaper, the *Virginian-Pilot,* of which we are proud, wrote and has continued to write excellent editorials urging the people to awaken to the need for action."[19] Jane Reif appreciated the intelligence, thoughtfulness, and liberalism of the *Pilot*'s contributions to the debate.[20]

Many of Norfolk's citizens not directly involved in the closing also perceived the *Pilot* as having figured importantly in moderating the crisis. One reader wrote to Chambers, "Your editorial policy was largely responsible for the crystallization of sane and purposeful action in regard to the opening of Public Schools in Norfolk. Without it, and the *Virginian-Pilot* . . . the groups in Norfolk working for the schools would not have succeeded, or at least for some time to come."[21]

More than three decades later, Chambers's surviving colleagues at the *Virginian-Pilot* contended that the paper's editorials had a significant influence on public opinion. The paper's publisher, Frank Batten, concluded that although typical day-to-day editorials do not influence the public to a large degree, the *Pilot*'s campaign had an impact on Norfolk's citizenry because the closing affected them so immediately and profoundly. He attributed the effectiveness of the *Pilot*'s arguments "in the midst of all that hatred" in part to their consistency and persistence throughout the years of the crisis and to the calm manner in which they were presented, which in his view had a calming influence on the community. He remained convinced that this quality itself played a role in the smooth, nonviolent integration of the schools.[22]

Luther Carter believed readers closely heeded the *Virginian-Pilot*'s editorials because of their uniqueness. He thought the iconoclasm of challenging the Byrd Machine and the sacrosanct southern tradition of segregation, particularly coming from an institution of the *Pilot*'s stature, drew and held the attention of the public. The long, steady campaign drilled the editorials' carefully reasoned message into the minds of this wide readership. And Chambers's astute strategy in not getting too far ahead of the people, but remaining intellectually honest, made the new ideas easier to digest, said Carter.[23]

Robert Mason, Chambers's successor as editor, believed that the newspaper had an important effect in educating Norfolk's citizenry and in mobilizing pro-school forces. He confirmed the perception that people read everything on the closing because it affected them all. The *Pilot* also provided a rallying point for the pro-school element, he said, and kept this constituency informed on action and reaction elsewhere in the country.[24]

Lenoir Chambers alone determined the *Pilot*'s editorial policy and, with the assistance of his staff of editorial associates—Harold Sugg, William Meacham, and later Robert Mason and Robert Smith—engaged in a tireless campaign that encouraged moderation and racial tolerance. The *Virginian-Pilot,* Virginia's second most widely circulated newspaper, was the only major daily newspaper in the state to oppose massive resistance and urge compliance with the Supreme Court's *Brown v. Board* decision.

Chambers's voice was heard throughout Virginia and indeed the South. His views were closely monitored by the principal architects of the state's resistance, including both Senator Harry Flood Byrd, Sr., and Governor J. Lindsay Almond. The editor's role was widely recognized by his peers and colleagues; and as a result of his persistent campaign, he received the Pulitzer Prize, the nation's highest award for editorial writing.

Chambers played an important role in moderating public opinion and encouraging the peaceful resolution of Norfolk's school crisis. Television journalism was in its infancy, and radio coverage of news and opinion was limited and superficial. Newspapers were the overwhelmingly dominant media of the day. During the massive-resistance era and especially during the school closing, the *Virginian-Pilot*'s editorials were read with unaccustomed and increasing frequency by the rank-and-file residents affected by the closing and by a watchful general public. Among so wide a readership, many persons would have been swayed to varying degrees by the reasoned and persistent arguments of Chambers, as some of the most prominent figures attested. It is likely that other opinion leaders and members of the elite known generally to read editorials were persuaded by the *Pilot* to temper their views and that they, in turn, influenced followers.[25]

To white southerners of the era, a segregated society and the subservience of blacks were the natural order of things, a way of life many whites had not questioned seriously if at all. When the comfortable status quo was threatened, most were inclined to defend it and would not have gone looking for justification for change. Whites who recognized and deplored the plight of blacks tended not to publicize their concerns, for fear of stirring up trouble; failed miserably by their political leadership, which exploited racial prejudice, these whites saw no prospect for early improvement in the lot of blacks.

In both of these situations—and especially with the preponderance of confirming and often incendiary sentiment coming at Virginia's pro-segregation element from like-minded peers, the politicians, and the predominant regional media of the time—a need existed for a strong voice on the side of public education, racial tolerance, and the law. Moreover, to be effective, the voice had to reach a wide audience.

Lenoir Chambers supplied that voice in Norfolk and throughout the region. He saw to it that the case for moderation, fairness, and responsible citizenship reached newsstands and doorsteps throughout the city, day after day, from the beginning of the crisis to its resolution five years later. From his position as editor of southeastern Virginia's leading newspaper, the scholarly Chambers provided the prestige needed to give weight to the voice.

The *Virginian-Pilot*'s unremitting campaign could only have raised the consciousness of thinking people on both sides of the issue and of many whose minds had been closed. The *Pilot*'s clear logic, unemotional laying out of facts, and exposure of sub-rosa political strategies could not have failed to point the way to some—probably many—who were undecided or who initially had leaned in the opposite direction.

The paper's position was widely discussed, even among those it infuriated. For many die-hard segregationists, put on early notice by such an authoritative source as the *Virginian-Pilot* that the law of the land might well prevail, the shock effect of the notion would have been eroded and the explosiveness of the situation defused long before the opening of the schools.

For readers who knew of his character and background—certainly a large number of the city's most powerful elite and of the general public—Lenoir Chambers was an especially credible and influential spokesperson. This audience could not easily dismiss his opinions and arguments. The genteel and impeccably mannered Chambers, who on occasion confided that he would have felt more comfortable living in the previous century, was a "son of the South," born into its aristocracy and steeped in its traditions. Chambers commanded and was accorded respect in the southern city of Norfolk. He invoked what was noble (perhaps, albeit, imagined) about the South—its manners and democratic heritage; and deplored its excesses—racism, intolerance, and emotionalism. When readers unfamiliar with his background called or wrote to complain about the *Pilot*'s editorial stance, they were dismayed to learn of the editor's southern roots and his authorship of a biography of "Marse Robert's" most revered lieutenant.

Chambers, although he would likely have objected to the appellation, was, along with Virginius Dabney, one of Virginia's leading intellectuals. His views on racial issues were singularly advanced in their time and context, and his editorials expounding those views rallied pro-school organizations and individuals opposing massive resistance.

To his additional credit, Chambers raised the quality of the debate on integration to a higher level. In painstaking detail, he informed his readers and encouraged them to form opinions based on objective evidence rather than emotional reaction.

The demise of massive resistance in Norfolk sealed its doom in Virginia. The peaceful integration of the state's schools portended the downfall of the entire South's resistance to the Supreme Court's decision. Francis Wilhoit observes that "the collapse of massive resistance in Virginia in 1959 was a decisive event in the history of the South's counterrevolution. And it is well to recall that the admission of black pupils to white schools, though doubtless resented by a majority of whites, took place without mob violence or abuse of black pupils."[26]

The mission on which Lenoir Chambers chose to embark at a crucial point in the history of the South and in which he prevailed against formidable opposition would make a difference well beyond the boundaries of the city and state in which he waged his campaign.

Chambers was a symbol of courage. Afforded complete editorial autonomy by the *Pilot*'s publisher, he could easily have chosen to pursue an editorial policy that would have conformed to the tenor of the times. The editor, despite tremendous pressures to do otherwise, stood alone.

16

Epilogue

The Editor and the Schools

L ENOIR CHAMBERS REMAINED very active after his retirement in 1962, frequently visiting the *Virginian-Pilot*'s editorial suite and co-writing with retired *Ledger-Star* news editor Joseph E. Shank and Harold Sugg *Salt Water & Printer's Ink,* a history of Norfolk's newspapers.

He retained a lively interest in current and community affairs, educating himself by constant and diverse reading, as he had throughout his professional career. Chambers served as a trustee for Norfolk Academy, the city's oldest private school, and for Woodberry Forest preparatory school, his alma mater. He was appointed to the Norfolk Library Board and was elected president of the Norfolk Forum, which sponsored speeches by notable literary, academic, and political figures. And despite some divisiveness his editorial campaign had created in the upper reaches of Norfolk society, he kept his membership in the city's two elite social organizations, the Virginia Club and the German Club.

Chambers also continued to play an active role in his profession, serving on the Nieman Fellowship selection committee and the jury for Pulitzer Prize candidates. His contributions to journalism earned wide recognition. The Columbia School of Journalism named him to its honors list, and the University of North Carolina awarded him an honorary doctor of laws degree.

Still uncomfortable addressing public audiences, he remained a sought-after lecturer, frequently speaking before historical and literary organizations in Virginia and throughout the South. Before he delivered the graduation speech at the University of North Carolina, in which he warned southerners to reach beyond the narrow confines of regionalism, his family watched him nervously pace his hotel room.[1]

On January 8, 1970, Chambers suffered a stroke while scraping ice from his windshield and never regained consciousness. He died two days later, at 78 years of age.

General application of the *Brown* ruling for which Chambers had fought proceeded gradually. Genuine change in the racial makeup of southern schools began when federal courts ordered busing, mandating that students attend schools outside their neighborhoods to prevent racial clustering. In 1968, nearly 80 percent of southern blacks attended schools in which nine out of ten students were black or Hispanic. Eight years later that percentage fell to 22.[2]

In Norfolk busing began in 1971, when a federal district court found that local officials had operated a racially segregated or "dual" school system. Black and white schools were paired, and about one-half of the system's elementary school students were bused, some traveling up to ninety minutes a day.

In 1975, although the courts ruled that the last vestiges of segregation in the schools had been effectively eliminated, Norfolk's school board elected to continue busing. Much of Norfolk's white population adamantly opposed this policy on the grounds that it was unfair to students and that it stimulated "white flight." Since the early 1970s, the city's economic base had weakened as white families moved to the suburbs of neighboring Virginia Beach, one of the country's fastest-growing metropolitan areas. Ten years after the implementation of busing, Norfolk's population had dropped by 11 percent; the school population had plummeted by 37 percent; and the percentage of white students in the system had declined significantly, from 57 to 43 percent.[3]

By 1982, Norfolk's school board, alarmed by the changing school demographics and responding to the increasingly vocal objections of busing opponents, was seriously weighing a new pupil-assignment strategy—"neighborhood schools"—in which students would attend the schools closest to their homes. To investigate the condition of Norfolk's public schools, the board hired sociologist David J. Armor, whose findings buttressed the neighborhood-school plan. Armor asserted a causal link between busing and white flight. Coalition for Quality Public Education spokesperson Gwendolyn Jones Jackson challenged Armor's conclusions, alleging bias on his part.[4]

The following year the school board, consisting of three black and four white members, voted unanimously to implement a neighborhood school plan in which four thousand black children would attend nearly all-black schools in their own inner-city neighborhoods. This would result in ten of the city's thirty-five grammar schools becoming at least 97 percent black. Approximately 40 percent of the city's black elementary school population would attend one of these segregated schools. Busing was slated to continue at junior and senior high schools.[5]

Critics of the school board argued that Norfolk's neighborhood-school plan was "resegregation," a return to the separate but equal policies of the previous era. They mounted a legal challenge to the plan, but a federal district court decided in favor of the school board, and the U.S. 4th Circuit

Court of Appeals upheld the lower court's decision. The board made a number of concessions in an effort to obtain support in the black community: limiting class size in the black schools to no more than twenty, developing exchange activities with white schools, and allowing black parents to transfer their children to white schools if they objected to their assigned schools.

The school board received the support of the Reagan administration, which viewed the experiment as an important national test case and a model for other communities that wished to end court-ordered busing. William Bradford Reynolds, the head of the Justice Department's Civil Rights Division, contended that the plan facilitated local control over education and would end white flight.

In 1986, the Supreme Court refused to grant an injunction sought by black parents preventing the school board from dismantling Norfolk's fifteen-year busing program. Justices Thurgood Marshall, Harry Blackmun, and John Paul Stevens dissented.

Five years later, the Norfolk Oversight Committee, which was charged with maintaining the fairness of school-choice assignments, voted to disband itself because of its narrow purview. Against the wishes of the school board, the committee had sought to examine variables in addition to funding, to assess better the quality of the educational experience all-black schools provided.[6]

In 1995 the jury on Norfolk's all-black schools was still out. School administrators had kept their bargain to better finance black schools, which received approximately 15 percent more instructional funding than their integrated counterparts. The ratio of white to black students had stabilized at 60 to 35, suggesting that white flight had been stemmed. While test scores had not risen, neither had they declined as significantly as had been expected in the wake of increasing poverty, an epidemic of crack-cocaine use and violence, and Navy and shipyard cutbacks. And although PTA membership had declined in the all-black schools, hours spent by black parents in school-centered activities had risen significantly. Despite these hopeful indicators, a recently released Harvard University study concludes that the only definite results of neighborhood schools "have been severe racial isolation and an increase in concentrated poverty."[7] Particularly disheartening is the fact that the system's lowest scoring eight schools on fourth-grade standardized tests were all-black.[8] Sadly, most of the students in Norfolk's all-black schools remain in the educational basement.[9]

What is Chambers's legacy to a new generation of journalists at the *Virginian-Pilot*'s successor, the *Virginian-Pilot and Ledger-Star,*[10] and to his city? Perhaps some hint of the answer to this question appears in an editorial written in the wake of the Circuit Court of Appeals's decision to allow the school board to proceed with its neighborhood school plan. Informing readers of the court's judgment and explaining in detail the three-judge panel's rationale for reaching its finding, the *Virginian-Pilot and Ledger-Star* urged Norfolk's citizens to prove that the neighborhood system could benefit all of the city's public schoolchildren, black and white. With an eye toward the South's long history of racial prejudice, the paper acknowledged the fear of many black parents that the schools would return to "those horrible days when blacks were discriminated against and often received a second-class education." "The board must confront this fear head on," the editorial continued, "and demonstrate that all the components of its new plan, including the majority/minority transfer option, will be carried out immediately. The board must make it clear, as it has before, that racial discrimination will not be tolerated and that predominantly black schools will not be shortchanged in any way."[11]

In this editorial the voice of Chambers can be clearly heard, stressing the value of public education, informing, teaching, and urging racial cooperation and fairness. Perhaps this voice is Lenoir Chambers's legacy to his city and to a new generation of journalists.

Notes

Preface

1. *Brown v. Board of Education of Topeka*, 347 US 483 (1954).
2. J. H. Wilkinson, *Harry Byrd and the Changing Face of Virginia Politics, 1945–1966* (Charlottesville: University Press of Virginia, 1968), 141.
3. C. V. Woodward, *The Strange Career of Jim Crow*, 3d edition (New York: Oxford University Press, 1974), 168.
4. L. Chambers, J. Shank, and H. Sugg, *Salt Water & Printer's Ink: Norfolk and Its Newspapers* (Chapel Hill: University of North Carolina Press, 1967), 387.

1. Closing of the Schools

1. *Southern School News*, September 1958.
2. H. Rorer, *History of Norfolk Public Schools, 1681–1968* unpublished manuscript, Old Dominion University Library, 1968, 292, 341.
3. B. Muse, *Virginia's Massive Resistance* (Bloomington: Indiana University Press, 1961), 75–78.
4. F. White, "Will Norfolk's Schools Stay Open?" *The Atlantic*, September 1959, 30.
5. Muse, *Virginia's Massive Resistance*, 92–93.
6. S. Barfield, interview by author, tape recording, 8 August 1990.
7. F. Batten, interview by author, tape recording, 25 September 1990.
8. Muse, *Virginia's Massive Resistance*, 116.
9. W. Dykeman and J. Stokely, "Report on 'The Lost Class of '59,' " *New York Times Magazine*, 4 January 1959, 20.
10. "How Norfolk's Schools Were Reopened," F. White Papers, Old Dominion University Library.
11. Muse, *Virginia's Massive Resistance*, 117; "80 Days Without Public Schools," *Newsweek*, 1 December 1958, 23–26.
12. B. Muse, *Ten Years of Prelude: The Story of Integration since the Supreme Court's 1954 Decision* (New York: Viking, 1964), 153.
13. Dykeman and Stokely, "Report on 'The Lost Class of '59,' " 54.
14. Muse, *Virginia's Massive Resistance*, 112.
15. *Southern School News*, November 1958, 13; Muse, *Ten Years of Prelude*, 151.

2. Divergent Views

1. L. Chambers to L. Wilson, 19 March 1959, Chambers Papers, Southern Historical Collection, University of North Carolina Library.
2. *Virginian-Pilot*, 28 September 1958.
3. Ibid., 24 September 1958.
4. Ibid., 25 September 1958.
5. Ibid., 23 September 1958.

6. Ibid., 21 September 1958.

7. Ibid., 29 September 1958.

8. H. Sugg, letter to author, 12 October 1990.

9. *Ledger-Dispatch,* 26 September 1958.

10. Ibid., 22, 23 September 1958.

11. Ibid., 22, 30 September 1958.

12. Ibid., 24 September 1958.

13. "Quest for a Personality," *Time,* 5 September 1960, 51.

14. R. Mason, telephone interview by author, tape recording, 5 December 1990.

15. Barfield, interview.

16. R. Mason, telephone interview by author, tape recording, 10 April 1989.

17. L. Chambers to L. Weary, 19 November 1958, Chambers Papers.

18. Batten, interview.

19. E. Burgess, interview by author, tape recording, 2 August 1990.

20. R. Mason, telephone interview by author, tape recording, 17 July 1990.

21. Ibid.

22. L. Chambers to J. Jones, 16 March 1956, Chambers Papers.

23. L. Chambers to G. Johnson, 7 January 1959, Chambers Papers.

24. Ibid.

25. Biographical Data, 1959, Chambers Papers.

26. Mason, interview, 17 July 1990.

27. Burgess, interview; R. Mason, *One of the Neighbors' Children* (Chapel Hill: Algonquin, 1987), 159.

28. R. Smith, telephone interview by author, tape recording, 17 April 1992.

29. J. Egerton, *Speak Now Against the Day: The Generation Before the Civil Rights Movement in the South* (New York: Knopf, 1994), 129–34; V. Dabney, *Liberalism in the South* (Chapel Hill: University of North Carolina Press, 1932), 349–51, 408.

30. J. Reif, *Crisis in Norfolk* (Richmond: Virginia Council on Human Relations, 1960), 13; E. Q. Campbell, *When a City Closes Its Schools* (Chapel Hill: Institute for Research in Social Sciences, 1960), 83.

31. D. J. Singal, *The War Within: From Victorian to Modernist Thought in the South, 1919–1945* (Chapel Hill: University of North Carolina Press, 1982), 301.

3. Lenoir Chambers: The Formative Years

1. *Virginian-Pilot,* 11 January 1970; L. Chambers to Morrow Press, 25 August 1956, Chambers Papers; J. Claiborne, *The Charlotte Observer: Its Time and Place, 1869–1986* (Chapel Hill: University of North Carolina Press, 1986), 47.

2. *Chapel Hill Weekly,* 14 January 1970; L. Chambers, *Stonewall Jackson* (New York: William Morrow, 1959), 463.

3. Burgess, interview; E. Burgess, letter to author, 5 December 1992.

4. *Charlotte Observer,* 18 May 1907.

5. *Charlotte Chronicle,* 18 May 1907.

6. *Washington Post,* undated, Chambers Papers.

7. *Tar-Heel,* undated, Chambers Papers.

8. L. Chambers to Morrow Press, 25 August 1959, Chambers Papers.

9. Ibid.

10. R. Baker, *A History of the Graduate School of Journalism, Columbia University* (New York: Columbia University, 1954), 83–85.

11. L. Chambers to Columbia University, 16 March 1956, Chambers Papers; L. Chambers to Morrow Press, 25 August 1959, Chambers Papers; M. Schuster to L. Chambers, 8 June 1933, Chambers Papers; G. Creel, *How We Advertised America: The First Telling of the Amazing Story of the Committee on Public Information that Carried the Gospel of Americanism to Every Corner of the Globe* (New York: Harper & Brothers, 1920).

12. Baker, *The Graduate School of Journalism,* 75–76; L. Chambers to Morrow Press, 25 August 1959, Chambers Papers.

13. L. Chambers to Columbia University, 16 March 1956, Chambers Papers; L. Chambers to Morrow Press, 25 August 1959, Chambers Papers; Baker, *The Graduate School of Journalism,* 75–76.

14. L. Chambers to G. Chambers, 13 October 1918, Chambers Papers.

15. *Stars and Stripes,* 7 May 1919.

16. L. Chambers to Morrow Press, 25 August 1959, Chambers Papers.

17. L. Chambers to G. Chambers, 11 August 1918, Chambers Papers.

18. Mason, *One of the Neighbors' Children,* 154.

19. L. Chambers to M. Schuster, 15 April 1933, Chambers Papers.

20. L. Chambers to G. Chambers, 20, 25 December 1918, Chambers Papers.

21. R. Draper, *The Letters of Ruth Draper: 1920–1956, a Self-portrait of a Great Actress,* ed. N. Warren (New York: Charles Scribner's Sons, 1979), 10, 20.

22. M. Zabel and R. Draper, *The Art of Ruth Draper: Her Dramas and Characters* (Garden City, N.Y.: Doubleday, 1960), 14.

23. Draper, *The Letters of Ruth Draper,* 19–20.

24. L. Chambers to G. Chambers, 19 July 1918, Chambers Papers.

25. L. Chambers to G. Chambers, 19 March 1919, Chambers Papers.

26. Chambers, *Stonewall Jackson,* 130.

27. L. Chambers to G. Chambers, 19 March 1919, Chambers Papers.

28. L. Chambers to G. Chambers, 19 July 1918, Chambers Papers.

29. *Charlottesville Daily Progress,* 16 March 1964; *University of Virginia College Topics,* 5 May 1915; W. Powell, ed., *Dictionary of North Carolina Biography* (Chapel Hill: University of North Carolina Press, 1991), 4:61.

30. L. Woolen, telephone interview by author, tape recording, 8 May 1992; Powell, *Dictionary of North Carolina Biography,* 4:61.

31. L. Chambers to G. Chambers, 22 March 1919, Chambers Papers.

32. L. Chambers to L. Chambers, Sr., 24 April 1919, Chambers Papers.

33. H. Gilrie to N. Lewis, 6 March 1919, Lewis Papers, Southern Historical Collection, University of North Carolina Library.

34. H. Calhoun to N. Lewis, 5 January 1919, Lewis Papers.

35. L. Chambers to L. Chambers, Sr., 24 April 1919, Chambers Papers.

36. Ibid.

37. Ibid.

38. L. Chambers to G. Chambers, 25 May 1919, Chambers Papers.

39. M. Stanley, telephone interview by author, tape recording, 8 May 1992.

40. "Inventory of Kemp Plummer Lewis Papers," Lewis Papers.

41. Woolen, interview, 8 May 1992.

42. N. Lewis, "Anarchy versus Communism in Gastonia." *The Nation,* 23 October 1929, 321–22; Egerton, *Speak Now Against the Day,* 60; B. Clayton, *W. J. Cash: A Life* (Baton Rouge: Louisiana State University Press, 1991), 49–50.

43. Powell, *Dictionary of North Carolina Biography,* 4:61–62; L. Green, "Nell Battle Lewis: Crusading Columnist, 1921–1938" (Master's thesis, East Carolina University, North Carolina, 1969).

44. Woolen, interview, 8 May 1992.
45. Dabney, *Liberalism in the South,* 400–01.

4. The Emergence of an Editor

1. R. Mason, telephone interview by author, tape recording, 19 November 1992.
2. G. Johnson to L. Chambers, 13 September 1924, Chambers Papers.
3. Powell, *Dictionary of North Carolina Biography,* 3:289–90.
4. R. Mason, interview, 19 November 1992.
5. *Greensboro Daily News,* 13 January 1970.
6. Burgess, interview.
7. E. Burgess, letter to author, 27 October 1992; S. Abeles, letter to author, 24 November 1992.
8. R. Draper to L. Chambers, 13 May 1926, Elisabeth Burgess, Norfolk, Virginia.
9. Ibid.
10. Burgess, letter to author, 27 October 1992.
11. J. Hohenberg, ed., *The Pulitzer Prize Story II: Award Winning News Stories, Columns, Editorials, and News Pictures, 1959–1980* (New York: Columbia University Press, 1980), 257.
12. Rorer, "History of Norfolk Public Schools," 74–79, 88.
13. L. Jaffe to G. Hall, 16 October 1929, Jaffe Papers, Manuscripts Division, Special Collections Department, University of Virginia Library.
14. G. Johnson to L. Jaffe, 14 October 1929, Jaffe Papers.
15. G. Hall to L. Jaffe, 18 October 1929, Jaffe Papers.
16. Ibid., 19 October 1929, Jaffe Papers; Clayton, *W. J. Cash: A Life,* 88.
17. Clayton, *W. J. Cash: A Life,* 158–61.
18. Egerton, *Speak Now Against the Day,* 277–80.
19. L. Jaffe to L. Chambers, 15 October 1929, Jaffe Papers; J. Kneebone, *Southern Liberal Journalists and the Issue of Race, 1920–1944* (Chapel Hill: University of North Carolina Press, 1985), 35.
20. G. Johnson to L. Jaffe, 14 October 1929, Jaffe Papers.
21. G. Tindall, *The Emergence of the New South, 1913–1945,* vol. 10 of *A History of the South* (Baton Rouge: Louisiana State University Press, 1967), 348–49; B. Stolberg, "Madness in Marion," *The Nation,* 23 October 1929, 462–64.
22. *Greensboro Daily News,* 3 October 1929.
23. M. Bonner, "Behind the Southern Textile Strikes," *The Nation,* 2 October 1929, 352.
24. *Greensboro Daily News,* 3 October 1929.
25. Stolberg, "Madness in Marion," 463.
26. *Greensboro Daily News,* 4 October 1929.
27. Tindall, *The Emergence of the New South,* 318–49; J. Hall et al., *Like a Family: The Making of a Southern Cotton Mill World* (Chapel Hill: University of North Carolina Press, 1987), 215–19.
28. G. Johnson to L. Jaffe, 16 October 1929, Jaffe Papers.
29. L. Jaffe to L. Chambers, 24 October 1929, Jaffe Papers.
30. L. Chambers to E. Roberts, 17 February 1937, Chambers Papers.
31. L. Jaffe to L. Chambers, 29 October 1929, Jaffe Papers.
32. G. Johnson to L. Jaffe, 4 December 1929, Jaffe Papers.
33. L. Jaffe to G. Johnson, 31 December 1929, Jaffe Papers.

34. L. Wilson to L. Chambers, 21 November 1929, Chambers Papers.
35. L. Chambers to J. Curtis, 6 March 1935, Chambers Papers.
36. A. Dill, letter to author, 20 November 1992.
37. H. Littledale to L. Chambers, 18 October 1934, Chambers Papers.
38. L. Reynolds to L. Chambers, 14 April 1936, Chambers Papers; T. Willis to L. Chambers, 15 May 1939, Chambers Papers.
39. Mason, *One of the Neighbors' Children,* 151.
40. A. Dill, telephone interview by author, tape recording, 20 November 1992.
41. Ibid.
42. Dill, letter; L. I. Jaffe, Jr., letter to author, 19 September 1995.
43. Dill, interview.
44. R. Glenn, letter to author, 24 November 1992; Mason, interview, 19 November 1992.
45. L. Chambers to G. Johnson, 11 March 1936, Chambers Papers; Chambers, Shank, and Sugg, *Salt Water & Printer's Ink,* 382.
46. L. Chambers to E. Roberts, 19 February 1937, Chambers Papers.
47. Mason, interview, 5 December 1990.

5. A Fish Out of His Pond

1. Mason, interview, 5 December 1990.
2. Dill, interview.
3. Ibid.
4. H. Byrd, Sr., to N. Leslie, Byrd Papers, Manuscripts Division, Special Collections Department, University of Virginia Library; *Who's Who in America, 1969–1973* (Chicago: Marquis, 1973).
5. L. Chambers to F. Spruill, 6 April 1950, Chambers Papers.
6. Mason, interview, 5 December 1990.
7. Batten, interview.
8. R. McPherson to H. Lewis, Chambers Papers.
9. L. Chambers to R. McPherson, 19 July 1948, Chambers Papers.
10. W. Martin to L. Chambers, 30 April 1942, Chambers Papers.
11. Burgess, interview; U.S. Marine Corps Citation, August 1945, Chambers Papers.
12. Burgess, interview; E. Lewis, *In Their Own Interests: Race, Class, and Power in Twentieth-Century Norfolk, Virginia* (Berkeley: University of California Press, 1991), 190.
13. Mason, *One of the Neighbors' Children,* 153; H. King to L. Chambers, 19 September 1957, Chambers Papers; F. Phillips to L. Chambers, 10 May 1949, Chambers Papers.
14. *New York Times,* 12 January 1970.
15. H. King to L. Chambers, 10 May 1949, Chambers Papers.
16. G. Johnson to L. Chambers, 3 November 1950, Chambers Papers.
17. Mason, interview, 19 November 1992.

6. Liberal Journalism in the South

1. N. Bartley, *The Rise of Massive Resistance: Race and Politics in the South During the 1950's* (Baton Rouge: Louisiana State University Press, 1969), 57.
2. M. Sosna, *In Search of the Silent South* (New York: Columbia University Press, 1977), 121.
3. Kneebone, *Southern Liberal Journalists,* 19.

4. A. Buni, *The Negro in Virginia Politics, 1902–1965* (Charlottesville: University Press of Virginia, 1967), 72.

5. *Virginian-Pilot,* 16 August 1926; *Journal and Guide,* 28 August 1926; *Virginian-Pilot,* 2 December 1927.

6. *Journal and Guide,* 4 September 1926.

7. *Virginian-Pilot,* 1, 2 December 1927.

8. *Bristol Herald-Courier,* 4 September 1926; *Bristol News Bulletin,* 18, 21 September 1926; *Bristol Herald-Courier,* 18 September, 1926; B. Phillips, telephone interview by author, 17 July 1995; D. Chalmers, *Hooded Americanism: The First Century of the Ku Klux Klan, 1865–1965* (Garden City: Doubleday, 1965), 243.

9. Chalmers, *Hooded Americanism,* 230.

10. E. Clarke to L. Jaffe, 15 November 1920, Jaffe Papers; Chalmers, *Hooded Americanism,* 31–38.

11. Citizen to L. Jaffe, 18 December 1924, Jaffe Papers.

12. "Reticence, Timidity Hamper Virginia's Press Jaffe Tells Virginia Editors," *Editor and Publisher,* 27 July 1929, 20.

13. W. Sloan and L. Anderson, *Pulitzer Prize Editorials: America's Best Editorial Writing, 1917–1993* (Ames: Iowa State University Press, 1994), 39.

14. Mason, *One of the Neighbors' Children,* 150; Chambers, Shank, and Sugg, *Salt Water & Printer's Ink,* 316–18; W. Brundage, *Lynching in the New South: Georgia and Virginia, 1880–1930* (Urbana: University of Illinois Press, 1993), 189–90.

15. Mason, *One of the Neighbors' Children,* 150; Chambers, Shank, and Sugg, *Salt Water & Printer's Ink,* 316–18; J. Hohenberg, ed., *The Pulitzer Prize Story: News, Stories, Editorials, Cartoons, and Pictures from the Pulitzer Prize Collection at Columbia University* (New York: Columbia University Press, 1959), 77–79.

16. H. Mencken, *The American Scene, a Reader* (New York: Knopf, 1965), 158.

17. Ibid., 159.

18. Ibid.; *Richmond Times-Dispatch,* 31 January 1956.

19. Dill, interview.

20. W. Manchester, *Disturber of the Peace: The Life of H. L. Mencken* (New York: Harper & Brothers, 1951), 240.

21. H. Mencken, *The Diary of H. L. Mencken,* ed. C. Fecher (New York: Knopf, 1989); Manchester, *Disturber of the Peace,* 88–111; Dill, letter.

22. Sosna, *In Search of the Silent South,* 203–4.

23. Ibid., 125–26.

24. Woodward, *The Strange Career of Jim Crow,* 38.

25. Sosna, *In Search of the Silent South,* 136; Lewis, *In Their Own Interests,* 189–90.

26. Sosna, *In Search of the Silent South,* 167; Kneebone, *Southern Liberal Journalists,* 215.

27. Sosna, *In Search of the Silent South,* 168; Kneebone, *Southern Liberal Journalists,* 221; V. Dabney, "Virginia's Peaceable, Honorable Stand," *Life,* 22 September 1958, 54–55; *Richmond Times-Dispatch,* 10 February, 20, 31 January, 29 February 1956; C. Putnam, *Race and Reason: A Yankee View* (Washington, D.C.: Public Affairs Press, 1961).

28. V. Dabney, *Across the Years, Memories of a Virginian* (Garden City: Doubleday, 1978), 232–33.

29. C. Eagles, *Jonathan Daniels and Race Relations: The Evolution of a Southern Liberal* (Knoxville: University of Tennessee Press, 1982), 194.

30. A. Hero, Jr., *The Southerner and World Affairs* (Baton Rouge: Louisiana State University Press, 1965), 395.

31. Kneebone, *Southern Liberal Journalists,* 25.

32. P. Fisher and R. Lowenstein, *Race and the News Media* (New York: Praeger, 1967), 63.

33. H. Carter, *Their Words Were Bullets: The Southern Press in War, Reconstruction, and Peace* (Athens: University of Georgia Press, 1969), 64.

34. Ibid., 65.

7. Chambers as Editor of the *Virginian-Pilot*

1. H. Sugg, *P. B. Young, Newspaperman: Race, Politics, and Journalism in the New South, 1910–1960* (Charlottesville: University Press of Virginia, 1988), 174; Chambers, Shank, and Sugg, *Salt Water & Printer's Ink,* 381–82; C. Porter, interview by author, tape recording, 18 May 1992.

2. L. Chambers to F. Graham, 17 April 1950, Chambers Papers.

3. L. Chambers to J. Dowd, 7 May 1950, Chambers Papers.

4. L. Chambers to H. Owens, 18 May 1950, Chambers Papers.

5. L. Chambers to F. Spruill, 6 April 1950, Chambers Papers.

6. H. Sugg, letter to author, 30 November 1990; *Who's Who in the South and Southwest 1976* (Chicago: Marquis, 1976); "Harold Sugg," 7 April 1950, Chambers Papers; L. Chambers to E. Jeffress, 16 August 1950, Chambers Papers.

7. L. Chambers to G. Johnson, 17 April 1950, Chambers Papers; L. Chambers to R. de Rosset, 7 January 1959, Chambers Papers.

8. L. Chambers to R. Mason, 13 August 1957, Chambers Papers; Mason, interview, 5 December 1990.

9. Chambers, Shank, and Sugg, *Salt Water & Printer's Ink,* 374; *Who's Who in the World, 1978* (Chicago: Marquis, 1978); W. Meacham to L. Chambers, 10 May 1927, Chambers Papers; Dabney, *Across the Years,* 134, 154; L. Jaffe to W. Meacham, 10 May 1927, Jaffe Papers.

10. Mason, interview, 5 December 1990.

11. H. Sugg, letter to author, 13 October 1990; Mason, interview, 5 December 1990; L. Chambers to G. Johnson, 17 April 1950, Chambers Papers.

12. Mason, *One of the Neighbors' Children,* 162.

13. S. Garrison, telephone interview by author, 27 September 1994.

14. S. Aprill, telephone interview by author, 24 September 1994.

15. Sugg, letter, 13 October 1990.

16. Mason, interview, 5 December 1990.

17. Smith, interview, 17 April 1992.

18. Mason, interview, 5 December 1990.

19. L. Chambers to R. de Rosset, 7 January 1959, Chambers Papers; Mason, *One of the Neighbors' Children; Who's Who in the South and Southwest,* 1973 (Chicago: Marquis, 1973).

20. R. Mason to L. Chambers, 5 February 1956, Chambers Papers.

21. Mason, interview, 17 July 1990.

22. L. Chambers to R. Mason, 13 August 1957, Chambers Papers.

23. Mason, interview, 19 November 1992.

24. Mason, *One of the Neighbors' Children,* 155.

25. Mason, interview, 17 July 1990, 19 November 1992.

26. "Tidewater Builders," 26 October 1957, Chambers Papers.

27. Sugg, letter, 13 October 1990.
28. L. Chambers to R. Mason, 13 August 1957, Chambers Papers.
29. Smith, interview, 17 April 1992.
30. Mason, interview, 19 November 1992.
31. Mason, *One of the Neighbors' Children,* 152; "Pulitzer Winners Formula: Write After Conferring," *Virginia Publisher and Printer,* June 1960, 4–6.
32. "Statement of Editorial Policy," August 1958, Chambers Papers.
33. Smith, interview, 17 April 1992.
34. Mason, interview, 5 December 1990.
35. Ibid., 19 November 1992.
36. Mason, *One of the Neighbors' Children,* 154; Mason, interview, 19 November 1992.
37. Mason, interview, 19 November 1992.
38. R. Glenn, letter to author, 10 November 1992.
39. Burgess, letter to author, 5 December 1992.
40. Mason, *One of the Neighbors' Children,* 158.
41. Mason, interview, 19 November 1992.
42. Glenn, letter, 24 November 1992.
43. Mason, interview, 19 November 1992.
44. Ibid.
45. Burgess, letter to author, 5 December 1992; R. Glenn, letter to author, 30 November 1992; Abeles, letter.
46. R. Glenn, letter to author, 23 November 1992.
47. Abeles, letter; Glenn, letter, 30 November 1992.
48. W. Fitzpatrick, letter to author, 11 December 1992.
49. Mason, interview, 19 November 1992.
50. Dill, interview.
51. Glenn, letter, 24 November 1992.
52. Ibid.
53. Dill, interview; E. Burgess, letter to author, 19 November 1992; Abeles, letter; Mason, interview, 19 November 1992.
54. Burgess, interview.
55. Dill, interview.
56. Abeles, letter.
57. Burgess, letter to author, 5 December 1992.
58. Burgess, interview; Burgess, letter to author, 5 December 1992.
59. Glenn, letter, 10 November 1992.
60. Ibid., 23 November 1992; Mason, *One of the Neighbors' Children,* 154.
61. Glenn, letter, 24 November 1992.
62. Mason, *One of the Neighbors' Children,* 154–55; Sugg, letter, 13 October 1990.
63. Mason, interview, 19 November 1992.
64. Ibid., 17 July 1990.
65. Dill, interview.
66. Mason, *One of the Neighbors' Children,* 154.
67. Mason, interview, 19 November 1992.
68. Mason, letter, 20 November 1992.
69. Glenn, letter, 24 November 1992; Mason, *One of the Neighbors' Children,* 153.
70. Burgess, letter to author, 5 December 1992.
71. Mason, interview, 19 November 1992.
72. Batten, interview.
73. Mason, interview, 17 July 1990.

74. L. Chambers to W. Abell, 6 September 1956, Chambers Papers, Southern Historical Collection, University of North Carolina Library.

75. Sugg, letter, 13 October 1990.

76. Smith, interview, 17 April 1992.

77. Sugg, letter, 13 October 1990; Pulitzer nomination, Chambers Papers.

78. Mason, interview, 17 July 1990.

79. Burgess, interview.

80. H. Sugg, letter to author, 2 October 1990.

81. Mason, interview, 5 December 1990.

82. Ibid.

83. Smith, interview, 17 April 1992, and R. Smith, telephone interview by author, 2 October 1995.

84. Mason, *One of the Neighbors' Children,* 151.

85. Batten, interview.

86. Mason, *One of the Neighbors' Children,* 153; Smith, interview, 17 April 1992.

87. L. Carter, telephone interview by author, tape recording, 10 October 1992.

88. Smith, interview, 17 April 1992.

89. Mason, interview, 17 July 1990.

90. Ibid., 5 December 1990.

91. Smith, interview, 17 April 1992.

92. Carter, interview.

93. H. Mencken, *Newspaper Days, 1899–1906* (New York: Knopf, 1941), 147.

94. Mason, interview, 17 July 1990.

95. Ibid., 10 April 1989.

96. Dill, interview.

97. Mason, *One of the Neighbors' Children,* 153; Mason, interview, 19 November 1992.

98. L. Chambers to J. Saunders, 11 May 1934, Chambers Papers.

99. L. Chambers to R. Mason, 31 January 1956, Chambers Papers.

100. L. Jaffe to W. Meacham, 2 July 1929, Jaffe Papers.

101. Chambers, Shank, and Sugg, *Salt Water & Printer's Ink,* 380; Mason, *One of the Neighbors' Children,* 146.

102. Mason, interview, 5 December 1990.

103. Batten, interview.

104. Ibid.

105. Smith, interview, 17 April 1992.

106. Burgess, interview.

107. L. Chambers to R. Mason, 13 August 1957, Chambers Papers.

8. Norfolk: The Setting for a Conflict

1. V. Key, *Southern Politics in State and Nation* (New York: Knopf, 1949), 32.

2. Muse, *Virginia's Massive Resistance,* 2–4; J. L. Buck, *The Development of Public Schools in Virginia, 1607–1952* (Richmond: Commonwealth of Virginia State Board of Education, 1952), 521–22.

3. N. Ford, "The Peaceful Resolution of Norfolk's Integration Crisis of 1958–1959" (Master's thesis, Old Dominion University, 1989), 2.

4. Reif, *Crisis in Norfolk,* 1.

5. Campbell, *When a City Closes Its Schools,* 1–2.

6. Ibid., 2.

7. Sugg, letter, 12 October 1990.

8. H. Sugg, *The Black Press in the South, 1865–1979* (Westport: Greenwood, 1983), 140.

9. G. Myrdal, *An American Dilemma: The Negro Problem and Modern Democracy* (New York: Harper & Row, 1944), 917; Sugg, *P. B. Young, Newspaperman,* 119.

10. Lewis, *In Their Own Interests,* 144.

11. Sugg, *The Black Press in the South,* 399.

12. Lewis, *In Their Own Interests,* 144.

13. Sugg, *P. B. Young, Newspaperman,* 44, 49.

14. L. Jaffe to W. Meacham, 9 November 1934, Jaffe Papers.

15. Sugg, *P. B. Young, Newspaperman,* 60–157; Lewis, *In Their Own Interests,* 67, 148; T. Wertenbaker, *Norfolk: Historic Southern Port* (Durham: Duke University Press, 1962), 337; Dabney, *Liberalism in the South,* 408.

16. Sugg, letter, 12 October 1990.

17. P. Young, Sr., to J. Thomas, 17 November 1929, Jaffe Papers.

18. Sugg, letter, 12 October 1990.

19. Mason, interview, 10 April 1989.

20. Porter, interview.

21. S. Boyle, *The Desegregated Heart: A Virginian's Stand in Time of Transition* (New York: William Morrow, 1962), 133–34.

22. Sugg, *P. B. Young, Newspaperman,* 57.

23. Reif, *Crisis in Norfolk,* 1.

24. Rorer, "History of Norfolk Public Schools," 291.

25. "How Norfolk's Schools Were Reopened," 25 February 1959, White Papers.

26. Reif, *Crisis in Norfolk,* 1.

27. Campbell, *When a City Closes Its Schools,* 2.

28. Rorer, "History of Norfolk Public Schools," 51, 327; Wertenbaker, *Norfolk,* 226–27; Sugg, *P. B. Young, Newspaperman,* 155–56.

29. P. Morgan, ed., *"Don't Grieve after Me," The Black Experience in Virginia 1619–1986* (Hampton, Va.: Hampton University Press, 1986), 52; C. J. Heatwole, *A History of Education in Virginia* (New York: Macmillan, 1916), 214.

30. Burgess, interview; Barfield, interview.

31. Campbell, *When a City Closes Its Schools,* 2.

32. Chambers, Shank, and Sugg, *Salt Water & Printer's Ink,* 279; Sugg, *P. B. Young, Newspaperman,* ix–x.

33. Sugg, *P. B. Young, Newspaperman,* 41.

34. Ibid., 85.

35. Lewis, *In Their Own Interests,* 167.

36. Ibid., 156.

37. Porter, interview.

38. Lewis, *In Their Own Interests,* 159–60; Porter, interview.

39. *Virginian-Pilot,* 16 June 1936.

40. Lewis, *In Their Own Interests,* 162; Rorer, "History of Norfolk Public Schools," 279–82; Sugg, *P. B. Young, Newspaperman,* 159–62; R. Mason, letter to author, 24 August 1995.

41. Lewis, *In Their Own Interests,* 164; Sugg, *P. B. Young, Newspaperman,* 159–63; Porter, interview.

42. Rorer, "History of Norfolk Public Schools," 279–82.

43. Porter, interview.

44. Lewis, *In Their Own Interests,* 160.

45. Wilkinson, *Harry Byrd and the Changing Face of Virginia Politics,* 59–60; Buni, *The Negro in Virginia Politics,* 174.

46. W. Prieur to H. Byrd, 11 July 1953, Byrd Papers.

47. Wilkinson, *Harry Byrd and the Changing Face of Virginia Politics,* 5; E. Ayers, *The Promise of the New South: Life After Reconstruction* (New York: Oxford University Press, 1992), 305–9.

48. R. L. Morton, *The Negro in Virginia Politics, 1865–1902* (Charlottesville: University of Virginia Press, 1919), 154–62.

49. Buni, *The Negro in Virginia Politics,* 1–33; C. V. Woodward, *Origins of the New South, 1877–1913* (Baton Rouge: Louisiana State University Press, 1951), 321–49.

50. Sugg, *P. B. Young, Newspaperman,* 126; Lewis, *In Their Own Interests,* 121.

51. Sugg, *P. B. Young, Newspaperman,* 128.

52. "How Norfolk's Schools Were Reopened," 25 February 1959, White Papers.

53. Lewis, *In Their Own Interests,* 135.

54. Wertenbaker, *Norfolk,* 234.

55. Chambers, Shank, and Sugg, *Salt Water & Printer's Ink,* 19; Wertenbaker, *Norfolk,* 235.

56. Chambers, Shank, and Sugg, *Salt Water & Printer's Ink,* 219–24.

57. Lewis, *In Their Own Interests,* 26–27.

58. Sugg, *The Black Press in the South,* 401, and idem, *P. B. Young, Newspaperman,* 41.

59. Sugg, *P. B. Young, Newspaperman,* 59.

60. Lewis, *In Their Own Interests,* 144.

61. Ibid., 191.

62. L. Carter, "Desegregation in Norfolk," *The South Atlantic Quarterly* 58, no. 4 (Autumn 1959): 514; Lewis, *In Their Own Interests,* 203.

63. Boyle, *The Desegregated Heart,* 249.

64. Carter, "Desegregation in Norfolk," 514–15.

9. The Issue of the Century

1. *Plessy v. Ferguson,* 163 US 537 (1896).

2. *Brown v. Board of Education,* 347 US 483, 74 S. Ct. 686, 98 L.Ed. 873 (1954).

3. Wilkinson, *Harry Byrd and the Changing Face of Virginia Politics,* 113.

4. F. Wilhoit, *The Politics of Massive Resistance* (New York: Braziller, 1973), 31.

5. Muse, *Ten Years of Prelude,* 21.

6. C. Phillips, "Virginia—The State and the State of Mind," *New York Times Magazine,* 28 July 1957, 49.

7. *Ledger-Dispatch,* 18 May 1954.

8. Ibid., 19–23 May 1954.

9. *Virginian-Pilot,* 18 May 1954.

10. Ibid., 19 May 1954.

11. Ibid., 22 May 1954.

12. V. Dabney, *Virginia, The New Dominion* (Charlottesville: University Press of Virginia, 1971), 531.

13. R. Gates, *The Making of Massive Resistance: Virginia's Politics of Public School Desegregation* (Chapel Hill: University of North Carolina Press, 1964), 30.

14. *Virginian-Pilot,* 22 May 1954.

15. Gates, *The Making of Massive Resistance,* 31; J. Ely, *The Crisis of Conservative*

Virginia: The Byrd Organization and the Politics of Massive Resistance (Knoxville: University Press of Tennessee, 1976), 5.

16. *Virginian-Pilot,* 8 June 1964.

17. Ford, "The Peaceful Resolution of Norfolk's Integration Crisis of 1958–1959," 13.

18. Ibid., 13.

19. Gates, *The Making of Massive Resistance,* 31.

20. Public Education Report, 1955, White Papers.

21. Dabney, *Virginia, The New Dominion,* 532; Gates, *The Making of Massive Resistance,* 51–52.

22. Wilhoit, *The Politics of Massive Resistance,* 36; *Virginian-Pilot,* 8 June 1964.

23. White, "Will Norfolk's Schools Stay Open?" 30; R. Smith, *They Closed Their Schools: Prince Edward County, Virginia, 1951–1964* (Chapel Hill: University of North Carolina Press, 1965), 87–112.

24. Ely, *The Crisis of Conservative Virginia,* 31.

25. Muse, *Virginia's Massive Resistance,* 47; Ely, *The Crisis of Conservative Virginia,* 46.

26. Muse, *Ten Years of Prelude,* 79.

27. Ibid., 178.

28. Gates, *The Making of Massive Resistance,* 53; Wilkinson, *Harry Byrd and the Changing Face of Virginia Politics,* 124.

29. Gates, *The Making of Massive Resistance,* 51.

30. Boyle, *The Desegregated Heart,* 189.

31. Public Education Report, 1955, White Papers.

32. *Brown v. Board of Education of Topeka,* 349 US 294 (1955).

33. Muse, *Ten Years of Prelude,* 25.

34. *Ledger-Dispatch,* 1 June 1955.

35. *Ledger-Dispatch,* 2 June 1955.

36. *Virginian-Pilot,* 1 June 1955.

37. Ibid.

38. *Virginian-Pilot,* 2 June 1955.

39. *Virginian-Pilot,* 3 June 1955.

40. Gates, *The Making of Massive Resistance,* 49; Bartley, *The Rise of Massive Resistance,* 95.

41. Statement of School Board, 1 July 1955, Schweitzer Papers, Old Dominion University Library.

42. J. Peltason, *Fifty-Eight Lonely Men: Southern Federal Judges and School Desegregation* (New York: Harcourt Brace & World, 1961), 77; W. Hoffman, interview by author, tape recording, 30 August 1990; *Virginian-Pilot,* 5 August 1990.

43. W. Prieur to H. Byrd, 4 February 1954, Byrd Papers.

44. Gates, *The Making of Massive Resistance,* 64–65.

10. Legislative Ploys

1. Public Education Report, 1955, White Papers.

2. *Ledger-Dispatch,* 14 November 1955.

3. Ibid., 15 November 1955.

4. *Virginian-Pilot,* 13 November 1955.

5. Ibid.

6. Ibid.

7. *Virginian-Pilot,* 15 November 1955.

8. *Virginian-Pilot and Ledger-Star,* 23 September 1990.

9. Dabney, *Virginia, The New Dominion,* 533.

10. Mason, interview, 17 July 1990.

11. *Virginian-Pilot,* 8 June 1964.

12. Constitution of Virginia, 1902.

13. Gates, *The Making of Massive Resistance,* 72.

14. Dabney, *Virginia, The New Dominion,* 533–34; Gates, *The Making of Massive Resistance,* 76–82.

15. Wilkinson, *Harry Byrd and the Changing Face of Virginia Politics,* 127.

16. Dabney, *Virginia, The New Dominion,* 534.

17. *Ledger-Dispatch,* 2 January 1956.

18. Ibid., 5 January 1956.

19. Ibid., 7 January 1956.

20. Ibid., 9 January 1956.

21. *Virginian-Pilot,* 5 January 1956.

22. Ibid., 3 January 1956.

23. Ibid., 7 January 1956.

24. Ibid., 5 January 1956.

25. Ibid., 4 January 1956.

26. Ibid., 8 January 1956.

27. Wilkinson, *Harry Byrd and the Changing Face of Virginia Politics,* 127.

28. Chambers, Shank, and Sugg, *Salt Water & Printer's Ink,* 384.

29. J. Kilpatrick, *The Sovereign States: Notes of a Citizen of Virginia* (Chicago: Henry Regnery, 1957), 51–98. Dabney, *Virginia, The New Dominion,* 534–35; Muse, *Ten Years of Prelude,* 70.

30. G. Tindall, *America, A Narrative History* (New York: Norton, 1984), 313–14; R. McGill, *The South and the Southerner* (Boston: Little, Brown and Company, 1963), 253.

31. H. S. Ashmore, *An Epitaph for Dixie* (New York: Norton, 1958), 87–88.

32. *Virginian-Pilot,* 8 June 1964.

33. *Race Relations Law Reporter,* April 1956, 462–64; Bartley, *The Rise of Massive Resistance,* 126; Dabney, *Virginia, The New Dominion,* 535.

34. Bartley, *The Rise of Massive Resistance,* 183.

35. *Race Relations Law Reporter,* April 1956, 447.

36. Wilhoit, *The Politics of Massive Resistance,* 139.

37. *Ledger-Dispatch,* 20 January 1956.

38. *Virginian-Pilot,* 4 February 1956.

39. Ibid.

40. Dabney, *Virginia, The New Dominion,* 531.

41. *Race Relations Law Reporter,* April 1956, 463.

42. *Richmond Times-Dispatch,* 25 February 1956.

43. Wilhoit, *The Politics of Massive Resistance,* 55.

44. Ibid., 76.

45. Mason, interview, 5 December 1990.

46. Wilkinson, *Harry Byrd and the Changing Face of Virginia Politics,* 152–54; Carter, "Desegregation in Norfolk," 508.

47. Wilkinson, *Harry Byrd and the Changing Face of Virginia Politics,* 154.

48. Dabney, *Virginia, The New Dominion,* 537.

49. *Race Relations Law Reporter,* April 1956, 436–37.

50. Ibid., 435.

51. Ibid., 436.

52. *Virginian-Pilot,* 8 June 1964.

53. Wilkinson, *Harry Byrd and the Changing Face of Virginia Politics,* 130; Gates, *The Making of Massive Resistance,* 130; *Virginian-Pilot,* 8 June 1964.

54. *Richmond Times-Dispatch,* 26 August 1956.

55. *Race Relations Law Reporter,* December 1956, 1091–113; Ely, *The Crisis of Conservative Virginia,* 45–46; Wilkinson, *Harry Byrd and the Changing Face of Virginia Politics,* 133.

56. *Ledger-Dispatch,* 27 August 1956.

57. Ibid., 28 August 1956.

58. Ibid.

59. *Virginian-Pilot,* 28 August 1956.

60. Ibid., 29 August 1956.

61. Ibid., 30 August 1956.

62. Ibid., 31 August 1956.

63. Muse, *Ten Years of Prelude,* 69.

64. Gates, *The Making of Massive Resistance,* 133; Wilkinson, *Harry Byrd and the Changing Face of Virginia Politics,* 133.

65. Dabney, *Virginia, The New Dominion,* 537–38.

66. *Race Relations Law Reporter,* October 1957, 1014–26; Peltason, *Fifty-Eight Lonely Men,* 65.

67. Ibid., 93.

68. Muse, *Ten Years of Prelude,* 162.

69. Bartley, *The Rise of Massive Resistance,* 214.

70. *Virginian-Pilot,* 8 June 1964; "Virginia, 'The Gravest Crisis,' " *Time,* 22 September 1958, 13–18.

71. Hoffman, interview.

72. *Adkins v. School Board of the City of Newport News* and *Beckett v. School Board of the City of Norfolk,* 148 F.Supp. 430 (1957).

73. *Race Relations Law Reporter,* April 1957, 336.

74. Ibid., 335.

75. *Ledger-Dispatch,* 12 February 1957.

76. *Virginian-Pilot,* 13 February 1957.

77. Ibid., 15 February 1957.

78. *Race Relations Law Reporter,* April 1957, 339.

79. H. Byrd to J. Kilpatrick, 21 March 1957, Kilpatrick Papers, Manuscripts Division, Special Collections Department, University of Virginia Library.

80. W. Prieur to H. Byrd, Sr., 18 January 1957, Byrd Papers.

81. Hoffman, interview.

82. Ibid.

83. W. Prieur to H. Byrd, 28 May 1957, Byrd Papers.

84. L. Chambers to H. Byrd, 23 May 1957, Chambers Papers.

85. H. Byrd to Lenoir Chambers, 28 May 1957, Chambers Papers.

86. W. Prieur to H. Byrd, 4 June 1957, Byrd Papers.

87. W. Prieur to H. Byrd, 7 March 1963, Byrd Papers.

88. D. Pace, "Lenoir Chambers Opposes Massive Resistance: An Editor Against Virginia's Democratic Organization, 1955–1959," *The Virginia Magazine of History and Biography,* October 1974, 422–23.

89. Mason, interview, 19 November 1992.

90. L. Chambers to W. Wing, 3 October 1958, Chambers Papers.

91. *Virginian-Pilot,* 21 August 1958.

92. Ely, *The Crisis of Conservative Virginia,* 63.

93. Ibid., 59–61; J. Williams, *Eyes on the Prize: America's Civil Rights Years, 1954–1965* (New York: Viking, 1987), 106–19.

94. Ely, *The Crisis of Conservative Virginia,* 61.

95. Ibid., 63.

96. Ibid., 70.

97. *Virginian-Pilot,* 12 January 1958.

98. *Ledger-Dispatch,* 11 January 1958.

99. Ibid.

100. *Virginian-Pilot,* 12 January 1958.

101. Ibid.

102. J. Almond, "We Are the Stewards of Our States' Inheritance," *The American Mercury,* May 1958, 57.

103. Ely, *The Crisis of Conservative Virginia,* 70-71.

104. *Race Relations Law Reporter,* August 1958, 768.

105. Ibid., April 1958, 341–43.

106. Buni, *The Negro in Virginia Politics,* 196–97; *Virginian-Pilot,* 1 February 1958; Ely, *The Crisis of Conservative Virginia,* 71-72.

107. *Race Relations Law Reporter,* April 1958, 274–75.

108. Peltason, *Fifty-Eight Lonely Men,* 78.

11. The Resistance in Norfolk

1. *Race Relations Law Reporter,* October 1958, 942.

2. W. Prieur to H. Byrd, 24 June 1958, Byrd Papers.

3. *Race Relations Law Reporter,* June 1958, 789–90.

4. *Southern School News,* July 1958; W. McKendree, interview by author, tape recording, 19 November 1990; Muse, *Virginia's Massive Resistance,* 112; Carter, interview.

5. Ford, "The Peaceful Resolution of Norfolk's Integration Crisis of 1958-1959," 35; McKendree, interview.

6. "The Lost Class of '59," 21 January 1959, Byrd Papers.

7. Ibid.

8. McKendree, interview; Carter, interview; R. Tonelson, interview by author, tape recording, 18 July 1990.

9. *Race Relations Law Reporter,* October 1958, 942–44.

10. Ibid., 944.

11. *Southern School News,* August 1958, 6.

12. *Race Relations Law Reporter,* October 1958, 944–45; Peltason, *Fifty-Eight Lonely Men,* 6.

13. *Race Relations Law Reporter,* October 1958, 945–46; *Southern School News,* September 1958, 1.

14. *Southern School News,* September 1958, 6.

15. *Race Relations Law Reporter,* October 1958, 946–55.

16. *Virginian-Pilot,* 26 August 1958.

17. *Virginian-Pilot and Ledger-Star,* 5 August 1990.

18. F. Powers, interview by author, tape recording, 4 October 1990.

19. Hoffman, interview; Burgess, interview.

20. Powers, interview.

21. *Race Relations Law Reporter,* December 1956, 1059.

22. *Southern School News,* September 1958, 6.

23. *Race Relations Law Reporter,* October 1958, 955–57.

24. Ibid., December 1958, 1156.

25. *Virginian-Pilot,* 30 August 1958.

26. White, "Will Norfolk's Schools Stay Open?" 31.

27. Defenders Resolution, 31 August 1958, Almond Executive Papers, Library of Virginia (formerly Virginia State Library); Muse, *Virginia's Massive Resistance,* 73–74.

28. *Southern School News,* October 1958, 3.

29. *Race Relations Law Reporter,* October 1958, 959.

30. *Southern School News,* October 1958, 3.

31. McKendree, interview.

32. Ibid.

33. D. Paschall to J. Almond, 29 September 1958, Almond Executive Papers; *Christian Science Monitor,* 8 October 1958.

34. *Christian Science Monitor,* 8 October 1958.

35. *Southern School News,* October 1958, 3.

36. Ely, *The Crisis of Conservative Virginia,* 75–76; *Race Relations Law Reporter,* Spring 1959, 65–78.

37. *Southern School News,* October 1958, 3; Ely, *The Crisis of Conservative Virginia,* 74.

38. *Virginian-Pilot,* 14 September 1958.

39. *Southern School News,* October 1958, 4.

40. Ibid., 3.

41. Ibid., 4.

42. *Race Relations Law Reporter,* October 1958, 962.

43. Ibid.

44. Ibid., 963.

45. *Virginian-Pilot,* 29 September 1958.

46. *Southern School News,* January 1959, 9; Muse, *Ten Years of Prelude,* 153, 156.

47. Batten, interview.

48. City Council Resolution, 30 September 1958, Almond Executive Papers.

49. *Southern School News,* November 1958, 13.

50. Reif, *Crisis in Norfolk,* 16.

51. *Virginian-Pilot,* 15 October 1958.

52. "How Norfolk's Schools Were Reopened," 25 February 1959, White Papers; Reif, *Crisis in Norfolk,* 18.

53. *Virginian-Pilot,* 10 October 1958.

54. Reif, *Crisis in Norfolk,* 16.

55. W. Duckworth to J. Almond, 6 October 1958, Almond Executive Papers.

56. J. Almond to W. Duckworth, 7 October 1958, Almond Executive Papers.

57. Muse, *Ten Years of Prelude,* 180.

58. *Virginian-Pilot,* 9 June 1964.

59. J. Almond to H. Byrd, 3 November 1958, Byrd Papers.

60. H. Byrd to J. Almond, 19 December 1958, Byrd Papers.

61. J. Almond to H. Byrd, 22 December 1958, Byrd Papers.

62. Muse, *Ten Years of Prelude,* 59.

63. *Virginian-Pilot,* 24 September 1958.

64. H. Byrd to J. Gravatt, 20 October 1958, Byrd Papers.

12. Advocacy for Reopening the Schools

1. *Southern School News,* November 1958, 13; Muse, *Virginia's Massive Resistance,* 47.
2. Porter, interview.
3. Ibid.; *Virginian-Pilot,* 18 February 1983.
4. M. Gordon, *A Documented History of the First Baptist Church* (Virginia Beach: Hill's Printing, 1988), 137–38; "How Norfolk's Schools Were Reopened," 25 February 1959, White Papers; Carter, "Desegregation in Norfolk."
5. "How Norfolk's Schools Were Reopened," 25 February 1959, White Papers; Muse, *Ten Years of Prelude,* 34.
6. Carter, "Desegregation in Norfolk," 513–14.
7. "How Norfolk's Schools Were Reopened," 25 February 1959, White Papers; Carter, "Desegregation in Norfolk"; Gordon, *A Documented History of the First Baptist Church,* 138.
8. Gordon, *A Documented History of the First Baptist Church,* 138.
9. L. Chambers to P. Young, 9 January 1959, Chambers Papers.
10. Carter, interview; L. Carter, letter to author, 30 September 1995.
11. *Southern School News,* November 1959, 13.
12. "How Norfolk's Schools Were Reopened," 25 February 1959, White Papers; Muse, *Virginia's Massive Resistance,* 89; Reif, *Crisis in Norfolk,* 13.
13. Muse, *Virginia's Massive Resistance,* 89.
14. "How Norfolk's Schools Were Reopened," 25 February 1959, White Papers.
15. Reif, *Crisis in Norfolk,* 9–10.
16. *Virginian-Pilot,* 30 September 1958.
17. Reif, *Crisis in Norfolk,* 10.
18. Ibid.
19. Carter, interview.
20. Reif, *Crisis in Norfolk,* 9.
21. Muse, *Ten Years of Prelude,* 163.
22. Tonelson, interview, 19 July 1991.
23. Reif, *Crisis in Norfolk,* 10.
24. F. Batten to P. Schweitzer, 28 October 1958, Schweitzer Papers.
25. Batten, interview.
26. Ibid.
27. Mason, interview, 17 July 1990.
28. Batten, interview.
29. P. Darden, interview by F. White, Jr., tape recording, 13 August 1975.
30. Ibid.
31. Key, *Southern Politics in State and Nation,* 26–27.
32. "What Massive Resistance Costs," *Business Week,* 4 October 1958, 32–34.
33. L. Chambers to K. Kramer, 14 October 1958, Chambers Papers.
34. "What Massive Resistance Costs," 32.
35. G. Friddell, *What Is It About Virginia?* (Richmond: Dietz Press, 1966), 44.
36. *Virginian-Pilot,* 16 October 1958.
37. L. McWhorten to P. Schweitzer, 23 January 1959, Schweitzer Papers.
38. Dykeman and Stokely, "Report on 'The Lost Class of '59,' " 55.
39. Reif, *Crisis in Norfolk,* 12.
40. *Virginian-Pilot,* 17 January 1959.
41. Ibid.

42. R. Martin, interview by author, tape recording, 20 August 1990; Mason, interview, 10 April 1989, 17 July 1990; Reif, *Crisis in Norfolk,* 11–12.

43. *Southern School News,* November 1958, 13.

44. Dykeman and Stokely, "Report on 'The Lost Class of '59,' " 55.

45. *Virginian-Pilot,* 4 October 1958.

46. Carter, interview.

47. Dykeman and Stokely, "Report on 'The Lost Class of '59,' " 54.

48. Ibid.; White, "Will Norfolk's Schools Stay Open?" 29–32; Reif, *Crisis in Norfolk,* 18.

49. Reif, *Crisis in Norfolk,* 20.

50. *Virginian-Pilot,* 23 October 1958.

51. Reif, *Crisis in Norfolk,* 21; Burgess, interview.

52. Mason, interview, 11 November 1992.

13. A City Divided and Beleaguered

1. *Southern School News,* November 1958; Peltason, *Fifty-Eight Lonely Men,* 214.

2. *Southern School News,* November 1958, 13.

3. *Virginian-Pilot,* 24 October 1958.

4. F. White to PTA Unit Presidents, undated, White Papers.

5. "Norfolk City Council of Parent-Teacher Associations Resolution," 9 February 1957, White Papers.

6. Muse, *Virginia's Massive Resistance,* 90.

7. R. Crawford to J. Almond, 24 February 1958, Almond Executive Papers.

8. Tonelson, interview, 18 July 1990.

9. Reif, *Crisis in Norfolk,* 8.

10. White, "Will Norfolk's Schools Stay Open?" 30.

11. *Southern School News,* December 1958, 6.

12. F. White to J. Almond, 17 December 1958, White Papers; Norfolk Committee for Public Schools Petition, 22 October 1958, White Papers.

13. Norfolk Committee for Public Schools Petition, 22 October 1958, White Papers.

14. Reif, *Crisis in Norfolk,* 5; "How Norfolk's Schools Were Reopened," 25 February 1959, White Papers.

15. *James v. Almond,* 170 F.Supp. 331 (1959).

16. Reif, *Crisis in Norfolk,* 175; Sugg, *P. B. Young, Newspaperman,* 175.

17. *Southern School News,* November 1958, 13.

18. White, "Will Norfolk's Schools Stay Open?" 32.

19. Reif, *Crisis in Norfolk,* 5.

20. *Harrison v. Day,* 106 S.E. 2d 636 (1959).

21. *Virginian-Pilot,* 9 June 1964.

22. Ibid.

23. *Ledger-Dispatch,* 30 October 1958.

24. *Virginian-Pilot,* 28 October 1958.

25. Reif, *Crisis in Norfolk,* 6–7.

26. *Southern School News,* November 1958, 13.

27. *Virginian-Pilot,* 31 October 1958.

28. *Southern School News,* December 1958, 7.

29. Muse, *Virginia's Massive Resistance,* 99; *Southern School News,* August 1958, 6.

30. *Southern School News,* August 1958, 6.

31. *Virginian-Pilot,* 2 November 1958.

32. Muse, *Virginia's Massive Resistance,* 99; *Southern School News,* August 1958, 6.

33. *Southern School News,* December 1958, 6.

34. Dabney, *Across the Years,* 235–36.

35. Peltason, *Fifty-Eight Lonely Men,* 216; *Southern School News,* December 1958, 6.

36. *Virginian-Pilot,* 16 November 1958.

37. Ibid.

38. Ibid.

39. Ibid., 18 November 1958.

40. *Southern School News,* December 1958, 6.

41. *Virginian-Pilot,* 13 November 1958.

42. Ibid., 12 November 1958.

43. Ibid., 18 November 1958.

44. *Southern School News,* December 1958, 6.

45. Ibid.

46. *Ledger-Dispatch,* 12 November 1958.

47. Ibid., 15 November 1958.

48. Ibid., 17 November 1958.

49. *Virginian-Pilot,* 14 November 1958.

50. Ibid.

51. *Virginian-Pilot,* 16 November 1958.

52. Ibid.

53. Guide Ballot, undated, White Papers.

54. *Virginian-Pilot,* 19 November 1958; Muse, *Virginia's Massive Resistance,* 93; Ely, *The Crisis of Conservative Virginia,* 80; W. Prieur to H. Byrd, 4 October 1956, Byrd Papers.

55. *Ledger-Dispatch,* 19 November 1958.

56. Ibid.

57. Ibid.

58. Reif, *Crisis in Norfolk,* 18.

59. *Race Relations Law Reporter,* Spring 1959, 43.

60. Reif, *Crisis in Norfolk,* 18.

61. W. Prieur to H. Byrd, Jr., 26 November 1958, Byrd Papers.

62. Reif, *Crisis in Norfolk,* 18.

63. Tonelson, interview, 18 July 1990.

64. Mason, interview, 17 July 1990.

65. W. Prieur to H. Byrd, 22 September 1959, Byrd Papers.

66. H. Byrd to W. Prieur, 20 October 1959, Byrd Papers.

67. F. White to W. Duckworth, 6 December 1958, White Papers.

68. F. White to J. Almond, 7 December 1958, White Papers.

69. Peltason, *Fifty-Eight Lonely Men,* 50.

70. *Southern School News,* January 1959, 9.

71. Peltason, *Fifty-Eight Lonely Men,* 49.

72. *Virginian-Pilot,* 19 December 1958.

73. Muse, *Ten Years of Prelude,* 180.

74. L. Thompson, "Virginia Education Crisis and Its Economic Aspects," *New South,* February 1959, 3–8.

75. Ibid., 3.

76. Batten, interview.

77. Carter, "Desegregation in Norfolk," 511; Wilkinson, *Harry Byrd and the Changing Face of Virginia Politics,* 145; Sugg, letter, 2 October 1990.

78. Batten, interview.

79. Ibid.

80. *Virginian-Pilot,* 9 June 1964.

81. Ely, *The Crisis of Conservative Virginia,* 85.

82. J. Almond to H. Byrd, 13 March 1959, Byrd Papers.

83. *Southern School News,* January 1959, 9.

84. Hoffman, interview.

85. *Virginian-Pilot,* 9 June 1964.

86. *Race Relations Law Reporter,* Spring 1959, 43.

87. Ely, *The Crisis of Conservative Virginia,* 82; Dabney, *Virginia, The New Dominion,* 541; Muse, *Virginia's Massive Resistance,* 119; *Race Relations Law Reporter,* Spring 1959, 45; Muse, *Ten Years of Prelude,* 181.

88. "How Norfolk's Schools Were Reopened," 25 February 1959, White Papers.

89. Martin, interview.

90. Ibid.

91. *Virginian-Pilot,* 14 January 1959.

92. J. Almond to W. Blount, 15 January 1959, Almond Executive Papers.

93. W. Hoffman, letter to author, 17 October 1995.

94. *Race Relations Law Reporter,* Spring 1959, 49.

95. Ibid.; "Desegregation—or No Public Schools," *New South,* March 1959, 3–10.

96. *Race Relations Law Reporter,* Spring 1959, 71.

97. Muse, *Virginia's Massive Resistance,* 122–23.

98. *Race Relations Law Reporter,* Summer 1959, 73.

99. *Virginian-Pilot,* 21 January 1959.

100. *Virginian-Pilot,* 9 June 1964; V. Dabney, "Next in the South's Schools: 'Limited Integration,' " *U.S. News & World Report,* 18 January 1960, 93.

101. *Virginian-Pilot,* 9 June 1964.

102. "Introduction to the Lost Class of '59," 21 January 1959, White Papers; "The Lost Class of '59," 21 January 1959, Byrd Papers.

103. Reif, *Crisis in Norfolk,* 22.

104. *Race Relations Law Reporter,* Spring 1959, 5–6.

105. *Ledger-Dispatch,* 20 January 1959.

106. Ibid.

107. Ibid.

108. *Virginian-Pilot,* 20 January 1959.

109. Ibid.

110. *Virginian-Pilot,* 24 January 1959.

111. Ibid., 25 January 1959.

112. Wilkinson, *Harry Byrd and the Changing Face of Virginia Politics,* 147.

113. Dabney, *Virginia, The New Dominion,* 147.

14. The Turning of the Tide

1. *Virginian-Pilot,* 26 January 1959.

2. Rorer, "History of Norfolk Public Schools."

3. *Virginian-Pilot,* 27 January 1959.

4. Batten, interview.

5. Darden, interview.

6. Martin, interview.

7. Barfield, interview.
8. Reif, *Crisis in Norfolk*, 14.
9. Muse, *Virginia's Massive Resistance*, 130.
10. *James v. Duckworth*, 170 F.Supp. 342 (1959).
11. *Race Relations Law Reporter*, Spring 1959, 55–56.
12. L. Chambers to L. Jaffe, Jr., 9 February 1947, Chambers Papers.
13. *Race Relations Law Reporter*, Spring 1959, 183.
14. Ibid., 184.
15. Ibid., 188.
16. Ibid.
17. Peltason, *Fifty-Eight Lonely Men*, 217.
18. *Virginian-Pilot and Ledger-Star*, 4 February 1991.
19. *Virginian-Pilot*, 6 February 1959.
20. *Virginian-Pilot*, 4 February 1959.
21. *Southern School News*, March 1959, 14.
22. Ibid., 15.
23. Ibid.
24. *Race Relations Law Reporter*, Spring 1959, 56.
25. Martin, interview.
26. Muse, *Virginia's Massive Resistance*, 140; Powers, interview; Hoffman, interview.
27. Reif, *Crisis in Norfolk*, 25.
28. Sugg, letter, 12 October 1990.
29. Porter, interview.
30. Carter, "Desegregation in Norfolk," 512; Tonelson, interview, 18 July 1990.
31. White, "Will Norfolk's Schools Stay Open?" 29.
32. Muse, *Virginia's Massive Resistance*, 142.
33. Carter, "Desegregation in Norfolk," 519.
34. *Ledger-Dispatch*, 2 February 1959.
35. Ibid.
36. *Ledger-Dispatch*, 3 February 1959.
37. Ibid.
38. *Virginian-Pilot*, 1 February 1959.
39. Batten, interview.
40. Burgess, interview; Smith, interview, 17 April 1992.
41. L. Chambers to P. Morgan, 8 May 1959, Chambers Papers.
42. J. Leslie to L. Chambers, 28 May 1959, Chambers Papers.
43. H. Byrd to L. Chambers, 26 December 1959, Byrd Papers.

15. The Influence of Lenoir Chambers

1. *Virginian-Pilot*, 3 May 1960.
2. G. Kirk to L. Chambers, 2 May 1960, Chambers Papers.
3. V. Dabney to L. Chambers, 6 May 1960, Chambers Papers.
4. Sugg, letter, 13 October 1990.
5. *Virginian-Pilot*, 3 May 1960.
6. *Virginian-Pilot and Ledger-Star*, 23 September 1990.
7. A. Jaffe to L. Chambers, 4 May 1960, Chambers Papers.
8. S. Barr to L. Chambers, 3 May 1960, Chambers Papers.
9. *New York Times*, 8 May 1960.

10. C. McKnight to L. Chambers, 3 February 1959, Chambers Papers.

11. C. McKnight to L. Chambers, 3 May 1960, Chambers Papers.

12. R. Estabrook to L. Chambers, 21 August 1958, Chambers Papers.

13. T. Young to H. Luce, 22 February 1956, Chambers Papers.

14. P. Young to L. Chambers, 24 December 1958, Chambers Papers.

15. T. Young to L. Chambers, 5 May 1960, Chambers Papers.

16. P. Schweitzer to L. Chambers, 3 May 1960, Chambers Papers.

17. Hoffman, interview.

18. L. McGonegal to L. Chambers, 31 March 1959, Chambers Papers.

19. "How Norfolk's Schools Were Reopened," 25 February 1959, White Papers.

20. Reif, *Crisis in Norfolk,* 4.

21. J. Nelson to L. Chambers, 3 May 1960, Chambers Papers.

22. Batten, interview.

23. Carter, interview.

24. Mason, interview, 17 July 1990.

25. E. Rogers and F. Shoemaker, *Communication of Innovations: A Cross-Cultural Approach,* 2d edition (New York: Free Press, 1971), 218, 343–44; W. Schramm and D. White, "Age, Education, and Economic Status as Factors in Newspaper Reading," in *Mass Communications,* ed. W. Schramm (Urbana: University of Illinois Press, 1960) 438–41; P. Lazarsfeld, B. Berelson, and H. Gaudet, *The People's Choice: How the Voter Makes Up His Mind in a Presidential Election* (New York: Columbia University Press, 1948), 151–52.

26. Wilhoit, *The Politics of Massive Resistance,* 149.

16. Epilogue: The Editor and the Schools

1. Burgess, letter, 5 December 1992.

2. T. Gest, "School Desegregation Grinds to a Halt in South," *U.S. News & World Report,* 21 May 1984, 49.

3. *Washington Post,* 9 February 1986.

4. *Washington Post,* 10 June 1982.

5. *Los Angeles Times,* 17 June 1986. *Virginian-Pilot and Ledger-Star,* 17 January 1993.

6. *Virginian-Pilot and Ledger-Star,* 4 December 1994.

7. *Virginian-Pilot and Ledger-Star,* 4 May 1994.

8. *Virginian-Pilot and Ledger-Star,* 7 April 1994.

9. *Virginian-Pilot and Ledger-Star,* 17 January 1993.

10. In 1996 the combined newspapers officially became the *Virginian-Pilot.*

11. *Virginian-Pilot and Ledger-Star,* 8 February 1986.

Bibliography

Personal Communications

Abeles, S. Letter to author, 24 November 1992.

Aprill, S. Telephone interview by author, 24 September 1994.

Barfield, S. Interview by author, tape recording, Norfolk, Virginia, 8 August 1990.

Batten, F. Interview by author, tape recording, Norfolk, Virginia, 25 September 1990.

Burgess, E. Interview by author, tape recording, Norfolk, Virginia, 2 August 1990.

———. Letter to author, 27 October 1992.

———. Letter to author, 19 November 1992.

———. Letter to author, 5 December 1992.

Carter, L. Telephone interview by author, tape recording, 10 October 1992.

———. Letter to author, 30 September 1995.

Darden, P. Interview by F. White, Jr., tape recording, Norfolk, Virginia, 13 August 1975.

Dill, A. Letter to author, 20 November 1992.

———. Telephone interview by author, tape recording, 20 November 1992.

Fitzpatrick, W. Letter to author, 11 December 1992.

Garrison, S. Telephone interview by author, 27 September 1994.

Glenn, R. Letter to author, 10 November 1992.

———. Letter to author, 23 November 1992.

———. Letter to author, 24 November 1992.

———. Letter to author, 30 November 1992.

Hoffman, W. Interview by author, tape recording, Norfolk, Virginia, 30 August 1990.

———. Letter to author, 17 October 1995.

Jaffe, L., Jr. Letter to author, 19 September 1995.

Martin, R., Jr. Interview by author, tape recording, Norfolk, Virginia, 20 August 1990.

Mason, R. Telephone interview by author, tape recording, 10 April 1989.

———. Telephone interview by author, tape recording, 17 July 1990.

———. Telephone interview by author, tape recording, 5 December 1990.

———. Letter to author, 18 November 1991.

———. Telephone interview by author, tape recording, 19 November 1992.

———. Letter to author, 20 November 1992.

———. Letter to author, 24 August 1995.

McKendree, W. Interview by author, tape recording, Norfolk, Virginia, 19 November 1990.

Phillips, B. Telephone interview by author, 17 July 1995.

Porter, C. Interview by author, tape recording, Norfolk Virginia, 18 May 1992.

Powers, F., Jr. Interview by author, tape recording, Norfolk, Virginia, 4 October 1990.
Smith, R. Telephone interview by author, tape recording, 17 April 1992.
———. Telephone interview by author, 2 October 1995.
Stanley, M. Telephone interview by author, tape recording, 8 May 1992.
Sugg, H. Letter to author, 2 October 1990.
———. Letter to author, 12 October 1990.
———. Letter to author, 13 October 1990.
———. Letter to author, 30 November 1990.
Tonelson, R. Interview by author, tape recording, Norfolk, Virginia, 18 July 1990.
Woolen, L. Telephone interview by author, tape recording, 8 May 1992.

Personal Papers and Documents

Almond, J. L. Papers. Letters Received and Sent, Governor's Office, Executive Department, Archives, Library of Virginia, Richmond.
Byrd, H. F., Sr. Papers (#9700). Special Collections Department, University of Virginia Library.
Chambers, L. Papers. Southern Historical Collection, Wilson Library, University of North Carolina at Chapel Hill.
Jaffe, L. I. Papers (#9924). Manuscripts Division, Special Collections Department, University of Virginia Library.
Kilpatrick, J. J. Papers (#6626). Manuscripts Division, Special Collections Department, University of Virginia Library.
Lewis, K. P. Papers. Southern Historical Collection, Wilson Library, University of North Carolina at Chapel Hill.
Schweitzer, P. T. Papers. Old Dominion University Library, Norfolk, Virginia.
White, F. P. Papers. Old Dominion University Library, Norfolk, Virginia.

Newspapers

Bristol Herald-Courier, 1926.
Bristol News Bulletin, 1926.
Chapel Hill Weekly, 1970
Charlotte Chronicle, 1907.
Charlotte Observer, 1907.
Charlottesville Daily Progress, 1964.
Christian Science News Monitor, 1958.
Greensboro Daily News, 1929, 1970.
Los Angeles Times, 1986.
New York Times, 1960, 1970.
Norfolk Journal and Guide, 1926.
Norfolk Ledger-Dispatch, 1954–1959.
Norfolk Virginian-Pilot, 1926, 1927, 1936, 1954–1960, 1964, 1970, 1983, 1990.
Norfolk Virginian-Pilot and Ledger-Star, 1986, 1990, 1991, 1993, 1994.
Richmond Times-Dispatch, 1956.
Southern School News, 1958, 1959.

Stars and Stripes, 1919.
University of North Carolina Tar Heel, undated.
University of Virginia College Topics, 1915.
Washington Post, undated, 1982, 1986.

Cases and Court Decisions

Adkins v. School Board of the City of Newport News and *Beckett v. School Board of the City of Norfolk,* 148 F.Supp. 430 (1957).
Brown v. Board of Education of Topeka, 347 US 483 (1954).
Brown v. Board of Education of Topeka, 349 US 294 (1955).
Harrison v. Day, 106 S.E. 2d 636 (1959).
James v. Almond, 170 F.Supp. 331 (1959).
James v. Duckworth, 170 F.Supp. 342 (1959).
Plessy v. Ferguson, 163 US 537 (1896).

Books, Theses, Periodicals, and Newspaper Series

Almond, J. L. "We Are the Stewards of Our States' Inheritance." *The American Mercury,* May 1958, 55–60.
Ashmore, H. S. *An Epitaph for Dixie.* New York: Norton, 1958.
Ayers, E. *The Promise of the New South: Life After Reconstruction.* New York: Oxford, 1992.
Baker, R. T. *A History of the Graduate School of Journalism, Columbia University.* New York: Columbia University, 1954.
Bartley, N. V. *The Rise of Massive Resistance: Race and Politics in the South During the 1950's.* Baton Rouge: Louisiana State University, 1969.
Bonner, M. "Behind the Southern Textile Strikes." *The Nation,* 2 October 1929, 351–52.
Boyle, S. P. *The Desegregated Heart: A Virginian's Stand in Time of Transition.* New York: William Morrow, 1962.
Brundage, W. *Lynching in the New South: Georgia and Virginia, 1880–1930.* Urbana: University of Illinois Press, 1993.
Buck, J. L. *The Development of Public Schools in Virginia, 1607–1952.* Richmond: Commonwealth of Virginia State Board of Education, 1952.
Buni, A. *The Negro in Virginia Politics, 1902–1965.* Charlottesville: University Press of Virginia, 1967.
Campbell, E. Q. *When a City Closes Its Schools.* Chapel Hill: Institute for Research in Social Sciences, 1960.
Carter, H. *Their Words Were Bullets: The Southern Press in War, Reconstruction, and Peace.* Athens: University of Georgia Press, 1969.
Carter, L. J. "Desegregation in Norfolk." *The South Atlantic Quarterly* 58, no. 4 (Autumn 1959): 507–20.
———. "Inside Byrd's Organization." *Virginian-Pilot,* 7 June 1964.
———. "State House Bid Delayed." *Virginian-Pilot,* 8 June 1964.
———. "The Senator Couldn't Be Reached." *Virginian-Pilot,* 9 June 1964.
Chalmers, D. *Hooded Americanism: The First Century of the Ku Klux Klan, 1865–1965.* Garden City: Doubleday, 1965.

Chambers, L. *Stonewall Jackson*. New York: William Morrow, 1959.

Chambers, L., J. Shank, and H. Sugg. *Salt Water & Printer's Ink: Norfolk and Its Newspapers*. Chapel Hill: University of North Carolina Press, 1967.

Claiborne, J. *The Charlotte Observer: Its Time and Place, 1869–1986*. Chapel Hill: University of North Carolina Press, 1986.

Clayton, B. *W. J. Cash: A Life*. Baton Rouge: Louisiana State University Press, 1991.

Creel, G. *How We Advertised America: The First Telling of the Amazing Story of the Committee on Public Information that Carried the Gospel of Americanism to Every Corner of the Globe*. New York: Harper & Brothers, 1920.

Dabney, V. *Liberalism in the South*. Chapel Hill: University of North Carolina Press, 1932.

———. "Virginia's Peaceable, Honorable Stand." *Life,* 22 September 1958, 54–55.

———. "Next in the South's Schools: 'Limited Integration.' " *U.S. News & World Report,* 18 January 1960, 92–94.

———. *Virginia, The New Dominion*. Charlottesville: University Press of Virginia, 1971.

———. *Across the Years, Memories of a Virginian*. Garden City: Doubleday, 1978.

"Desegregation—or No Public Schools." *New South,* March 1959, 3–10.

Draper, R. *The Letters of Ruth Draper: 1920–1956, a Self-portrait of a Great Actress*. Edited by N. Warren. New York: Charles Scribner's Sons, 1979.

Dykeman, W., and J. Stokely. "Report on 'The Lost Class of '59.' " *New York Times Magazine,* 4 January 1959, 20, 54–55.

Eagles, C. *Jonathan Daniels and Race Relations: The Evolution of a Southern Liberal*. Knoxville: University of Tennessee Press, 1982.

Egerton, J. *Speak Now Against the Day: The Generation Before the Civil Rights Movement in the South*. New York: Knopf, 1994.

"80 Days Without Public Schools." *Newsweek,* 1 December 1958, 23–26.

Ely, J. *The Crisis of Conservative Virginia: The Byrd Organization and the Politics of Massive Resistance*. Knoxville: University Press of Tennessee, 1976.

Fisher, P. L., and R. L. Lowenstein. *Race and the News Media*. New York: Praeger, 1967.

Ford, N. P. "The Peaceful Resolution of Norfolk's Integration Crisis of 1958–1959." Master's thesis, Old Dominion University, Norfolk, Virginia, 1989.

Friddell, G. *What Is It About Virginia?* Richmond: Dietz Press, 1966.

Gates, R. L. *The Making of Massive Resistance: Virginia's Politics of Public School Desegregation*. Chapel Hill: University of North Carolina Press, 1964.

Gest, T. "School Desegregation Grinds to a Halt in South." *U.S. News & World Report,* 21 May 1984, 49.

Gordon, M. L. *A Documented History of the First Baptist Church*. Virginia Beach: Hill's Printing, 1988.

Green, L. L. "Nell Battle Lewis: Crusading Columnist, 1921–1938." Master's thesis, East Carolina University, Greenville, North Carolina, 1969.

Hall, J., J. Leloudis, R. Korstad, M. Murphy, L. A. Jones, and C. Daly. *Like a Family: The Making of a Southern Cotton Mill World*. Chapel Hill: University of North Carolina Press, 1987.

Heatwole, C. J. *A History of Education in Virginia*. New York: Macmillan, 1916.

Hero, A. O., Jr. *The Southerner and World Affairs*. Baton Rouge: Louisiana State University Press, 1965.

Hohenberg, J., ed. *The Pulitzer Prize Story: News, Stories, Editorials, Cartoons, and*

Pictures from the Pulitzer Prize Collection at Columbia University. New York: Columbia University Press, 1959.

———, ed. *The Pulitzer Prize Story II: Award Winning News Stories, Columns, Editorials, and News Pictures, 1959–1980.* New York: Columbia University Press, 1980.

Key, V. O. *Southern Politics in State and Nation.* New York: Knopf, 1949.

Kilpatrick, J. J. *The Sovereign States: Notes of a Citizen of Virginia.* Chicago: Henry Regnery, 1957.

Kneebone, J. *Southern Liberal Journalists and the Issue of Race, 1920–1944.* Chapel Hill: University of North Carolina Press, 1985.

Lazarsfeld, P., B. Berelson, and H. Gaudet. *The People's Choice: How the Voter Makes Up His Mind in a Presidential Election.* New York: Columbia University Press, 1948.

Lewis, E. *In Their Own Interests: Race, Class, and Power in Twentieth-Century Norfolk, Virginia.* Berkeley: University of California Press, 1991.

Lewis, N. "Anarchy versus Communism in Gastonia." *The Nation,* 23 October 1929, 321–22.

Manchester, W. *Disturber of the Peace: The Life of H. L. Mencken.* New York: Harper & Brothers, 1951.

Mason, R. *One of the Neighbors' Children.* Chapel Hill: Algonquin, 1987.

McGill, R. *The South and the Southerner.* Boston: Little, Brown and Company, 1963.

Mencken, H. L. *Newspaper Days, 1899–1906.* New York: Knopf, 1941.

———. *The American Scene, a Reader.* New York: Knopf, 1965.

———. *The Diary of H. L. Mencken.* Edited by C. Fecher. New York: Knopf, 1989.

Morgan, P., ed. *"Don't Grieve after Me," The Black Experience in Virginia 1619–1986.* Hampton, Va.: Hampton University Press, 1986.

Morton, R. L. *The Negro in Virginia Politics, 1865–1902.* Charlottesville: University of Virginia Press, 1919.

Muse, B. *Virginia's Massive Resistance.* Bloomington: Indiana University Press, 1961.

———. *Ten Years of Prelude: The Story of Integration since the Supreme Court's 1954 Decision.* New York: Viking, 1964.

Myrdal, G. *An American Dilemma: The Negro Problem and Modern Democracy.* New York: Harper & Row, 1944.

Odum, H. W. *Southern Regions of the United States.* Chapel Hill: University of North Carolina Press, 1936.

Pace, D. "Lenoir Chambers Opposes Massive Resistance: An Editor Against Virginia's Democratic Organization, 1955–1959." *The Virginia Magazine of History and Biography,* October 1974, 415–29.

Peltason, J. W. *Fifty-Eight Lonely Men: Southern Federal Judges and School Desegregation.* New York: Harcourt, Brace & World, 1961.

Phillips, C. "Virginia—The State and the State of Mind." *New York Times Magazine,* 28 July 1957, 18–19, 49, 51.

Powell, W. S., ed. *Dictionary of North Carolina Biography.* Vols. 3, 4. Chapel Hill: University of North Carolina Press, 1988, 1991.

"Pulitzer Winners Formula: Write After Conferring." *Virginia Publisher and Printer,* June 1960, 3–6.

Putnam, C. *Race and Reason: A Yankee View.* Washington, D.C.: Public Affairs Press, 1961.

"Quest for a Personality." *Time,* 5 September 1960, 51.

Race Relations Law Reporter, February 1956–Summer 1959.

Reif, J. *Crisis in Norfolk.* Richmond: Virginia Council on Human Relations, 1960.

"Reticence, Timidity Hamper Virginia's Press Jaffe Tells Virginia Editors." *Editor and Publisher,* 27 July 1929, 20.

Rogers, E. M., and F. F. Shoemaker. *Communication of Innovations: A Cross-Cultural Approach.* 2d edition. New York: Free Press, 1971.

Rorer, H. S. "History of Norfolk Public Schools, 1681–1968." Unpublished manuscript. Old Dominion University Library, Norfolk, Virginia, 1968.

Schramm, W., and D. M. White. "Age, Education, and Economic Status as Factors in Newspaper Reading." In *Mass Communication,* edited by W. Schramm. Urbana: University of Illinois Press, 1960.

Singal, D. J. *The War Within: From Victorian to Modernist Thought in the South, 1919–1945.* Chapel Hill: University of North Carolina Press, 1982.

Sloan, W. D., and L. B. Anderson. *Pulitzer Prize Editorials: America's Best Editorial Writing, 1917–1993.* Ames: Iowa State University Press, 1994.

Smith, R. *They Closed Their Schools: Prince Edward County, Virginia, 1951–1964.* Chapel Hill: University of North Carolina Press, 1965.

Sosna, M. *In Search of the Silent South.* New York: Columbia University Press, 1977.

Stolberg, B. "Madness in Marion." *The Nation,* 23 October 1929, 462–64.

Sugg, H. L. *The Black Press in the South: 1865–1979.* Westport: Greenwood, 1983.

———. *P. B. Young, Newspaperman: Race, Politics, and Journalism in the New South, 1910–1960.* Charlottesville: University Press of Virginia, 1988.

Thompson, L. A. "Virginia Education Crisis and Its Economic Aspects." *New South,* February 1959, 3–8.

Tindall, G. B. *The Emergence of the New South, 1913–1945.* Vol. 10 of *A History of the South.* Baton Rouge: Louisiana State University Press, 1967.

———. *America, A Narrative History.* New York: Norton, 1984.

"Virginia, 'The Gravest Crisis.' " *Time,* 22 September 1958, 13–18.

Wertenbaker, T. J. *Norfolk: Historic Southern Port.* Durham: Duke University Press, 1962.

"What Massive Resistance Costs." *Business Week,* 4 October 1958, 32–34.

White, F. "Will Norfolk's Schools Stay Open?" *The Atlantic,* September 1959, 29–32.

Wilhoit, F. M. *The Politics of Massive Resistance.* New York: Braziller, 1973.

Wilkinson, J. H. *Harry Byrd and the Changing Face of Virginia Politics, 1945–1966.* Charlottesville: University Press of Virginia, 1968.

Williams, J. *Eyes on the Prize: America's Civil Rights Years: 1954–1965.* New York: Viking, 1987.

Woodward, C. V. *Origins of the New South, 1877–1913.* Baton Rouge: Louisiana State University Press, 1951.

———. *The Strange Career of Jim Crow.* 3d edition. New York: Oxford University Press, 1974.

Zabel, M., and R. Draper. *The Art of Ruth Draper: Her Dramas and Characters.* Garden City, N.Y.: Doubleday, 1960.

Index

Gordon, Douglas, 26
Graham, Frank Porter, 9
Graves, John Temple, Sr., 34–35
Graves, John Temple, II, 29
Graves, Louis, 9
Gray, Garland ("Peck"), 66, 68, 78
Gray Commission, 67–68, 72, 78
Gray Report. *See* Gray Commission
Greenberg, Jack, 67
Greensboro Daily News, 19

Haardt, Sara Powell, 32
Hall, Grover, 20–21, 29
Hampton Institute, 58
Hanckel, Allan R., 60
Harrell, Lydon C., 104
Harris, Julia Collier, 17
Harris, Julian LaRose, 17, 20, 29
Harrison, Albertis S., Jr., 67, 90–91, 93, 104, 112
Harrison v. Day, 104, 112, 114
Hayes, George E. C., 67
Haynsworth, Clement F., 104
Hebert, George J., 41
Herndon, Angelo, 33
Hero, Alfred, 34
Hill, Oliver W., 66, 87
Hoffman, Walter E. ("Beef"): and Seashore State Park, 70; disaffection with Byrd, 70, 81–82; and *Beckett v. School Board* and *Adkins v. School Board,* 80–81; order to act on black transfers, 86; order regarding school board denial of transfer of black students, 88–89; threatened, 88–89; and injunction barring school board from pupil assignment, 90–91; court of appeals upholds order admitting black students, 91; appointment to three-judge panel in *James v. Almond,* 104; delay in release of *James v. Almond* opinion, 112; as author of *James v. Almond* decision, 114; and *James v. Duckworth,* 119; on Chambers's influence, 130–31
Huber, Paul S., Jr., 128
Hughes, Massie F., 100, 127

I'Anson, Lawrence W., 117
Interposition, 75–76

Jackson, Gwendolyn Jones, 136
Jackson, Thomas Jonathan ("Stonewall"), 11, 123
Jacob, Clyde H., 107
Jaffe, Alice, 128

Jaffe, Louis, Jr., 119
Jaffe Louis, Sr.: intellectual and moral influence on Chambers, 8, 23; search for associate editor, 20–23; background and temperament, 24, 49, 51, 53; in Europe, 30; and Ku Klux Klan and anti-lynching campaign, 30–31, 57; and Mencken, 32–33; and Dabney, 33; death, 41; and P. B. Young, 57; championing of improved race relations, 57–58, 128
James, Ellis, 104
James, Ruth Pendleton, 104
James v. Almond, 104–5, 112, 114
James v. Duckworth, 119
Jefferson, Thomas, 75
Jeffress, E. B., 21
Jeffries, Jack, 63
Jews, 98
Johnson, Gerald W., 8–9, 18–21, 28
Johnson, Jack, 63

Kelley, George M., 109
Key, V. O., Jr., 55, 99
Kilpatrick, James Jackson ("Jack"), 35, 43, 67, 75, 81, 106–7
King, Helen Brinkley, 28
Kneebone, John T., 30
Krock, Arthur, 24
Ku Klux Klan, 9, 30–31

Lacy, Drury, 11
League of Women Voters, 98, 127
Ledger-Dispatch. See Norfolk Ledger-Dispatch
Leslie, Joseph A., Jr.: on massive resistance and school closing, 1, 5–6; racial views, 6; connections to Byrd organization, 6; as associate editor of *Ledger-Dispatch,* 26–27; and Chambers, 26–27, 123; as editor of *Ledger-Dispatch,* 41; and reversal of *Ledger-Dispatch* editorial stance on resistance, 123; criticism of Hoffman, 130–31
Lewis, Earl, 61
Lewis, Henry S., 53
Lewis, Ivey, 15
Lewis, Kemp Plummer, 15
Lewis, Nell Battle, 15–17, 19–20
Lewis, Richard Henry, 15, 16
Littledale, Harold A., 24
Little Rock, Arkansas, school desegregation, ix, 84
Little Rock Bills, 85
"Lost Class of '59, The," television documentary, 115
Luce, Henry R., 129

About the Author

Alexander Leidholdt is an assistant professor in the Department of Communication at Purdue University. He received his bachelor's degree from Virginia Wesleyan College, his master's degree from Clarion University, an education specialist's degree from Indiana University, and his doctorate from Old Dominion University.